PHILIP'S

C000108876

STRE

Bristol

Avonmouth, Filton, Keynsham

www.philips-maps.co.uk

First published in 2008 by

Philip's, a division of
Octopus Publishing Group Ltd
www.octopusbooks.co.uk
2-4 Heron Quays, London E14 4JP
An Hachette Livre UK Company

First edition 2008
First impression 2008

ISBN 978-0-540-09200-0

© Philip's 2008

Ordnance Survey®

This product includes mapping data licensed
from Ordnance Survey®, with the
permission of the Controller of Her Majesty's
Stationery Office.© Crown copyright 2008.
All rights reserved.
Licence number 100011710

Data for the speed cameras provided by
PocketGPSWorld.com Ltd.

Ordnance Survey and the OS symbol are
registered trademarks of Ordnance Survey,
the national mapping agency of Great Britain

Photographic acknowledgements:
VIII and IX by James Hughes

Printed by Toppan, China

Contents

II   **Key to map symbols**

III   **Key to map pages**

IV   **Route planning**

VIII   **Illustrated guide to visitor attractions**

2   **Street maps** at 4½ inches to 1 mile

84   **Street maps of central Bristol**
at 7 inches to 1 mile

88   **Index**

118   **List of numbered locations**

Key to map symbols

Roads

(12) **Motorway** with junction number

A42 **Primary route** – dual, single carriageway

A42 **A road** – dual, single carriageway

B1289 **B road** – dual, single carriageway

Through-route – dual, single carriageway

Minor road – dual, single carriageway

Rural track, private road or narrow road in urban area

Path, bridleway, byway open to all traffic, road used as a public path

Road under construction

Pedestrianised area

Gate or obstruction to traffic restrictions may not apply at all times or to all vehicles

P P&R **Parking, Park and Ride**

(30) (30)) **Speed cameras** – single, multiple

Railways

Railway

Miniature railway

Metro station, private railway station

Emergency services

Ambulance station, coastguard station

Fire station, police station

H ✚ **Hospital, Accident and Emergency entrance to hospital**

General features

✚ PO **Place of worship, Post Office**

i **Information centre** (open all year)

Bus or coach station, shopping centre

Important buildings, schools, colleges, universities and hospitals

Woods, built-up area

Tumulus FORT **Non-Roman antiquity, Roman antiquity**

Leisure facilities

 Camping site, caravan site

 Golf course, picnic site

Boundaries

● ● ● ● ● ● ● ● **Postcode boundaries**

— · — **County and unitary authority boundaries**

Water features

 River Ouse **Tidal water, water name**

Non-tidal water – lake, river, canal or stream

< | **Lock, weir**

Enlarged mapping only

Railway or bus station building

Place of interest

Parkland

Scales

Blue pages: 4½ inches to 1 mile 1:14 080

| 0 | 220 yds | ¼ mile | 660 yds | ½ mi |

| 0 | 125m | 250m | 375m | ½ km |

Red pages: 7 inches to 1 mile 1: 9051

| 0 | 110 yds | 220 yds | 330 yds | ¼ mile |

| 0 | 125m | 250m | 375m | ½km |

 62 **Adjoining page indicators** The colour of the arrow and the band indicates the scale of the adjoining page (see above)

Abbreviations

Acad	Academy	Mkt	Market
Allot Gdns	Allotments	Meml	Memorial
Cemy	Cemetery	Mon	Monument
C Ctr	Civic Centre	Mus	Museum
CH	Club House	Obsy	Observatory
Coll	College	Pal	Royal Palace
Crem	Crematorium	PH	Public House
Ent	Enterprise	Recn Gd	Recreation Ground
Ex H	Exhibition Hall	Resr	Reservoir
Ind Est	Industrial Estate	Ret Pk	Retail Park
IRB Sta	Inshore Rescue Boat Station	Sch	School
Inst	Institute	Sh Ctr	Shopping Centre
Ct	Law Court	TH	Town Hall/House
L Ctr	Leisure Centre	Trad Est	Trading Estate
LC	Level Crossing	Univ	University
Liby	Library	Wks	Works
		YH	Youth Hostel

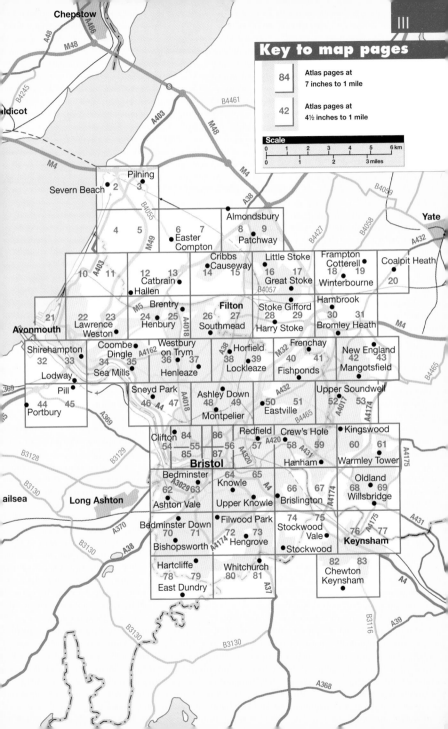

Chepstow

Yate

Key to map pages

| 84 | Atlas pages at 7 inches to 1 mile |
| 42 | Atlas pages at 4½ inches to 1 mile |

Scale
0 1 2 3 4 5 6 km
0   1   2   3 miles

Severn Beach 2 **Pilning** 3

Almondsbury 8 9 **Patchway**

4 5 6 **Easter Compton** 7

Cribbs Causeway 14 15 **Little Stoke** 16 17 **Frampton Cotterell** 18 19 **Coalpit Heath**

10 11 **Catbrain** 12 13 **Great Stoke** **Winterbourne** 20

Hallen B4057

Brentry **Filton** **Stoke Gifford** 28 29 **Hambrook** 30 31

21 **Lawrence Weston** 22 23 24 25 26 27 **Southmead** **Harry Stoke** **Bromley Heath**

Avonmouth **Henbury**

Shirehampton 32 33 **Coombe Dingle** 34 35 **Westbury on Trym** 36 37 **Horfield** 38 39 **Frenchay** 40 41 **New England** 42 43 **Mangotsfield**

Lodway **Sea Mills** **Henleaze** **Lockleaze** **Fishponds**

Pill **Sneyd Park** 46 44 47 **Ashley Down** 48 49 50 51 **Upper Soundwell** 52 53

44 45 **Montpelier** **Eastville**

Portbury

Clifton 84 86 **Redfield** **Crew's Hole** **Kingswood**
54 55 56 57 **Hanham** 58 59 60 61
85 87 **Bristol** **Warmley Tower**

Long Ashton **Bedminster** 62 63 **Knowle** 64 65 66 67 **Oldland** 68 69 **Willsbridge**
Ashton Vale **Upper Knowle** **Brislington**

Bedminster Down 70 71 **Filwood Park** 74 **Stockwood Vale** 75 76 77 **Keynsham**
Bishopsworth 72 73 **Hengrove** **Stockwood**

Hartcliffe 78 79 **Whitchurch** 80 81 82 83 **Chewton Keynsham**
East Dundry

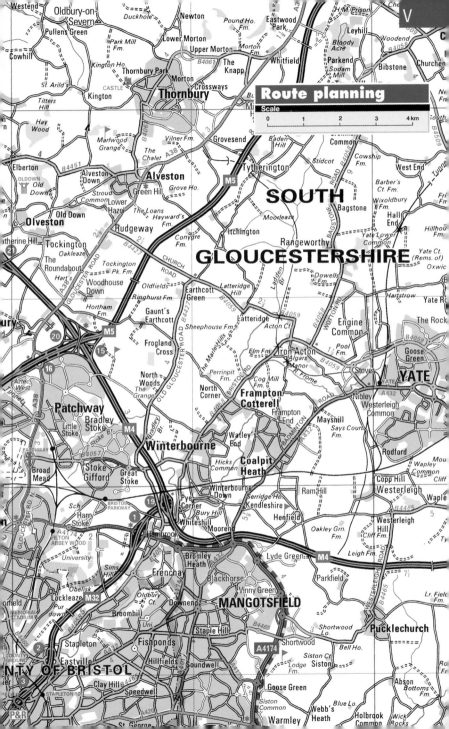

Visitor attractions

Museums and Galleries

Blaise Castle House Museum *Blaise Castle Estate, Henbury Road, Henbury, Bristol* Built in 1796–8 for John Harford, a wealthy Bristol merchant and banker, the building has some original interiors and serves as a local and social history museum, with home and costume galleries, toys, model train collection and Victorian School Room. ☎0117 903 9818 🖥www.bristol.gov.uk 24 C2

Bristol City Museum and Art Gallery *Queens Road, Bristol* The region's largest museum has a broad collection of exhibits from nationally important art to palaeontology, natural history, geology, archaeology, glassware, decorative arts and a freshwater aquarium. Wide range of public events, craft sessions and children's holiday activities. ☎0117 922 3571 🖥www.bristol.gov.uk 84 C3

British Empire and Commonwealth Museum *Station Approach, Temple Meads, Bristol* Housed in Brunel's 19th-century Bristol Temple Meads railway station, this award-winning museum explores the 500-year legacy and history of the British Empire, concentrating on Bristol's role in shipping, trade, slavery, the railways and manufacturing. ☎0117 925 4980 🖥www.empiremuseum.co.uk 87 C1

Georgian House Museum *7 Great George Street, Bristol* Built in 1790 for a West India merchant John Pinney, the house is arranged to show how life was lived above and below stairs in the 18th century, with an exhibition on the life of

▼ *Bristol Cathedral (Church of England)*

Pinney's slave, Pero. Limited accessibility. ☎0117 921 1362 🖥www.bristol.gov.uk 85 C2

Kingswood Heritage Museum *Tower Lane, Warmley, Bristol* Housed in William Champion's 18th-century brass works, this small museum has a variety of displays on local industry and social history. 🖥www.kingswoodmuseum.org.uk ☎0117 960 5664 61 A2

Historic Sites

The New Room *36 The Horsefair, Bristol* The oldest Methodist chapel in the world, this building was completed in 1739 and is a beautiful example of a building designed to suit John Wesley's style of preaching, which had originally been developed out of doors. The double decker pulpit is typical of the era. Above the chapel are rooms in which Welsey and other preachers stayed and also a museum display. ☎0117 926 4740 86 B3

The Red Lodge *Park Row, Bristol* Known for its magnificent Tudor rooms, the building was built in 1580 as a lodge for a Great House on the site of the present Colston Hall and was added to in Georgian times. Exhibitions tell its history and there is a recreation of an Elizabethan knot garden. Limited accessibility. ☎0117 921160 🖥www.bristol.gov.uk 84 C3

Temple Church *Temple Street, Bristol* Begun in the mid-12th century for Robert of Gloucester, a son of Henry I, the original church was an oval shape, reflecting the Temple at Jerusalem. It was rebuilt in a more usual rectangle in the early 14th century but the huge tower has been leaning since the late 14th century. The building was ruined by bombing in World War II. 🖥www.english-heritage.org.uk 87 B2

Places of Worship

Cathedral of the Holy and Undivided Trinity (C of E) *College Green, Bristol* The Abbey of St Augustine was founded here in c.1140, and dissolved just under 400 years later, becoming a cathedral in 1542. The cathedral is a fine example of a hall church, a kind not usually found in England, with the nave, choir and aisles all the same height. The nave, incomplete at the time of the Dissolution, was demolished but rebuilt to Medieval designs in the mid-19th century. Among modern highlights are the Saxon sculpture of the Harrowing of Hell and the 1960s South Choir Aisle window. ☎0117 926 4879 🖥www.bristol-cathedral.co.uk 85 C2

Cathedral of St Peter and St Paul, Clifton (RC) *Clifton Park, Bristol* Built in the 1970s, the Roman Catholic cathedral is centred around the hexagonal Sanctuary, and the effect of natural daylight from the roof is stunning. Concerts are regularly held here. ☎0117 973 8411 🖥www.cliftoncathedral.org.uk 84 A4

St Mary Redcliffe *Colston Parade, Redcliffe, Bristol* The tallest building in Bristol, St Mary Redcliffe was described by Queen Elizabeth I as 'the fairest, goodliest, and most famous parish church in England.' The earliest parts of the building date to the 12th century, but most date from the 15th-century. 🖥www.stmaryredcliffe.co.uk 87 B1

Other Sights

Brunel's SS Great Britain *Great Western Dockyard, Gas Ferry Road, Bristol* The first iron-hulled, steam-powered ocean-going ship was built to Isambard Kingdom Brunel's designs in 1843 to serve the growing transatlantic passenger trade, although she was used more for trips to Australia. After a period as a troop ship and bulk coal carrier, she was scuttled in the Falkland Islands, before being rescued in 1970 and returned to her original dock. Subjected to an extensive restoration and conservation programme, she is now one of the city's prime visitor attractions. The nearby Maritime Heritage Centre forms part of the same attraction. ☎0117 929 1843 🖥www.ssgreatbritain.org 85 B1

Cabot Tower *Brandon Hill, Bristol* Built by William Venn Gough, the Cabot Tower dates back to 1897 and commemorates John Cabot, who set sail from the city 400 years earlier. Its spiral staircase leads to two viewing platforms that offer views over the city from the vantage point of Brandon Hill. It is built from red sandstone and covered with cream Bath stone. 85 B2

Clifton Suspension Bridge *Leigh Woods, Bristol* Begun in 1831 by Isambard Kingdom Brunel and finished to his designs in 1864, the bridge spans the beautiful Avon Gorge. Guided tours. 🖥www.clifton-suspension-bridge.org.uk ☎0117 974 4664 54 A3

Clifton Observatory, Camera Obscura and Cave *Litfield Place, Clifton Down, Bristol* The only camera obscura open to the public in England and housed in a converted 'snuff mill', this monument offers views over the Clifton Suspension Bridge. The image is projected from a lens in the roof onto a concave table. ☎0117 974 1379 54 B3

Severn Bridges Visitor Centre *Shaft Road, Severn Beach* Exhibition of boat, rail and road crossings of the estuary and the building of the Second Severn Crossing in 1996. Nearby is the Severn Beach Sea Walk with spectacular views of both Severn crossings. ☎01454 633 511 2 B4

Wills Memorial Building *Park Street, Queens Road, Bristol* Designed in 1912 by Sir George Oatley, the Wills Memorial

Building is one of the last magnificent Gothic buildings to be constructed in England. The building is known locally as 'The University' and its most prominent feature is the 215-foot Wills Tower which affords amazing views of Bristol and dominates the city. 84 C3

Green Spaces

Ashton Court Estate *Rownham Hill, off Kennel Lodge Road, Bristol* Also known as Ashton Park, these 850 acres of woods and grassland boast breathtaking views over Bristol and red and fallow deer in a deer park dating back to 1392. Activities include pitch and putt, orienteering, mountain biking, walking trails and horse riding. It is the site of the annual International Balloon Fiesta and the Kite Festival.
🖳 www.forestofavon.org/ashtoncourt.html 📞 0117 963 9176 62 A4

Avon Gorge An outstandingly beautiful area, running approximately 3 km (2 miles) north-west of the docks and beyond to Pill. The limestone acres of the gorge are also of scientific interest for their plant and invertebrate species and breeding birds, including peregrine falcons. 🖳 www.nationaltrust.org.uk 🖳 www.bristol.gov.uk 54 A3

Blaise Castle Estate *Kingsweston Road, Bristol* The grounds of John Harford's House (see under museums), consists of 650 acres of parkland and gardens laid out by Humphry Repton. The 'Castle' is a small Gothic folly built at the top of Blaise Hill in 1766. Among the best areas are the wooded limestone gorge, woodlands and chalk grassland on Kingsweston Down. The Blaise Hamlet Cottages (National Trust) are nearby and there are children's play areas and a horse-riding trail. 🖳 www.bristol.gov.uk 📞 0117 353 2268 24 C1

Willsbridge Valley Nature Reserve *Long Beach Road, Bristol* A 22-acre reserve in the peaceful valley of the Siston Brook on the edge of the city. Nature activities, sculpture trail, a wide array of wildlife and walking trails. The Willsbridge Mill – a restored 19th-century corn mill and barn – houses the visitor centre (open during term time). Wildlife events are open to the public throughout the year, and there are weekend festivals. 📞 0117 932 6885 🖳 www.avonwildlifetrust.org.uk 69 A2

Leigh Woods *off the A369 Bristol to Portishead Road* An ancient broadleaved woodland with views of the Avon Gorge, rare trees, woodland sculptures, trails, Stoneleigh Camp and a replica timber-framed barn. 🖳 www.forestry.gov.uk 🖳 www.nationaltrust.org.uk 54 A4

Other Activities

Arnolfini *Narrow Quay, Bristol* This contemporary arts centre has exhibitions,

▲ *Avon Gorge and Clifton Suspension Bridge*

film, live art, dance, music and literature. 📞 0117 017 2300 🖳 www.arnolfini.org.uk 87 A1

Ashton Gate Stadium *Ashton Road, Bedminster, Bristol* Home of Bristol City Football Club 📞 0117 963 0600 🖳 www.bcfc.co.uk 62 B3

At-Bristol *Anchor Road, Harbourside, Bristol* A hands-on science centre with interactive exhibits and special exhibitions, experiments and activities, as well as a planetarium. 📞 0845 345 1235 🖳 www.at-bristol.org.uk 85 C2

Avon Valley Country Park *Pixash Lane, Bath Road, Keynsham, Bristol* Also known as Avon Valley Adventure and Wildlife Park, with children's play areas, birds, boating, fishing, assault course, miniature railway, quad bikes, riverside trail, pets corner and farm and other animals. 🖳 www.avonvalleycountrypark.co.uk 📞 0117 986 4929 77 C2

Avon Valley Railway *Bitton Station, Bath Road, Bitton, Bristol* Steam train rides and children's days out. 📞 0117 932 5538 🖳 www.avonvalleyrailway.org 69 A1

Bristol Hippodrome *St Augustines Parade, Bristol* Bristol's major venue for stage shows and musicals. 📞 0117 302 3333 🖳 www.bristolhippodrome.org.uk 85 C2

Bristol Harbour Railway *Prince's Wharf, Wapping Road* Small railway running along the harbour to the SS Great Britain during summer weekends. (Telephone to check times). 📞 0117 9251470 🖳 www.bristol.gov.uk 85 C1

Bristol Zoo Gardens *Guthrie Road, Clifton, Bristol* Set in a 12-acre site, with a wide variety of animals including monkeys, lemurs, gorillas, penguins, bugs, seals, tortoises, mammals and reptiles in beautiful grounds. 📞 0117 973 8951 🖳 www.bristolzoo.org.uk 54 B4

Broadmead Shopping Centre *Broadmead, Bristol* More than 300 shops. Parts of the medieval St John's Priory are included within the site. 📞 0117 925 7053 🖳 www.bristolbroadmead.co.uk 86 B3

Colston Hall *13 Colston Street, Bristol* Venue for classical, folk, rock and pop concerts. 🖳 www.colstonhall.org 📞 0117 922 3682 86 A3

Gloucestershire County Cricket Club *The County Ground, Nevil Road, Bristol* 📞 0117 9108000 🖳 www.gloscricket.co.uk 49 A4

The Mall Galleries *25 Union Gallery, Broadmead, Bristol* More than 80 shops. 📞 0117 929 0569 🖳 www.themall.co.uk/my-mall/bristol/index.aspx 86 B3

St George's *Great George Street, Bristol* One of Bristol's premier concert venues. 🖳 www.stgeorgesbristol.co.uk 📞 0117 929 4929 85 C2

The Mall *Merlin Road, Cribbs Causeway, Bristol* More than 130 stores, 17 restaurants and cafes and other facilities. 🖳 www.mallcribbs.com 📞 0117 903 0303 14 B2

The Memorial Stadium *Filton Avenue, Horfield, Bristol* Home of Bristol Rovers Football Club and Bristol Rugby 🖳 www.bristolrovers.premiumtv.co.uk 38 B2 📞 0117 977 2000

Spike Island Artspace *133 Cumberland Road, Bristol* National centre for the production and exhibition of contemporary visual art, in the Cumberland Basin. Studios, exhibition space. 📞 0117 929 2266 🖳 www.spikeisland.org.uk 85 B1

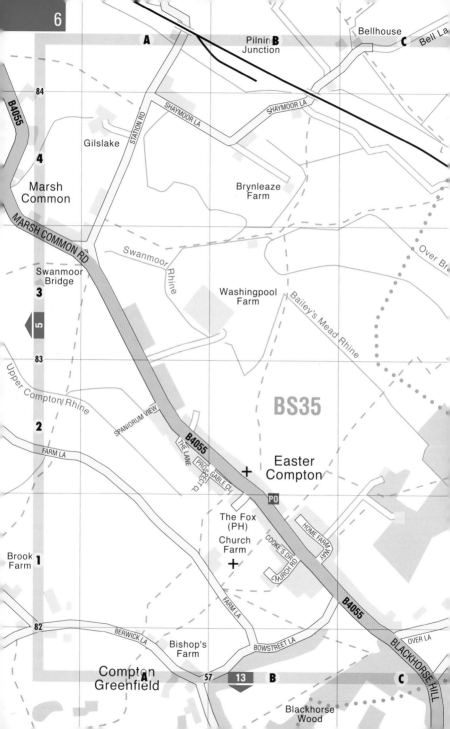

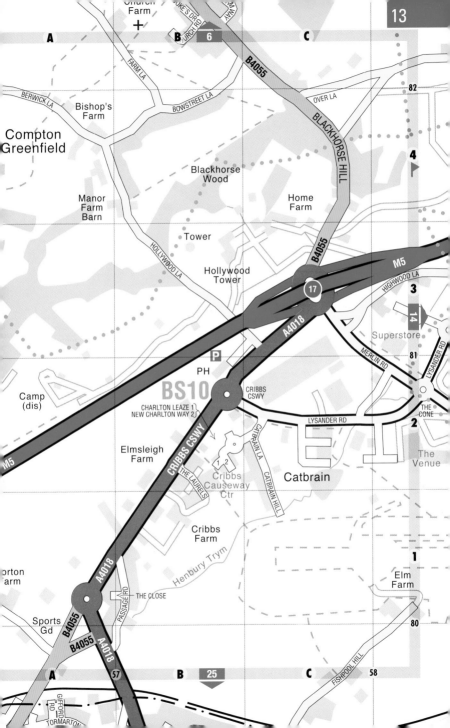

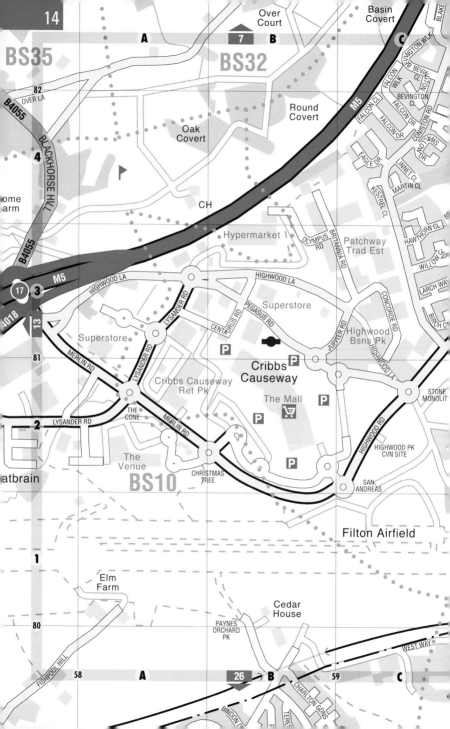

BS35

BS32

BS10

A · 7 · B · C

Over Court

Basin Covert

BLAKE

LEVINGTON WLK

BEVINGTON WLK

BEVINGTON CL

FALCON CL

BEVINGTON CL

SWALLOW CL

CONISTON RD

BEVINGTON CL

82

OVER LA

B4055

FALCON CL

FALCON DR

FALCON DR

Round Covert

M5

Oak Covert

4

BLACKHORSE HVLT

ome arm

B4055

EAGLE DR

LINNET CL

MARTIN CL

KESTREL CL

HAWTHORN CL

WILLOW CL

LARCH WAY

BIRCH C

CH

Hypermarket

OLYMPUS RD

BRITANNIA RD

Patchway Trad Est

M5

HIGHWOOD LA

HIGHWOOD LA

17

3

A4018

M5

13

HIGHWOOD LA

LYSANDER RD

CENTAURUS RD

PEGASUS RD

Superstore

JUPITER RD

CONCORDE RD

Highwood Bsns Pk

HIGHWOOD LA

81

MERLIN RD

Superstore

LYSANDER RD

P

Cribbs Causeway

P

STONE MONOLIT

atbrain

2

LYSANDER RD

THE CONE

Cribbs Causeway Ret Pk

MERLIN RD

The Mall

🛒

P

HIGHWOOD RD

HIGHWOOD PK CVN SITE

The Venue

CHRISTMAS TREE

P

SAN ANDREAS

Filton Airfield

1

Elm Farm

Cedar House

80

PAYNES ORCHARD PK

WEST WAY

FISHPOOL HILL

58

A · 26 · B · 59 · C

CHARLTON GDNS

BINDON

TERE

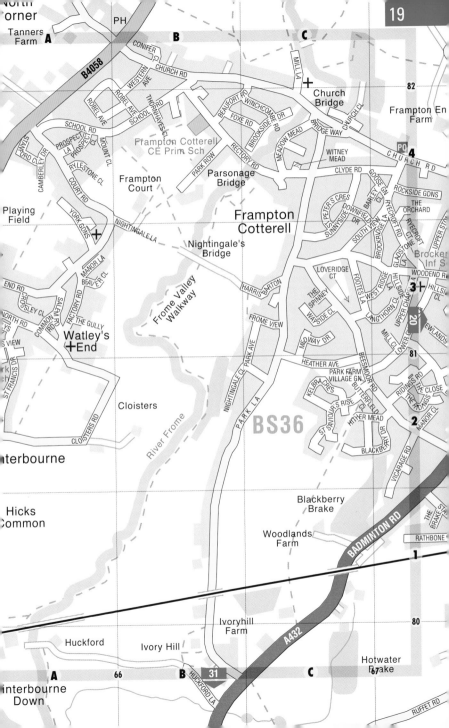

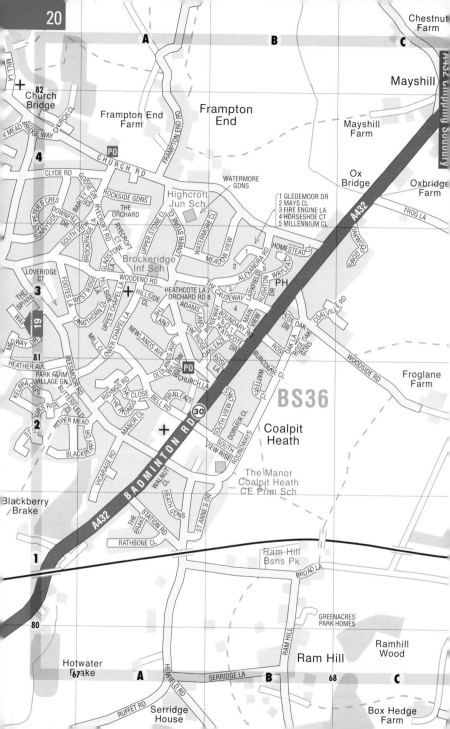

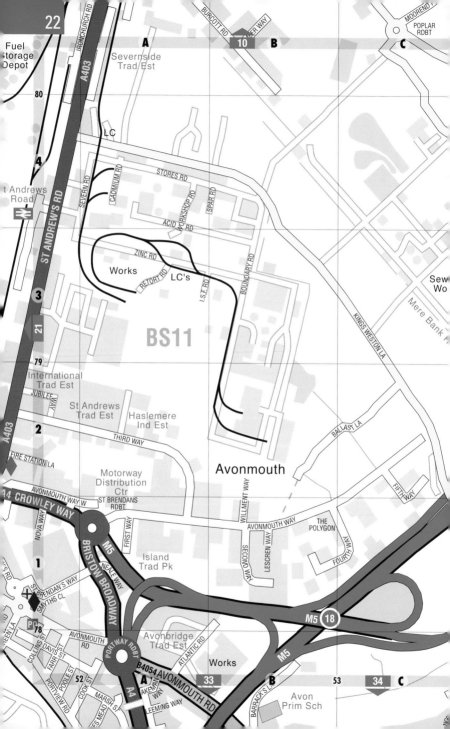

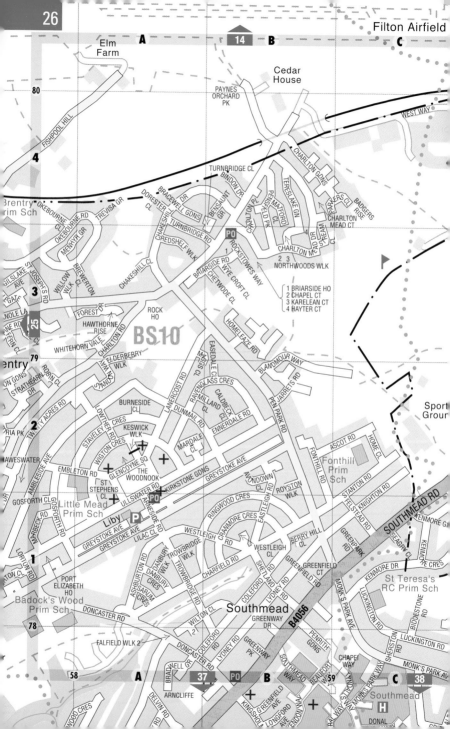

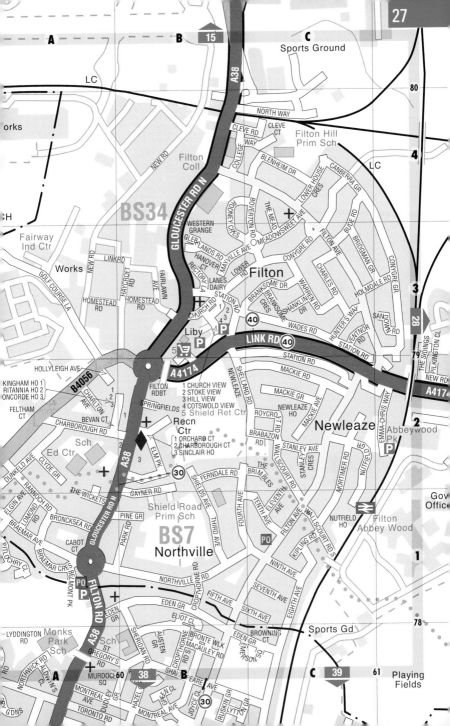

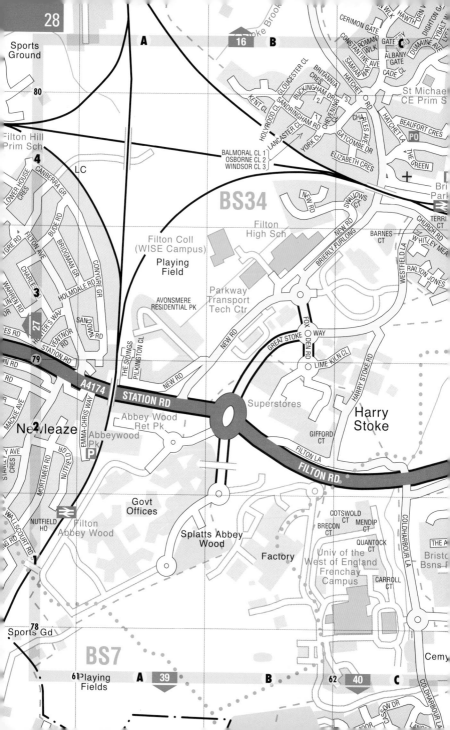

Sports
Ground

A

16 **B**

80

Filton Hill
Prim Sch

4

LC

CANBERRA GR

LOWER HOUSE
CRES

BUDE RD

FILTON AVE

BRIDGMAN GR

CONYGRE GR

HOLMDALE RD

CHARLES RD

WARREN RD

3

TIGRE RD

VENTNOR
RD

SAN...
...WN
RD

HUNTER'S WAY

STATION RD

27

79

N RD

ES RD

A4174 **STATION RD**

PILKINGTON CL

THE SIDINGS

NEW RD

Newleaze

2

MACKIE AVE

STANLEY AVE
CRES

MORTIMER RD

NUTFIELD

NUTFIELD
GR

EMMA-CHRIS WAY

WALSCOURT RD

RING RD

Abbey Wood
Ret Pk

Abbeywood
Pk **P**

79

NUTFIELD
HO

Filton
Abbey Wood

Govt
Offices

Splatts Abbey
Wood

Factory

Sports Gd **78**

BS7

A **39**

Playing
Fields

61

CERIMON GATE

ROMAN
WLK

HAWTH

DIGHTON G...

TYBALT W...

CONSTANTINE AVE

GATE

C

ALBANY
GATE

DUMAINE CL

CADE CL.

SAMIAN WAY

HATCHE...

St Michael
CE Prim S

GLOUCESTER CL

BRITANNIA
CRES

BUCKINGHAM DR

KENT CL

SANDRINGHAM RD

CHEVENING
CL

CHARLES AVE

BEAUFORT CRES

HATCHE...

HOLYROOD CL

LANCASTER CL

YORK CL

GATCOMBE DR

ELIZABETH CRES

THE GREEN

PO

BALMORAL CL **1**
OSBORNE CL **2**
WINDSOR CL **3**

BS34

NEW RD

SWALLOWS
CT

Bri
Park

Filton
High Sch

BARNES
CT

NEW RD

BRIERLY FURLONG

WESTFIELD LA

CHURCH RD

TERRI
CT

WHITLEY MEA

RALTON JONES

Filton Coll
(WISE Campus)

Playing
Field

AVONSMERE
RESIDENTIAL PK

Parkway
Transport
Tech Ctr

FOX
DEN RD

GREAT STOKE

WAY

LIME KILN CL

HARRY STOKE RD

Superstores

Harry
Stoke

GIFFORD
CT

FILTON RD

FILTON LA

COTSWOLD
CT

BRECON
CT

MENDIP
CT

COLDHARBOUR LA

THE A...

Bristo
Bsns...

QUANTOCK
CT

Univ of the
West of England
Frenchay
Campus

CARROLL
CT

Cemy

62 **40** **C**

...SON DR

COLDHARBOUR...

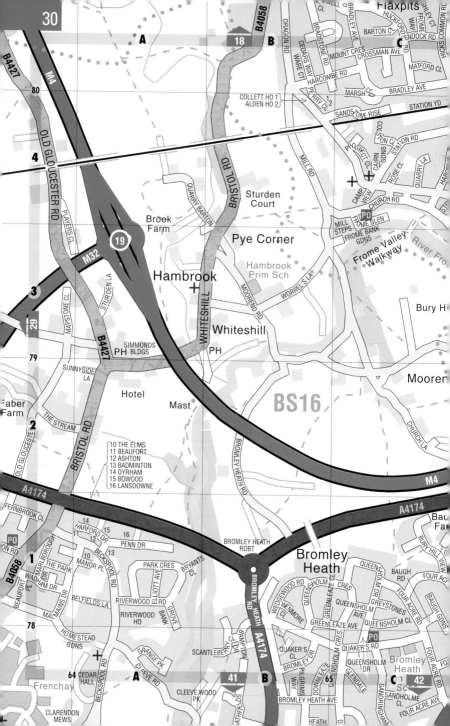

32

SEA BANK RD

RIVER RD

River Avon

River Quay

Nelson Point

Avonmouth Dock

Mill

The Royal Portbury Dock

Gordano Quay

St George's Quay

ST GEORGE'S RD

SHEEPHOUSE CVN PK

Marsh Lane Ind Est

NORMANS WAY

BS20

MARSH LA

REDLAND AVE

Wr Twr

THE DROVE

FIRST AVE

ROYAL PORTBURY DOCK RD

GARONOR WAY

GORDANO WAY

PORTBURY WAY

BANYARD RD

BRADLEY RD

ROYAL PORTBURY DOCK RD

Drove Rhyne

Court House Farm

MARSH LA

BEECHWOO

NAPIER SQ

QUEEN ST

CLAYTON ST

GLO

Ave

A **B** 21 **C** P

78

4

3

77

2

1

76

50 **A** 44 **B** 51 **C**

A369 M5

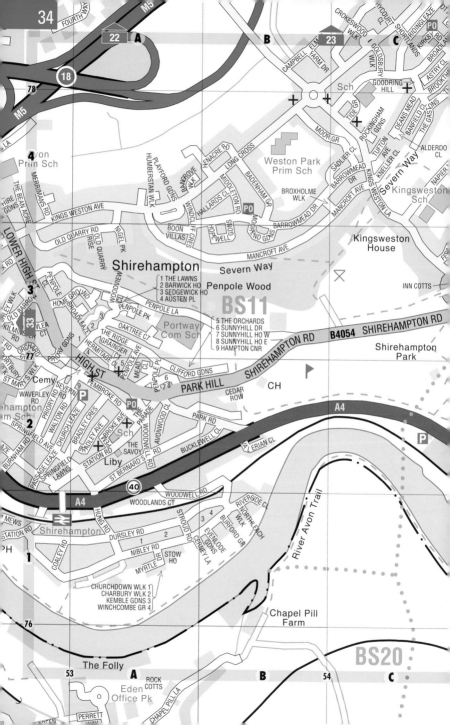

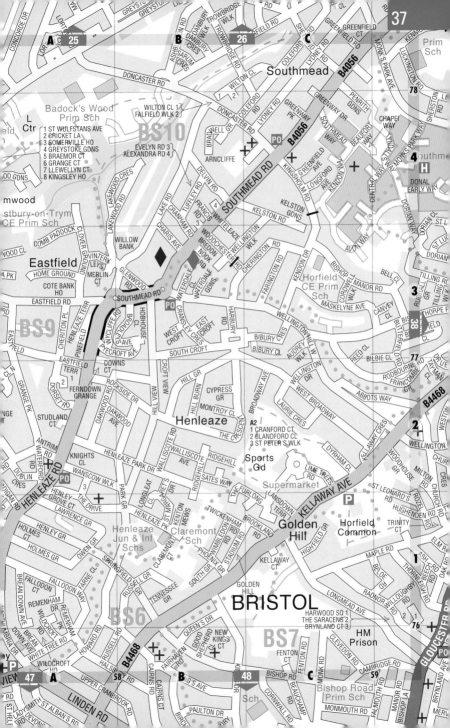

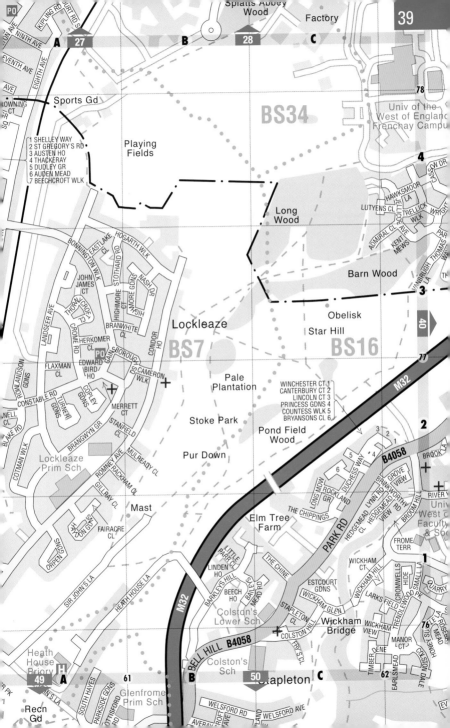

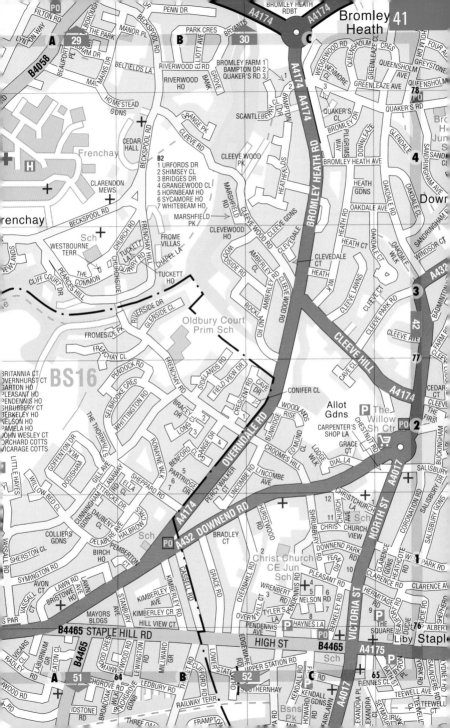

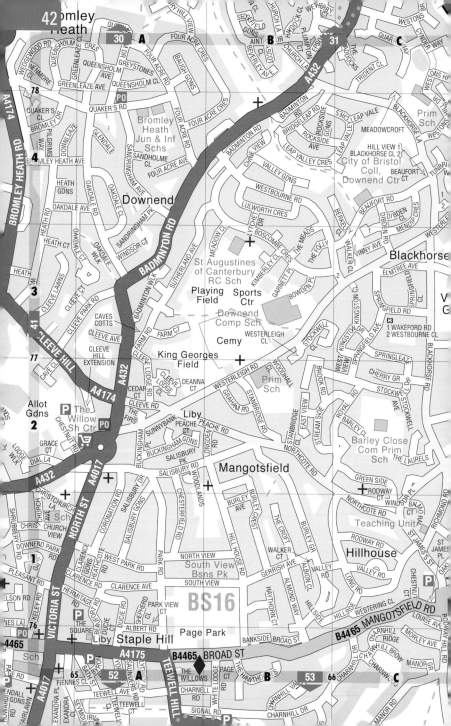

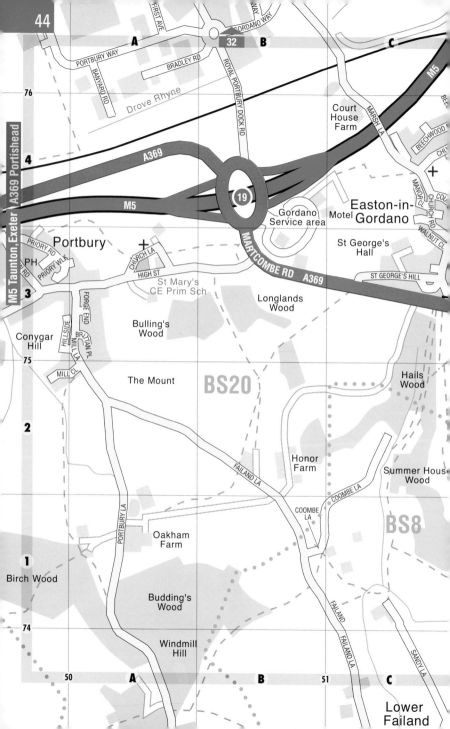

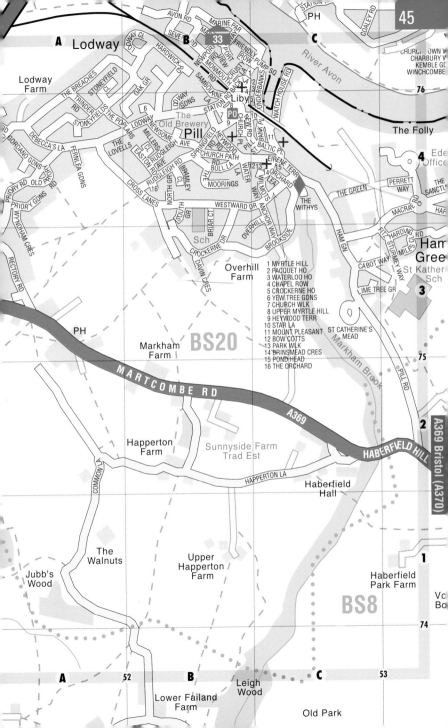

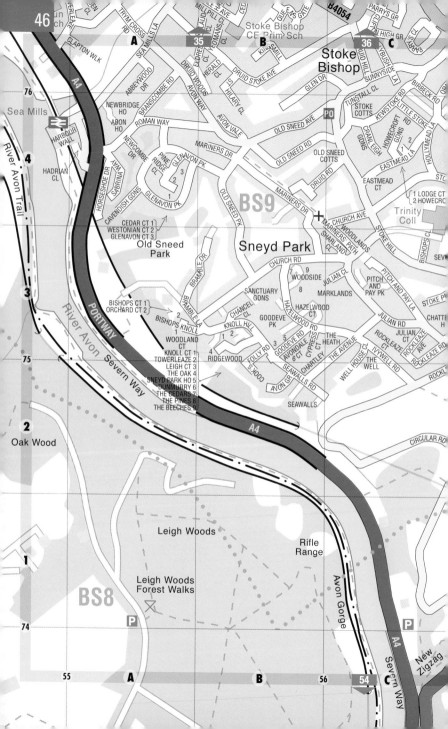

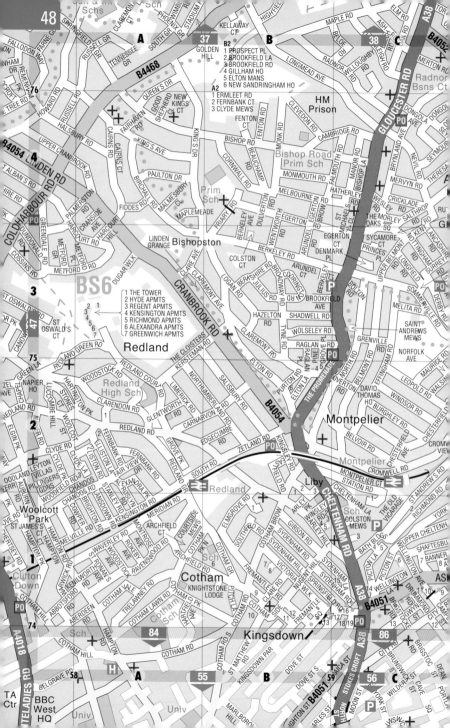

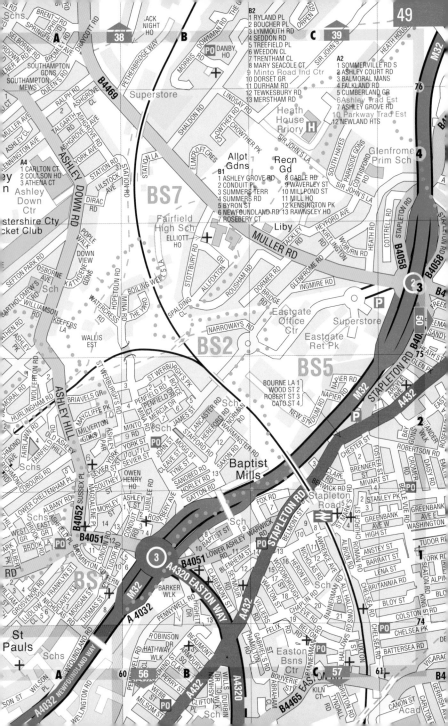

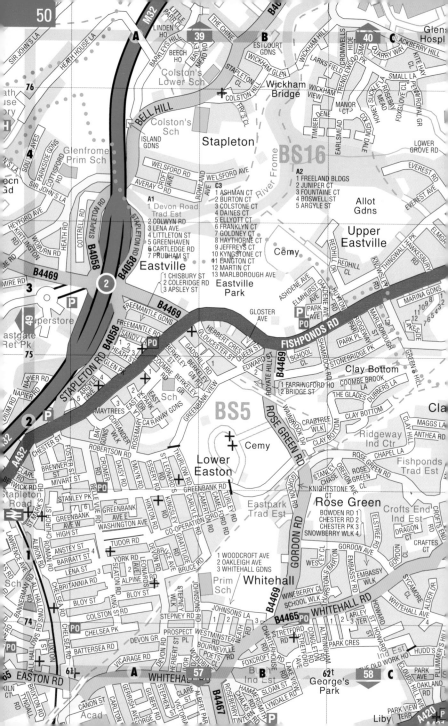

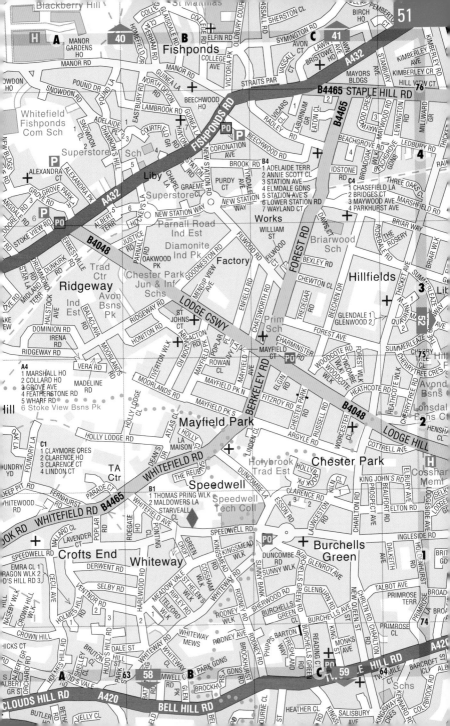

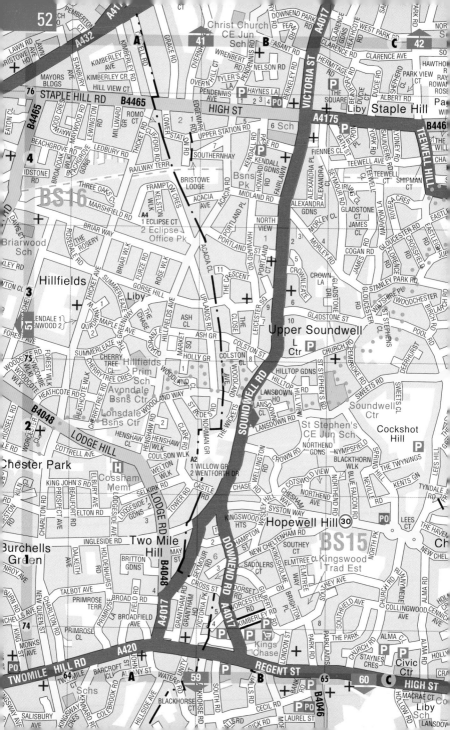

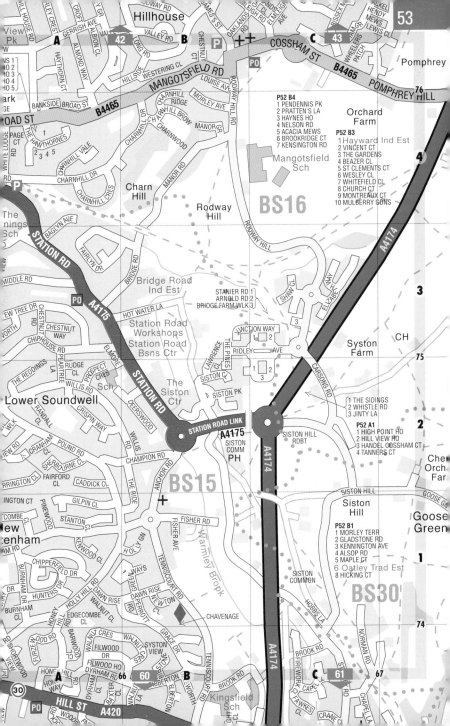

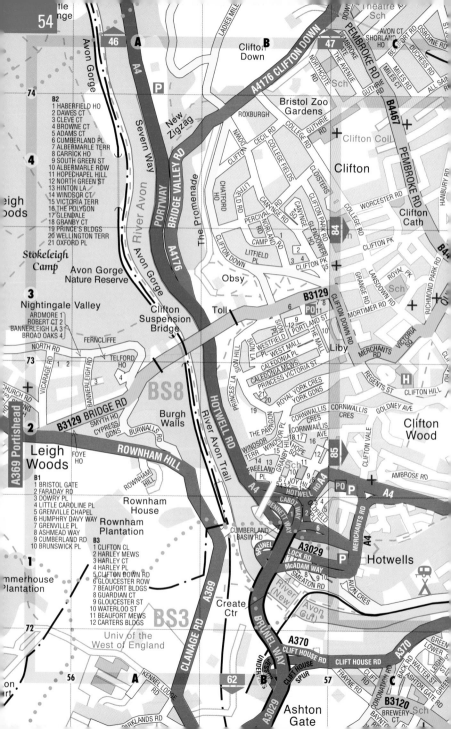

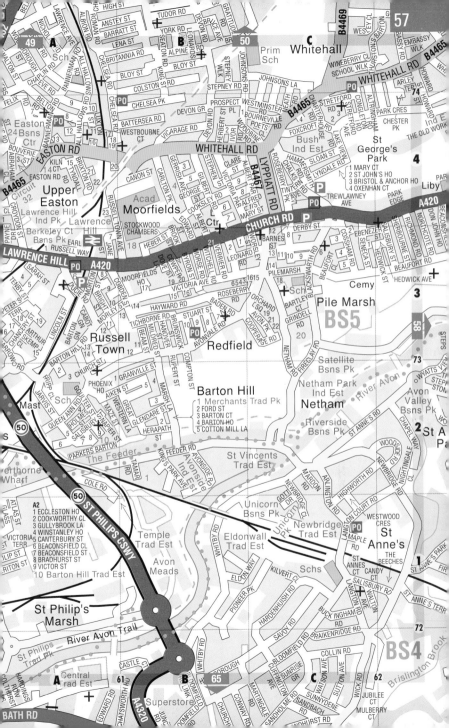

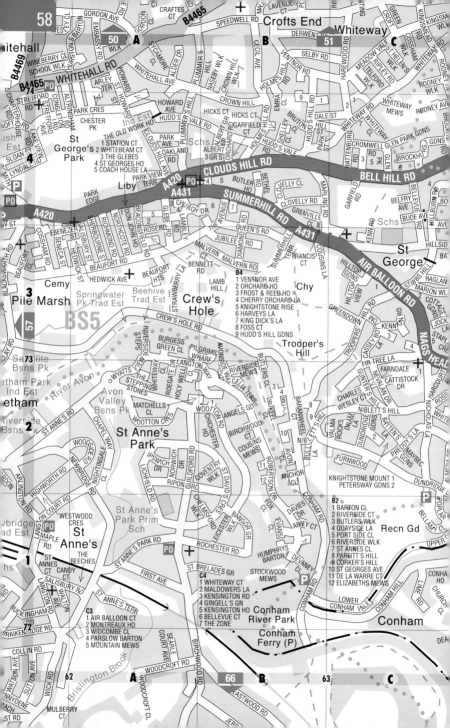

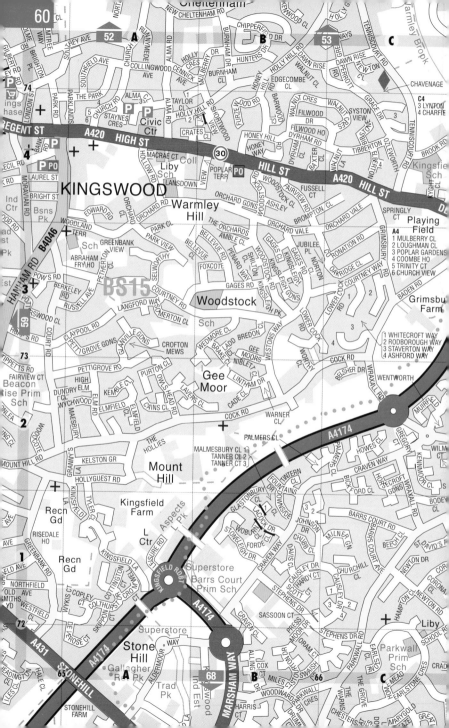

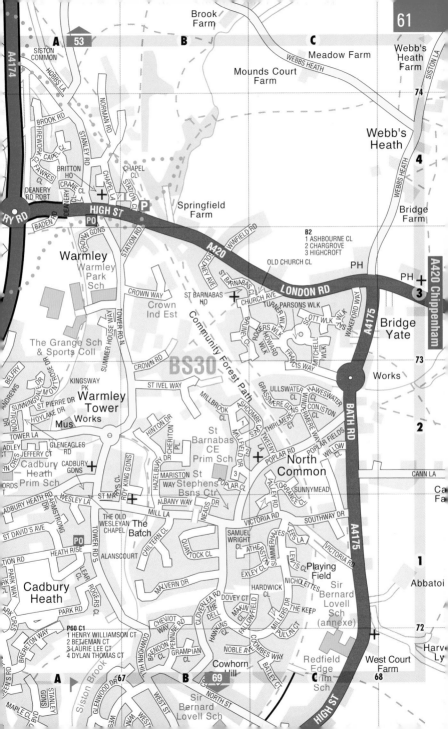

Brook Farm

A **B** **C**

SISTON
COMMON

Meadow Farm

Webb's
Heath
Farm

Mounds Court
Farm

A4174

74

HOBBS LA

NORMAN RD

Webb's
Heath

BROOK RD

FIREWORK CL

CAP CL

STANLEY RD

CANE CL

FAWKES
CL

BRITTON
HO

CRANE CL

CHAPEL
CL

CHAPEL LA

STATION CL

WEBBS HEATH

4

DEANERY
RD RDBT

RY RD

BADEN

DEANERY

HIGH ST

P

PO

Springfield
Farm

Bridge
Farm

CROWN GDNS

Warmley

Warmley
Park
Sch

STATION RD

BOLTNEY AVE

WINFIELD RD

A420

ST BARNABAS CL

OLD CHURCH CL

B2
1 ASHBOURNE CL
2 CHARGROVE
3 HIGHCROFT

PH

PH

A420 Chippenham

3

CROWN WAY

ST BARNABAS
HO

LONDON RD

CHURCH AVE

TURNER WLK

PARSONS WLK

OTT WLK

WLK

WAKEFORD WAY

Bridge
Yate

Crown
Ind Est

Community Forest Path

BRUNEL CL

ROGERS WLK

HOWARD
WLK

MITCHELL WLK

WLK

A4175

73

The Grange Sch
& Sports Coll

SUMMER HOUSE WAY

TOWER RD N

CROWN RD

FRANCIS WAY

Works

BS30

2

BELFRY

MONTROSE DR

KINGSWAY
PK

ST IVEL WAY

MILLBROOK CL

SPICOMBE GDNS

ULLSWATER

GRASSMERE GDNS

RAWESWATER

WINDERMERE WAY

CONISTON

ANDREWS

SUNNINGDALE

ST PIERRE DR

**Warmley
Tower
Works**

Mus

HOYLAKE DR

HINTON DR

CHERITON
DR

1

THIRLMERE

TWEEN WAY

POPLAR FIELDS

WILLOW CL

TOWER LA

GLENEAGLES
RD

HAZELBURY DR

St
Barnabas
CE
Prim Sch

MILLFIELD DR

POPLAR RD

**North
Common**

ADLEY

JEFFERY CT

Cadbury
Heath
Prim Sch

CADBURY
GDNS

ROY KING GDNS

MARISTON
WAY

St
Stephens
Bsns Ctr

POPLAR CL

ORANGE CL

ALLEY RD

SUNNYMEAD

CANN LA

Ca
Fa

CRES

ORDS

ADBURY HEATH RD

ARMSTRONG

WESLEY LA

ST MARYS CL

ALBANY WAY

NEADS RD

VICTORIA RD

ES LA

SOUTHWAY DR

A4175

ST DAVID'S AVE

MILL LA

THE OLD
WESLEYAN
CHAPEL

The
Batch

CHILTERN CL

SAMUEL
WRIGHT
CL

ATHE

SISTON CL

SUMMERHAYES

LEWIS CL

VICTORIA RD

TION RD

HEATH RISE

ALANSCOURT

QUANTOCK CL

EXLEY CL

Playing
Field

Sir
Bernard
Lovell Sch
(annexe)

Abbatoi

PARK CRES

Cadbury
Heath

TOWER RD S

EARL CL

MALVERN DR

NICHOLETTES

HARDWICK
CL

MILLERS DR

THE KEEP

ARK CRES

ROGERS CL

PARK RD

CHEVIOT
WAY

CLOVERLEA RD

DOVEY CT

THE DELL

MAKIN CL

FALLOWFIELD

HARV
LY

72

BRERETON WAY

P60 C1
1 HENRY WILLIAMSON CT
2 BETJEMAN CT
3 LAURIE LEE CT
4 DYLAN THOMAS CT

CHIPPENHAM RD

BRENDON
CL

GRAMPIAN
CL

HAWKINS
CL

NOBLE AV

COOMBES WAY

PULLIN CT

BATLEY CT

Redfield
Edge
Prim
Sch

West Court
Farm

A **B** **C**

67

GLENWOOD RD

Siston Brook

NORTH ST

WEST ST

WEST ST

Cowhorn
Hill

69

Sir
Bernard
Lovell Sch

HIGH ST

68

STANLEY
GDNS

MAPLE CL

BLVD

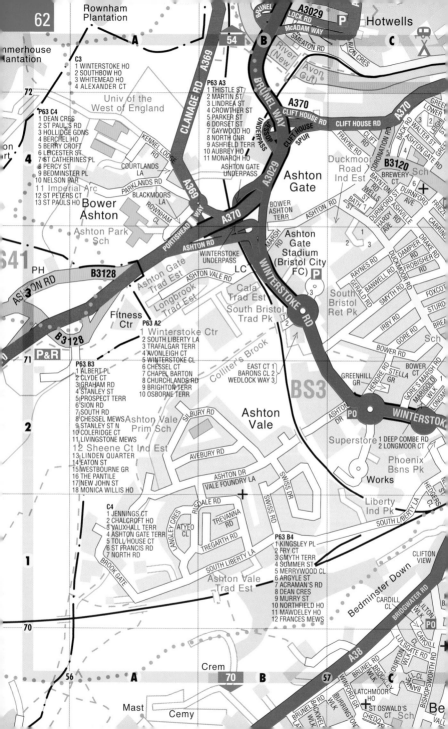

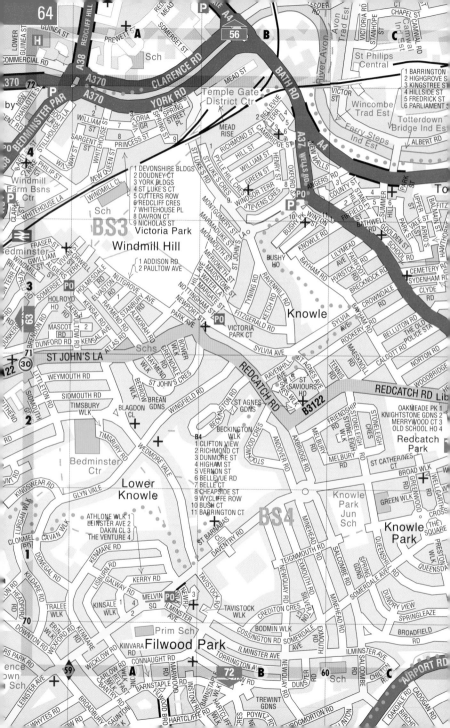

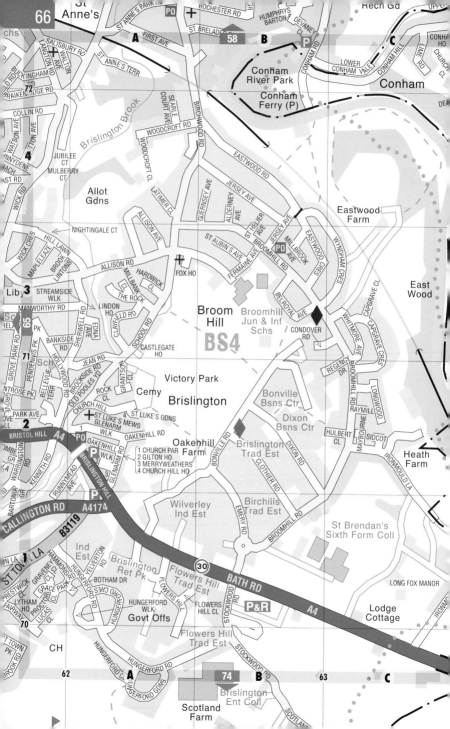

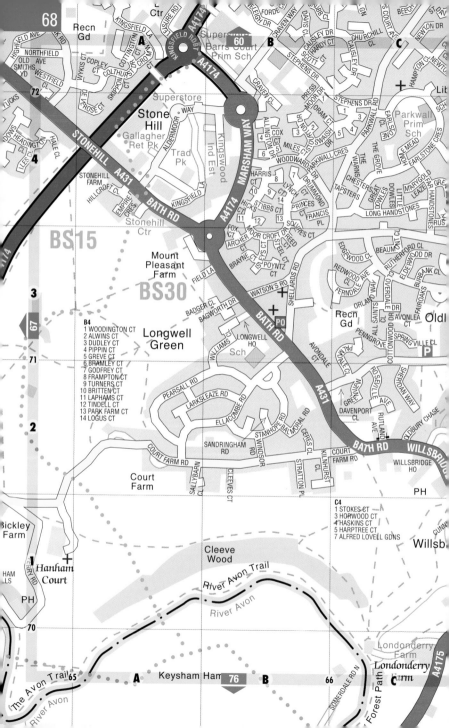

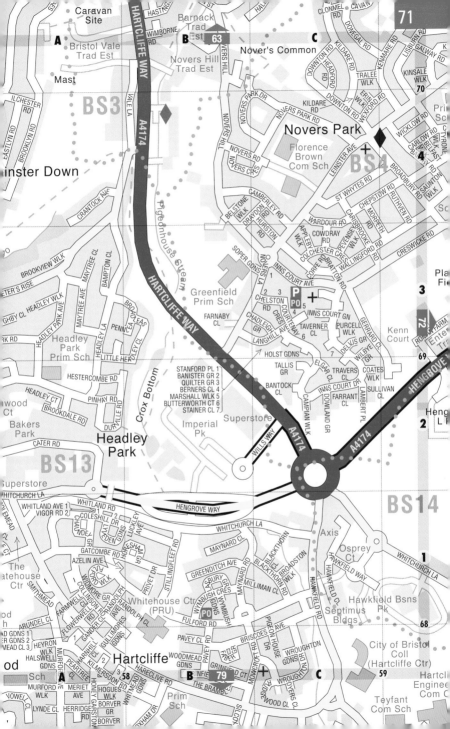

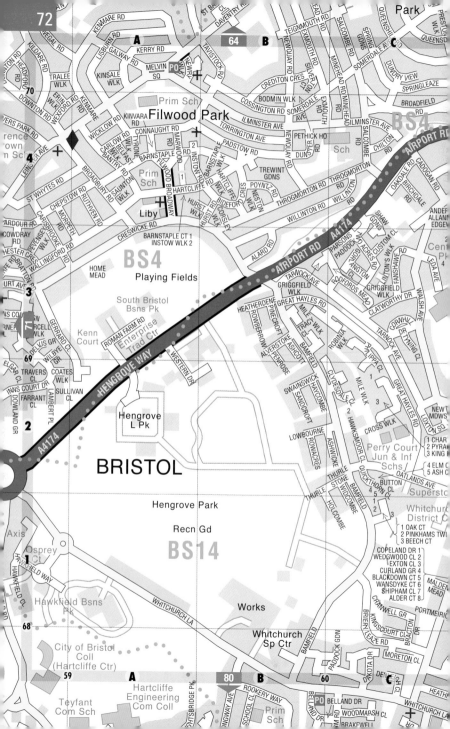

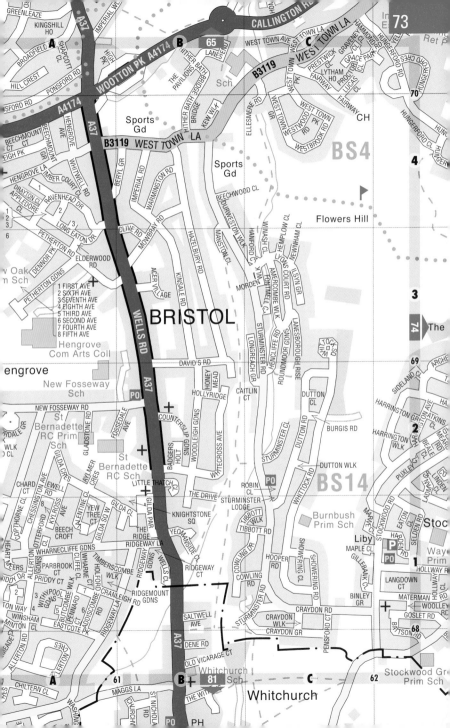

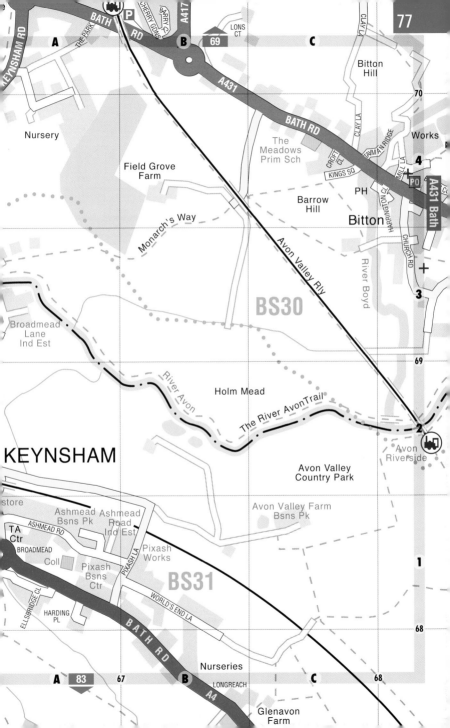

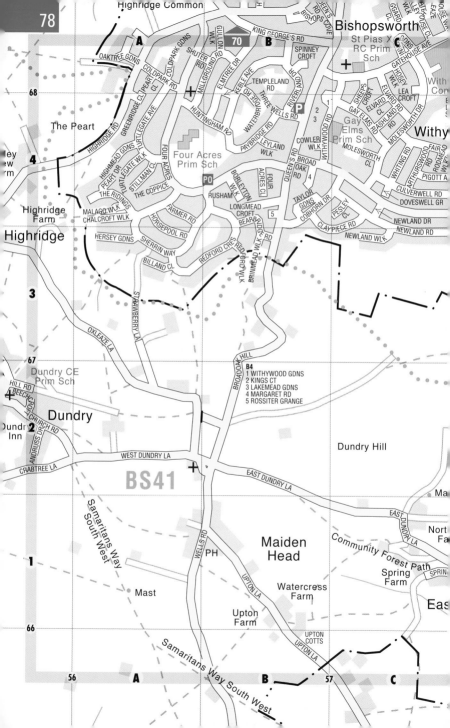

Highridge Common

Bishopsworth

St Pias X RC Prim Sch

King George's Rd

70

A

B

C

Oaktree Gdns

Coldpark Gdns

Shuter Rd

Coldpark Rd

Coldpark Cl

Peart Cl

Millground Rd

Elmtree Dr

Gullon Wlk

Keble Ave

Spinney Croft

Gatehouse Ave

Hosey Wlk

Lea Croft

Elvard Rd

With Com

With

Templeland Rd

Three Wells Rd

Waterborough Rd

Sheeps Croft

Elvard Cl

Ashland Rd

Molesworth Dr

Greenridge Cl

Highridge Rd

Highmead Gdns

Peart Dr

Turtlegate Ave

Turtlegate Wlk

Four Acres

Stillman Cl

Huntingham Rd

Paybridge Rd

Leyland Wlk

Queen's Rd

Withywood Rd

Gay Elms Rd

Cowler Wlk

Broad

Molesworth Cl

Ashland Rd

Fairo

Whiting Rd

Arthurshood Rd

Rodmea

Pigott A

68

The Peart

Four Acres Prim Sch

Culverwell Rd

Doveswell Gr

Withy

4

The Ridings

The Coppice

Farmer Rd

Rusham

Bobleyton Wlk

Four Acres Cl

Oak Rd

Taylor Gdns

Cobhorn Dr

Pesley Cl

Highridge Farm

Malago Wlk

Chalcroft Wlk

Longmead Croft

Bearb

Clay Piece Rd

Newland Dr

Newland Wlk

Newland Rd

Highridge

Hersey Gdns

Sherrin Way

Horsepool Rd

Billand Cl

Redford Cres

Redford Wlk

Brinmead Wlk

Bridge Rd

3

Oxleaze La

Strawberry La

Broadoak Hill

67

Dundry CE Prim Sch

Hill Rd

Beechcroft

Church Rd

Dundry

Andruss Dr

2

Dundry Inn

Crabtree La

West Dundry La

East Dundry La

Dundry Hill

East Dundry La

Nort Fa

Ma

BS41

Maiden Head

Community Forest Path

Spring Farm

SPRIN

1

Samaritans Way South West

Wells Rd

PH

Watercress Farm

Eas

Mast

Upton La

Upton Farm

66

Samaritans Way South West

Upton Cotts

Upton La

56

A

B

57

C

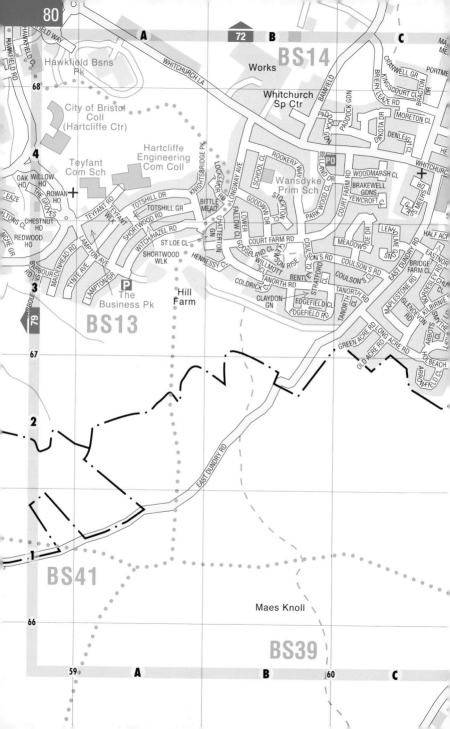

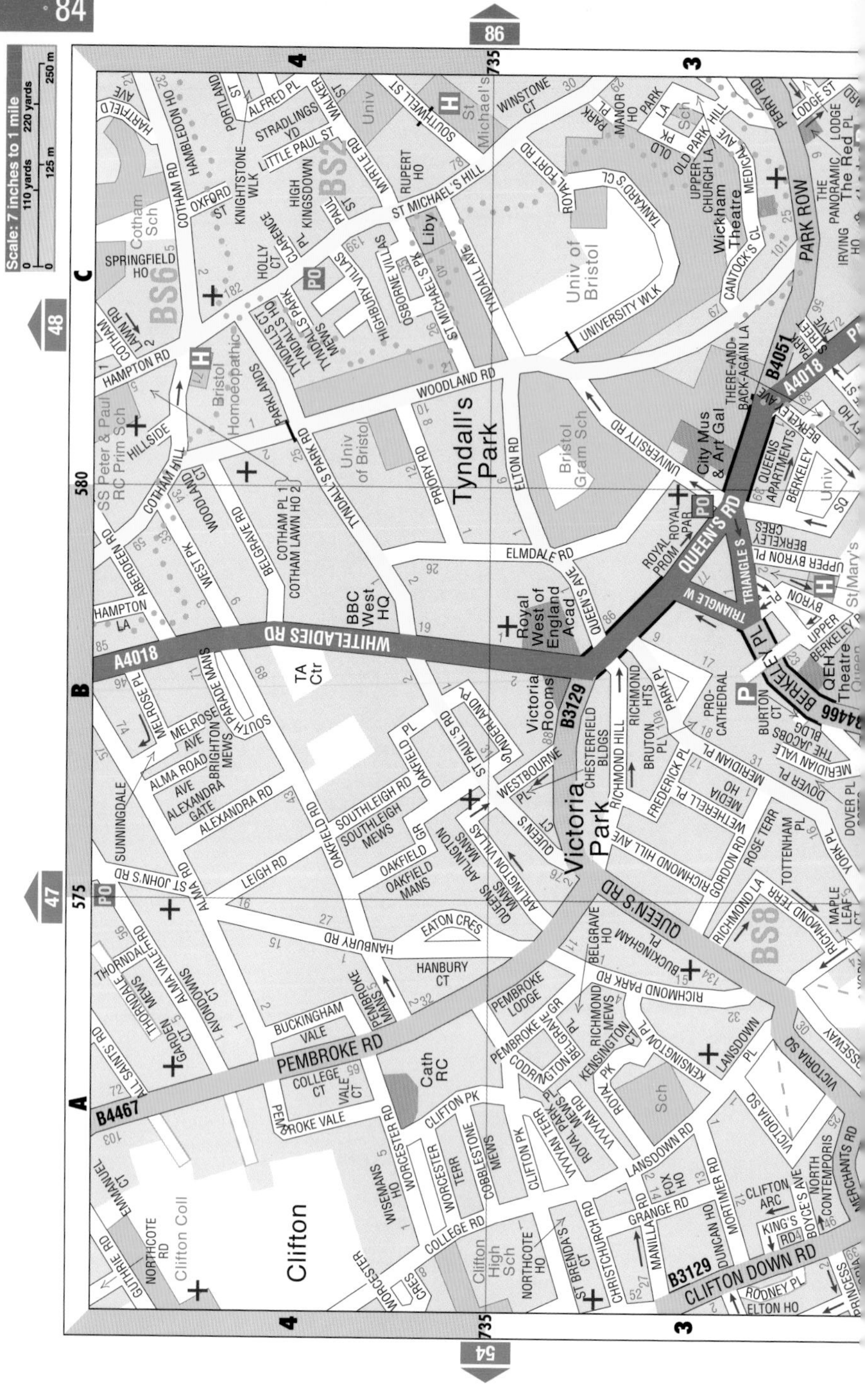
Scale: 7 inches to 1 mile
110 yards
220 yards
125 m
250 m
86
48
47
54
580
575
735
A
B
C
3
4
Tyndall's Park
Victoria Park
Clifton
Clifton Coll
Univ of Bristol
Bristol Gram Sch
City Mus & Art Gal
Wickham Theatre
Royal West of England Acad
Victoria Rooms
BBC West HQ
TA Ctr
Bristol Homoeopathic
SS Peter & Paul RC Prim Sch
Cotham Sch
Cath RC
Clifton High Sch
QEH Theatre
St Michael's
PRO-CATHEDRAL
Liby
Univ
Sch
BS2
BS6
BS8
A4018
B4051
B3129
B4467
B4466
WHITELADIES RD
QUEEN'S RD
PEMBROKE RD
CLIFTON DOWN RD
PARK ROW
WOODLAND RD
UNIVERSITY RD
UNIVERSITY WLK
TYNDALL'S PARK RD
ST MICHAEL'S HILL
COTHAM HILL
HAMPTON RD
ELMDALE RD
ELTON RD
PRIORY RD
BELGRAVE RD
WEST PK
HANBURY RD
LEIGH RD
OAKFIELD RD
ALEXANDRA RD
ALMA RD
ST JOHN'S RD
RICHMOND PARK RD
LANSDOWN RD
VICTORIA SQ
MERCHANTS RD
WESTBOURNE PL
RICHMOND HILL
TRIANGLE S
TRIANGLE W
UPPER BYRON PL
BERKELEY SQ
PERRY RD
LODGE ST
ALFRED PL
PORTLAND ST
STRADLINGS YD
LITTLE PAUL ST
HIGH KINGSDOWN
KNIGHTSTONE WLK
OXFORD ST
HAMBLEDON HO
COTHAM RD
SPRINGFIELD HO
COTHAM LAWN RD
HILLSIDE
WOODLAND CT
ABERDEEN RD
HAMPTON LA
MELROSE PL
MELROSE AVE
SOUTH PARADE MANS
BRIGHTON MEWS
ALMA ROAD AVE
ALEXANDRA GATE
SUNNINGDALE
THORNDALE
THORNDALE MEWS
ALMA VALE RD
AVONDOWN CT
GARDEN CT
ALL SAINTS' RD
BUCKINGHAM VALE
COLLEGE CT
VALE CT
PEMBROKE VALE
WORCESTER RD
WORCESTER TERR
COBBLESTONE MEWS
CLIFTON PK
VYVYAN TERR
VYVYAN RD
ROYAL PARK
CODRINGTON PL
KENSINGTON PL
BUCKINGHAM PL
BELGRAVE HO
HANBURY CT
EATON CRES
PEMBROKE LODGE
OAKFIELD GR
OAKFIELD MANS
ARLINGTON VILLAS
SOUTHLEIGH RD
SOUTHLEIGH MEWS
ST PAUL'S RD
CHESTERFIELD BLDGS
BRUTON PL
FREDERICK PL
MERIDIAN PL
WETHERELL PL
RICHMOND HILL AVE
GORDON RD
ROSE TERR
TOTTENHAM PL
RICHMOND TERR
RICHMOND LA
YORK PL
DOVER PL
CANTOCK'S CL
TANKARD'S CL
ROYAL FORT RD
WINSTONE CT
SOUTHWELL ST
MYRTLE RD
RUPERT HO
HIGHBURY VILLAS
OSBORNE VILLAS
TYNDALL'S PARK MEWS
PARKLANDS
COTHAM PL
COTHAM LAWN HO
GRANGE RD
CHRISTCHURCH RD
MORTIMER RD
DUNCAN HO
NORTHCOTE RD
NORTHCOTE HO
GUTHRIE RD
EMMANUEL CT
COLLEGE RD
WISEMANS HO
CLIFTON ARC
BOYCE'S AVE
KING'S RD
RODNEY PL
ELTON HO
PRINCESS
BURTON CT
THE JACOBS BLDG
MEDIA HO
THE PANORAMIC
LODGE
The Red
IRVING HO

87
725
62
63
54
575
580

2
1

One-way streets

House numbers
HIGH ST   59

COLLEGE GN
A4018
MARK LA
CHANTRY ST
DENMARK ST
ORCHARD ST
TRINITY ST
FROG LA
The Bristol Hippodrome
CANONS RD
Anchor Sq
Millennium Sq
Cath CE Sch
At-Bristol
i Sq
Mus

The Council House
1 DENMARK AVE
2 ORCHARD AVE
3 HOBB'S LA
4 ORCHARD LA
5 GAUNT'S LA
6 PROTHEROES HO
EXPLORE LA
Liby

Canon's Marsh

MILLENNIUM PROM
WATERLEY HO
CATHEDRAL WLK
WAVERLEY
HARBOUR WAY
CANONS WAY
Bristol Rly Mus

THE QUAYS
PERRETTS CT
66
OSBORNE RD
WEST END
ALLINGTON RD
A370

DEAN'S CT
BIGWOOD LA
Mus
CHARLOTTE ST S
GEORGE ST
BRANDON STEEP
ST GEORGES RD
BRANDON COTTS
DENERY
LOWER COLLEGE ST
LAMB ST
LOWER PARK ST
ANCHOR RD
COLLEGE ST
ST DAVIDS MEWS
CHARTER HO
BALMORAL
BS1

1 PENNON RISE
2 LIBERTY GDNS
3 MERCHANTS ROW
4 LANDMARK CT
HARBOUR WLK

Brandon Hill

JACOB'S WELLS RD
ROSEBERY TERR
JOHN CARR'S TERR
GORSE LA
BELLEVUE
BELLEVUE CTS
BELLEVUE CRES
BELLEVUE CT
CONSTITUTION HILL
HILL VIEW
QUEENS PAR
JACOB'S RD
YORK PL
PARTITION ST
PETER'S CT
SOUTHERNHAY
SOUTHERNHAY AVE
HARBOURS EDGE
CAPRICORN PL
LIME KILN
GASFERRY RD
CANON'S RD
Coll
St George CE Prim Sch
St George's Ho
B4466
1 SOUTHERNHAY CRES
2 SOUTHERNHAY

Severn Way
Floating Harbour
River Avon Trail
Maritime Heritage Ctr
S.S. Gt Britain
Spike Island
Spike Island Artspace
HANOVER PL
SYDNEY ROW
133
WESTGATE
CALEDONIA PL
CUMBERLAND RD
CAMDEN RD
PARK RD
119
THE PARISH
612
37
36
37
BS3
CORONATION RD
BEAULEY RD
COOPERAGE LA
A370

Clifton Wood
A2
1 CHARLES CT
2 BEAR YARD MEWS
3 TRINITY PL
4 AMBRA VALE W
5 AMBRA VALE
6 ROYAL YORK MEWS
7 ROYAL YORK HO
CLIFTON HILL
GOLDNEY AVE
Chesterfield H
LOWER CLIFTON HILL
CLIFTONWOOD RD
CLIFTON WOOD CRES
CLIFTON WOOD
CLIFTONWOOD TERR
CLIFTON VIEW
CHURCH RD
RANDALL RD
ST EDWARD'S RD
CAPITAL EDGE
THE LEADING EDGE
HOTWELL RD
30
924
82

AMBRA VALE E
AMBRA TERR
AMBROSE RD
ROSEMONT TERR
CROSBY ROW
AMBRA CT
GOLDNEY RD
ELLENBOROUGH HO
ARGYLE PL
CLIFTONWOOD TERR
PEMBROKE
ROWNHAM MEAD

HOTWELL RD
184
HOTWELLS HO
POOLES WHARF CT
PEMBROKE PL
DOCK GATE LA
POOLES WHARF
9
7 MERCHANTS CT
8 ROWNHAM CT
9 OSBORNE WALLIS HO

PORTLAND
MARDYKE FERRY RD
HOPE CT
WESTBROOKE CT
WEARE CT
CUMBERLAND CL
CANADA WAY
NAPIER CT
GEFLE CL
MEREDITH CT
JOHN CABOT CT

ROYAL YORK VILLAS
YORK PL
ST S ST
HENSMAN'S HILL
CORNWALLIS CRES
CORNWALLIS GR
CORNWALLIS HO
ST VINCENT'S RD
POLYGON RD
DOWRY RD
DOWRY SQ
MILLSBOROUGH
HOTWELL RD
CLIFTON VALE
CLIFTON VALE CL
CAMDEN TERR
A4
725
Hotwells
MERCHANTS RD
A3029
CHARLES PL
SANDFORD RD
OLDFIELD RD
CUMBERLAND BASIN RD
BRUNEL LOCK RD
NOVA SCOTIA PL
AVON CRES
A4176
25

3 OLDFIELD PL
4 HUMPHRY DAVY WAY
5 CHRISTINA TERR
6 BRITANNIA BLDGS
1 McADAM WAY
2 ASHTON AVE

The River Avon (New Cut)
213

One-way streets

56

49

595

48

590

84

735

3

St Pauls

Kingsdown

Andalusia Acad

Cabot Prim Sch

The Old Malthouse

The Old School House

Bishop Terr

Broadmead Expansion due to open 2008

Due to open 2008

Quakers' Friars

Castle Park

Castle Weir

The Horsefair

Old King Street Ct

Wesley's New Room

The Arcade The Mall Galleries

Bristol Royal Hospital for Children

Bristol Royal Infirmary

Dental & Eye Hospital

The Guildhall

Univ

Broad Weir

Temple Way

Midland Mkt

Kingsland Trad Est

Amb HQ

Drill Hall

BS5

BS2

BS2

BS9

A4032

A420

A4044

A38

A4044

A38

B4051

B4051

NEWFOUNDLAND WAY

WELLINGTON RD

ST NICHOLAS RD

NEWFOUNDLAND ST

STOKES CROFT

ST JAMES' BARTON

THE HAYMARKET

MARLBOROUGH ST

UPPER MAUDLIN ST

PERRY RD

COLSTON ST

LEWINS MEAD

RUPERT ST

BOND ST

LOWER CASTLE ST

WEST ST

LAMB ST

PENN ST

NORTH ST

DIGHTON ST

JAMAICA ST

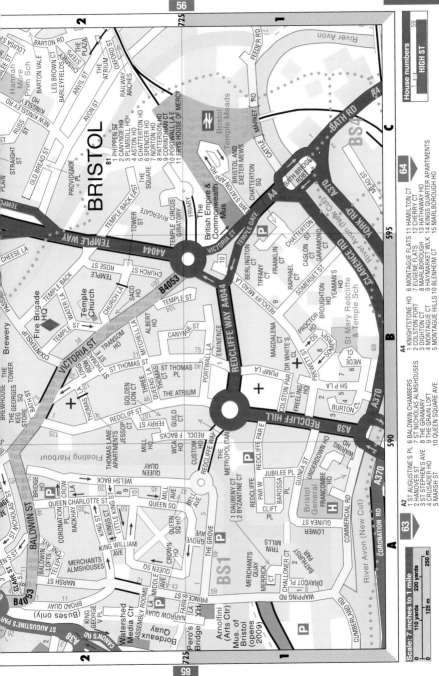

BRISTOL

B1
1 PHIPPEN ST
2 CANYNGE HO
3 PLIMSOLL HO
4 ASTON HO
5 CHATTERTON HO
6 SPENCER HO
7 NORTON HO
8 PATTERSON HO
9 CATTERSON HO
10 PORTWALL LA E
11 FRYS HOUSE OF MERCY

A4
1 KNIGHTSTONE HO
2 COLSTON FORT
3 DIGHTON CT
4 MONTAGUE CT
5 MONTAGUE HILLS
6 MONTAGUE FLATS
7 EUGENE FLATS
8 MARLBOROUGH
9 HAYMARKET WLK
10 BLENHEIM CT
11 HAMILTON CT
12 CHERRY CT
13 HATHAWAY HO
14 KINGS QUARTER APARTMENTS
15 MARLBOROUGH HO

A2
1 ST AUGUSTINE'S PL
2 HANOVER ST
3 ST STEPHEN'S AVE
4 CRUSADER HO
5 MARSH ST
6 BALDWIN CHAMBERS
7 ST NICHOLAS ALMSHOUSES
8 THE GRANARY
9 THE GRAIN LOFT
10 QUEEN SQUARE AVE

1 DAUBENY CT
2 BYZANTINE CT

House numbers
HIGH ST   59

64

63

Scale: 7 inches to 1 mile
0   110 yards   220 yards
0   125 m   250 m

Street names are listed alphabetically and show the locality, the Postcode district, the page number and a reference to the square in which the name falls on the map page

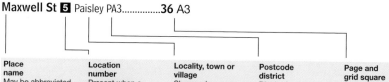

Place name	Location number	Locality, town or village	Postcode district	Page and grid square
May be abbreviated on the map	Present when a number indicates the place's position in a crowded area of mapping	Shown when more than one place has the same name	District for the indexed place	Page number and grid reference for the standard mapping

Towns and villages are listed in CAPITAL LETTERS
Public and commercial buildings are highlighted in magenta. **Places of interest** are highlighted in blue with a star ★

Abbreviations used in the index

Acad	Academy	Ct	Court	Hts	Heights	Pl	Place
App	Approach	Ctr	Centre	Ind	Industrial	Prec	Precinct
Arc	Arcade	Ctry	Country	Inst	Institute	Prom	Promenade
Ave	Avenue	Cty	County	Int	International	Rd	Road
Bglw	Bungalow	Dr	Drive	Intc	Interchange	Recn	Recreation
Bldg	Building	Dro	Drove	Junc	Junction	Ret	Retail
Bsns, Bus	Business	Ed	Education	L	Leisure	Sh	Shopping
Bvd	Boulevard	Emb	Embankment	La	Lane	Sq	Square
Cath	Cathedral	Est	Estate	Liby	Library	St	Street
Cir	Circus	Ex	Exhibition	Mdw	Meadow	Sta	Station
Cl	Close	Gd	Ground	Meml	Memorial	Terr	Terrace
Cnr	Corner	Gdn	Garden	Mkt	Market	TH	Town Hall
Coll	College	Gn	Green	Mus	Museum	Univ	University
Com	Community	Gr	Grove	Orch	Orchard	Wk, Wlk	Walk
Comm	Common	H	Hall	Pal	Palace	Wr	Water
Cott	Cottage	Ho	House	Par	Parade	Yd	Yard
Cres	Crescent	Hospl	Hospital	Pas	Passage		
Cswy	Causeway	HQ	Headquarters	Pk	Park		

Index of towns, villages, streets, hospitals, industrial estates, railway stations, schools, shopping centres, universities and places of interest

Abb–Ale

5102 Apartments
BS1 . . . .**86** B4

A

Abbey Cl BS31 . . . .**76** B2
Abbey Ct BS4 . . . .**58** B1
Abbeydale BS36 . . . . . .**18** C2
Abbey Pk BS31 . . . .**76** B2
Abbey Rd BS9 . . . .**36** B3
Abbeywood Dr BS9 . .**35** B1
Abbeywood Pk
BS34 . . . .**28** A2
Abbey Wood Ret Pk
BS34 . . . .**28** A2
Abbots Ave BS15 . . . .**67** B4
Abbots Cl BS14 . . . . . .**80** C3
Abbotsford Rd BS6 .**47** C1
Abbots Rd BS15 . . . . .**67** B2
Abbots Way BS9 . . . .**38** A2
Abbotswood BS15 . .**59** C3
Abbott Rd BS35 . . . . . .**2** B1
Aberdeen Rd BS6 . . .**84** B4

Abingdon Rd BS16 . . .**51** B3
Ableton Ct BS35 . . . . . .**2** B2
Ableton La
Hallen BS10 . . . .**11** B4
Severn Beach BS35 . . . .**2** B1
Ableton Wlk BS9 . . . .**35** B1
Abon Ho BS9 . . . . . .**46** A4
Abraham Cl BS5 . . . . .**57** A4
Abraham Fry Ho
BS15 . . . .**60** A3
Acacia Ave BS16 . . . .**52** B4
Acacia Cl BS16 . . . . . .**52** B3
Acacia Ct BS31 . . . . . .**82** A4
Acacia Mews **5**
BS16 . . . .**52** B4
Acacia Rd BS16 . . . . .**52** B4
Acer Village BS14 . . . .**73** B3
Acid Rd BS11 . . . .**22** A4
Acorn Gr BS13 . . . . . .**70** A2
Acraman's Rd **7**
BS3 . . . .**63** B4
Acresbush Cl BS13 . .**70** C1
Acton Rd BS16 . . . . . .**51** B3
Adams Cl **8** BS8 . . . .**54** B2
Adams Hay **6** BS4 . .**65** C1
Adams Land BS36 . .**20** A3

Adderly Gate BS16 . . .**43** A3
Addiscombe Rd
BS14 . . . .**73** A1
Addison Rd BS3 . . . .**64** A3
Adelaide Pl
Bristol, Fishponds
BS16 . . . .**51** A4
12 Bristol, Upper Easton
BS5 . . . .**57** A4
Adelaide Terr **1**
BS16 . . . .**51** B4
Adelante Cl BS34 . . .**29** B4
Admiral Cl BS16 . . . .**40** A3
Adryan Ct **6** BS5 . . .**57** B3
Agate St BS3 . . . .**63** A3
Aiken St BS5 . . . .**57** A2
Aintree Dr BS16 . . . . .**31** A1
Alard Rd BS4 . . . .**72** B3

Albany Gate BS34 . . . .**16** C1
Albany Rd BS6 . . . . . .**49** A1
Albany St BS15 . . . . .**59** B4
Albany Way BS30 . . . .**61** B1
Albermarle Row **10**
BS8 . . . .**54** B2
Albermarle Terr **7**
BS8 . . . .**54** B2
Albert Cres BS2 . . . . .**57** A1
Albert Gr BS5 . . . .**58** B4
Albert Gr S BS5 . . . . .**58** B4
Albert Ho BS1 . . . . . .**87** B2
Alberton Rd BS16 . . .**40** B2
Albert Par BS5 . . . . . .**57** C4
Albert Park Pl BS6 . .**49** A1
Albert Pk BS6 . . . .**49** A1
Albert Pl
1 Bristol, Bedminster
BS3 . . . .**63** B3
Bristol, Eastfield BS9 . .**36** C3
Albert Rd
Bristol, Hanham
BS15 . . . .**59** C1
Bristol, St Philip's Marsh
BS2 . . . .**64** C4

Albert Rd continued
Bristol, Staple Hill
BS16 . . . .**52** C4
Keynsham BS31 . . . . . .**76** A1
Severn Beach BS35 . . . .**2** B2
Albert St BS5 . . . .**57** B4
Albert Terr BS16 . . . .**51** A4
Albion Cl BS16 . . . . .**42** B1
Albion Rd BS5 . . . . . .**49** C1
Albion Pl **16** BS2 . . .**86** C3
Albion St **6** BS5 . . . .**57** B4
Albion Terr BS34 . . . .**8** C1
Alcove Rd BS16 . . . . .**51** A3
Alden Ho BS36 . . . . . .**30** B4
Aldercombe Rd BS9 .**35** B4
Alder Ct BS14 . . . .**73** A1
Alderdown Cl BS11 . .**34** C4
Alder Dr BS5 . . . .**50** C1
Aldermoor Way
BS30 . . . .**68** A4
Alderney Ave BS4 . . .**66** B4
Alders The BS9 . . . . . .**35** B4
Alderton Rd BS7 . . . .**38** A4
Aldwick Ave BS13 . . .**79** B3
Alexander Ct **4**
BS3 . . . .**62** C3

Alexandra Apartments
BS6 . . . . .48 A3
Alexandra Cl BS16 . . . .52 B4
Alexandra Ct BS16 . . . .51 A4
Alexandra Gate BS8 .84 B4
Alexandra Gdns
BS16 . . . . .52 B4
Alexandra Pk
Bristol, Cotham
BS6 . . . . .48 A2
Bristol, Ridgeway
BS16 . . . . .51 A4
Alexandra Pl BS16 . . .52 B4
Alexandra Rd
Bristol BS8 . . . . .84 B4
Bristol, Eastfield
BS10 . . . . .37 B4
Bristol, Hanham
BS15 . . . . .59 C1
Bristol, Highridge
BS13 . . . . .70 B3
Frampton Cotterell
BS36 . . . . .20 B3
Alford Rd BS4 . . . . . . .65 B2
Alfred Hill BS2 . . . . . . .86 A4
Alfred Lovell Gdns 7
BS30 . . . . .68 C4
Alfred Par BS2 . . . . . . .86 A4
Alfred Pl BS2 . . . . . . .84 C4
Alfred Rd
Bristol, Westbury Park
BS6 . . . . .47 B4
Bristol, Windmill Hill
BS3 . . . . .63 C3
Alfred St
Bristol, Moorfields
BS5 . . . . .57 C4
Bristol, Newton BS2 . . .56 C2
Algiers St BS3 . . . . . . .63 C3
Allanmead Rd BS14 . .73 A4
Allerton Cres BS14 . . .81 A4
Allerton Gdns BS14 . . .73 A1
Allerton Rd BS14 . . . . .73 A1
Allfoxton Rd BS7 . . . . .49 B3
All Hallows Ct 11
BS5 . . . . .57 A4
All Hallows Rd BS5 . .57 A4
Allington Dr BS30 . . . .68 B4
Allington Rd BS3 . . . . .85 C1
Allison Ave BS4 . . . . . .66 A4
Allison Rd BS4 . . . . . . .66 A3
All Saints Cl BS30 . . . .68 C3
All Saints' Ct BS1 . . . .86 A3
All Saints Ho BS2 . . . .86 B4
All Saints' La BS1 . . . . .87 A2
All Saints' Rd BS8 . . . .84 A4
All Saints' St BS1 . . . .86 A3
Alma Cl BS15 . . . . .60 A4
Alma Ct BS8 . . . . .47 C1
Alma Rd
Bristol BS8 . . . . .84 B4
Bristol, Kingswood
BS15 . . . . .52 C1
Alma Road Ave BS8 . .84 B4
Alma St BS8 . . . . .47 C1
Alma Vale Rd BS8 . . . .84 A4
Almeda Rd BS5 . . . . . . .58 C2
Almondsbury Bsns Ctr
BS32 . . . . .9 B3
*Almondsbury CE Prim
Sch* BS32 . . . . .8 B4
Almondsbury Intc
BS32 . . . . .9 C4
Almond Way BS16 . . .42 B1
Almorah Rd BS3 . . . . . .64 A3
Alpha Rd BS3 . . . . .63 C4
Alpine Rd BS5 . . . . .50 A1
Alsop Rd 4 BS15 . . . .52 B1
Alton Rd BS7 . . . . .38 B1
Altringham Rd BS5 . . .57 C4
Alverstoke BS14 . . . . .72 B3
Alveston Wlk BS9 . . . .35 A3
Alwins Ct 2 BS30 . . . .68 B4

Amberley Cl
Bristol BS16 . . . . .41 C3
Keynsham BS31 . . . . . .82 C4
Amberley House Sch
BS8 . . . . .47 B1
Amberley Rd
Bristol, Kingswood
BS16 . . . . .41 C3
Bristol, Patchway
BS34 . . . . .15 C4
Amble Cl BS15 . . . . . . .60 B3
Ambleside Ave
BS10 . . . . .25 C2
Ambra Ct BS8 . . . . .85 A2
Ambra Terr BS8 . . . . . .85 A2
Ambra Vale BS8 . . . . . .85 A2
Ambra Vale E BS8 . . . .85 A2
Ambra Vale S 5
BS8 . . . . .85 A2
Ambra Vale W 4
BS8 . . . . .85 A2
Ambrose Rd BS8 . . . . .85 A2
Amercombe Wlk
BS14 . . . . .73 C3
Anchor Cl BS5 . . . . .58 B2
Anchor Ho BS4 . . . . . . .65 A2
Anchor Rd
Bristol BS1 . . . . .85 C2
Bristol, Kingswood
BS15 . . . . .53 B2
Anchor Way BS20 . . . .45 C4
Andalusia Acad BS2 .86 A4
Andereach BS14 . . . . .73 A4
Andover Rd BS4 . . . . . .64 B2
Angels Gd BS4 . . . . . . .58 B2
Angers Rd BS4 . . . . . . .64 C4
Anglesea Pl 15 BS8 . .47 B2
Annie Scott Cl 2
BS16 . . . . .51 B4
Ansteys Cl BS15 . . . . . .59 A1
Anstey's Ct BS15 . . . . .59 B1
Anstey's Rd BS15 . . . . .59 B1
Anstey St BS5 . . . . .49 C1
Anthea Rd BS5 . . . . . . .50 C2
Antona Ct BS11 . . . . . .33 C3
Antona Dr BS11 . . . . . .33 C3
Antrim Rd BS9 . . . . .37 A2
Anvil St BS2 . . . . .87 C2
Apex Ct BS32 . . . . .9 B3
Appleby Wlk BS4 . . . . .71 C3
Appledore Cl BS14 . . .73 A4
Applegate BS10 . . . . . .25 C3
Applin Gn BS16 . . . . . .43 B2
Apseleys Mead BS32 . .9 A2
**Apsley Garden
Apartments** BS6 . . . .48 C2
Apsley Mews BS8 . . . .47 B2
Apsley Rd BS8 . . . . . . .47 B1
Apsley St BS5 . . . . .50 A3
Arbutus Dr BS9 . . . . . . .35 B4
Arcade The BS1 . . . . . . .86 B3
Archer Ct BS30 . . . . . . .68 B3
Arches The 1 BS5 . . . .57 A3
Archfield Ct BS6 . . . . . .48 A1
Archfield Rd BS6 . . . . .48 A1
Ardagh Ct BS7 . . . . . . .38 B3
Arden Cl BS32 . . . . .16 C2
Ardenton Wlk BS10 . .25 B3
Ardern Cl BS9 . . . . .35 A4
Argus Ct BS3 . . . . .63 B2
Argus Rd BS3 . . . . .63 B3
Argyle Ave BS5 . . . . . . .50 A2
Argyle Pl BS8 . . . . .85 A2
Argyle Rd
Bristol BS2 . . . . .86 B4
Bristol, Chester Park
BS16 . . . . .51 C2
Argyle St
5 Bristol, Eastville
BS5 . . . . .50 A2
6 Bristol, Southville
BS3 . . . . .63 B4
Arley Cotts 5 BS6 . . .48 B1

Arley Ct 4 BS6 . . . . . .48 B1
Arley Hill BS6 . . . . .48 B1
Arley Pk BS6 . . . . .48 B1
Arley Terr BS5 . . . . .50 C1
Arlingham Way BS34. . .8 A1
Arlington Mans BS8 . .84 B4
Arlington Rd BS4 . . . . .57 C1
Arlington Villas BS8 . .84 B3
Armada Ho BS2 . . . . . . .86 A4
Armada Pl BS1 . . . . . . .86 B4
Armidale Ave 4
BS6 . . . . .48 C1
Armidale Cotts 5
BS6 . . . . .48 C1
Armoury Sq BS5 . . . . . .56 C4
Armstrong Dr BS30 . . .61 A1
Arnall Dr BS10 . . . . . . .25 A1
Arncliffe BS10 . . . . .37 B4
Arneside Rd BS10 . . . . .26 A1
Arnold Rd BS16 . . . . . . .53 C3
Arnolfini (Arts Ctr) ★
BS1 . . . . .87 A1
Arno's St BS4 . . . . .64 C3
ARNO'S VALE 65 A4
Arrowfield Cl BS14 . . .80 C2
Arthurs Ct BS16 . . . . . .43 B2
Arthur Skemp Cl
BS5 . . . . .57 A3
Arthur St
7 Bristol, Moorfields
BS5 . . . . .57 B4
Bristol, St Philip's Marsh
BS2 . . . . .56 C1
Arthurswood Rd
BS13 . . . . .78 C4
Arundel Cl BS13 . . . . . .71 A1
Arundel Ct BS7 . . . . . . .48 B3
Arundel Rd BS7 . . . . . .48 B3
Arundel Wlk BS31 . . . .75 C1
Ascot Cl BS16 . . . . .31 A1
Ascot Rd BS10 . . . . . . .26 C2
Ashbourne Cl 1
BS30 . . . . .61 B2
Ashburton Rd BS10 . .26 A1
Ash Cl
Bristol, Hillfields
BS16 . . . . .52 A3
Bristol, Little Stoke
BS34 . . . . .16 B3
Ashcombe Cres
BS30 . . . . .61 C2
Ashcott BS14 . . . . .72 B3
Ashcroft Ave BS31 . . .75 C1
Ashcroft Rd BS9 . . . . . .35 B3
Ash Ct BS14 . . . . .72 C2
Ashdene Ave BS5 . . . . .50 B3
Ashdown Ct BS9 . . . . . .36 B4
Asher La BS2 . . . . .86 C3
Ashfield Pl BS6 . . . . . . .49 A1
Ashfield Rd BS3 . . . . . .63 A3
Ashfield Terr 9
BS3 . . . . .63 A3
Ashford Rd BS34 . . . . .15 B3
Ashford Way BS15 . . . .60 C3
Ash Gr BS16 . . . . .52 B3
Ashgrove Ave BS7 . . . .49 A4
Ashgrove Ct BS7 . . . . . .49 A4
Ashgrove Rd
Bristol, Ashley Down
BS7 . . . . .49 A4
Bristol, Bedminster
BS3 . . . . .63 A3
Ash La BS32 . . . . .7 B2
Ashland Rd BS13 . . . . .78 C4
Ashley BS15 . . . . .60 B4
Ashley Court Rd 2
BS7 . . . . .49 A4
Ashley Ct 1 BS2 . . . . .49 A1
ASHLEY DOWN 48 C4
*Ashley Down Jun & Inf
Schs* BS7 . . . . .38 B1
Ashley Down Rd
BS7 . . . . .49 A4

Ashley Grove Rd
7 Bristol BS2 . . . . .49 A1
1 Bristol BS2 . . . . .49 B1
Ashley Hill BS6, BS7 . .49 A2
Ashley Ho BS34 . . . . . . .8 A1
Ashley Par BS2 . . . . . . .49 A2
Ashley Pk BS6 . . . . .49 A3
Ashley Rd BS6 . . . . .48 C1
Ashley St BS2 . . . . .49 B1
Ashley Trad Est 6
BS2 . . . . .49 A2
Ashman Cl BS5 . . . . . . .56 C4
Ashman Ct 1 BS6 . . . .48 C4
Ashmead Bsns Pk
BS31 . . . . .77 A1
Ashmead Ho 12 BS5 .57 B3
Ashmead Rd BS31 . . . .77 A1
Ashmead Road Ind Est
BS31 . . . . .77 A1
Ashmead Way 8
BS1 . . . . .54 B1
Ash Rd BS7 . . . . .38 A1
Ash Ridge Rd BS32 . . . .8 C3
Ashton BS16 . . . . .30 A1
Ashton Ave BS1 . . . . . . .85 A1
Ashton Dr BS3 . . . . .62 B2
ASHTON GATE 62 B4
Ashton Gate Prim Sch
BS3 . . . . .62 C4
Ashton Gate Rd BS3 .62 C4
*Ashton Gate Stadium
(Bristol City FC)*
BS3 . . . . .62 B3
Ashton Gate Terr 4
BS3 . . . . .62 C4
Ashton Gate Trad Est
BS3 . . . . .62 A3
Ashton Gate Underpass
BS3 . . . . .62 B4
Ashton Park Sch
BS3 . . . . .62 A3
Ashton Rd BS3 . . . . . . .62 B4
ASHTON VALE 62 B2
Ashton Vale Prim Sch
BS3 . . . . .62 A3
Ashton Vale Rd BS3 .62 A3
Ashton Vale Trad Est
BS3 . . . . .62 B1
Ashton Way BS31 . . . .76 A2
Ashville Rd BS3 . . . . . . .62 C4
Ashwell Cl BS14 . . . . . .74 A2
Ashwicke BS14 . . . . . . .72 C2
Ash Wlk BS10 . . . . .25 C3
Aspects L Pk BS15 . . . .60 A1
Assembly Rooms La
BS1 . . . . .87 A2
Aston Ho 4 BS1 . . . . . .87 B1
Astry Cl BS11 . . . . .23 B1
At-Bristol ★ BS1 . . . . .85 C2
Atchley St 18 BS5 . . . .57 A3
Athena Ct 3 BS7 . . . . .49 A4
Atherston BS30 . . . . . . .61 C1
Athlone Wlk BS4 . . . . . .64 A1
Atkins Cl BS14 . . . . . . .74 A2
Atlantic Rd BS11 . . . . .33 B4
Atlas Cl BS5 . . . . .51 B2
Atlas Rd BS3 . . . . .64 A3
Atlas St BS2 . . . . .57 A1
Atrium The
Bristol BS1 . . . . .87 B2
Bristol BS2 . . . . .87 C2
Atwell Dr BS32 . . . . .8 C1
Atwood Dr BS11 . . . . . .23 C2
Ateyo Cl BS3 . . . . .62 A1
Aubrey Ho 10 BS3. . . .63 A3
Aubrey Rd BS3 . . . . . . .63 A3
Auburn Ave BS30 . . . . .69 A3
Auburn Rd BS6 . . . . . . .47 C1
Auden Mead BS7 . . . . .38 C4
Audrey Wlk BS9 . . . . . .37 C3
Augustus Ho BS15 . . . .59 A2
Austen Gr BS7 . . . . .38 C4
Austen Ho BS7 . . . . . . .38 C4
Austen Pl BS11 . . . . . . .34 A3

Aust La BS9 . . . . .36 C4
Avalon La BS5 . . . . .59 A2
Avalon Rd BS5 . . . . .59 A2
Avebury Rd BS3 . . . . . .62 B2
Avening Rd BS15 . . . . .58 C4
Avenue The
Bristol, Ashley Down
BS7 . . . . .48 C3
Bristol, Clifton BS8 . . . .47 B1
Bristol, Crew's Hole
BS5 . . . . .58 B4
Bristol, Frenchay
BS16 . . . . .28 C3
Bristol, Little Stoke
BS34 . . . . .16 A4
Bristol, Patchway
BS34 . . . . .8 C2
Bristol, Sneyd Park
BS9 . . . . .46 C3
Keynsham BS31 . . . . . .76 A2
Averay Rd BS16 . . . . . .50 A4
Avonbank Ind Est
BS11 . . . . .33 A3
Avonbridge Trad Est
BS11 . . . . .33 B4
Avon Bsns Pk BS16 . .51 B3
Avon Cl
Bristol BS5 . . . . .58 B2
Keynsham BS31 . . . . . .76 B2
Avon Cres BS1 . . . . . . .85 A1
Avon Ct
Bristol, Clifton BS8 . . . .47 B1
Bristol, Fishponds
BS16 . . . . .41 A1
Avondale Bsns Ctr
BS15 . . . . .52 A2
Avondale Ct
Bristol BS9 . . . . .46 B3
Bristol, Oldland BS30 . .68 B4
Avondown Cl BS10 . . .26 B2
Avondown Ct BS3 . . . .63 B2
Avondowns Ct BS8 . .84 A4
Avon Gorge Ind Est
BS11 . . . . .33 B3
*Avon Gorge Nature
Reserve* ★ BS8 . . . . . .54 A3
Avon Gr BS9 . . . . .46 B2
Avonlea BS15 . . . . .59 B1
Avonlea Ct BS30 . . . . . .68 C3
Avonleaze BS9 . . . . .35 A1
Avonleigh Ct 4 BS3 .63 A2
Avonleigh Rd BS3 . . . . .63 A2
Avonmead BS2 . . . . . . .86 B4
Avon Meads BS2 . . . . . .57 B1
Avon Mill La BS31 . . . .76 B2
AVONMOUTH 22 B2
*Avonmouth CE Prim
Sch* BS11 . . . . .33 B4
Avonmouth Rd
Avonmouth BS11 . . . . .21 C1
Bristol BS11 . . . . .33 B4
Avonmouth Sta
BS11 . . . . .21 C1
Avonmouth Way
Avonmouth BS11 . . . . .22 B1
Bristol BS11 . . . . .24 C3
Avonmouth Way W
BS11 . . . . .21 C1
Avon Pk BS5 . . . . .57 C3
Avon Prim Sch
BS11 . . . . .33 C4
Avon Rd
Bristol BS13 . . . . .70 C2
Keynsham BS31 . . . . . .76 B1
Pill BS20 . . . . .33 B1
Avon Riverside Est
BS11 . . . . .33 A3
Avonside Ind Est
BS2 . . . . .57 B2
Avonside Rd BS2 . . . . .57 B2
Avonside Way BS4 . . . .58 B2

Avonsmere Residential
Pk BS34 . . . . .28 A3
Avon St BS2 . . . . .87 C2
Avon Trad Est BS2 . .56 C1
Avon Vale BS4 . . . . .46 B4
Avonvale Rd BS5 . . . . .57 B3
Avon Valley Bsns Pk
BS4 . . . . .58 A2
Avon Valley Ctry Pk★
BS31 . . . . .77 C2
Avon Valley Farm Bsns
Pk BS31 . . . . .77 C1
Avon Valley Rly★
Bitton BS30 . . . . .77 C3
Bristol BS30 . . . . .69 B3
Avon View BS15 . . . . . .67 A3
Avon Way
Bristol BS9 . . . . .46 A4
Bristol, Southmead
BS10 . . . . .37 C3
Avonwood Cl BS11 . . .34 A2
Awdelett Cl BS11 . . . .23 C1
Axbridge Rd BS4 . . . .64 B2
Axis BS11 . . . . .71 C1
Aylesbury Cres BS3 . .63 A1
Aylesbury Rd BS3 . . . .63 A1
Aylmer Cres BS14 . . . .73 A2
Aylminton Wlk BS11 .23 C2
Azelin Ave BS13 . . . . . .71 A1
Aztec Ctr The BS32 . . . .8 B2
Aztec West BS32 . . . . . .8 B2

B

Backfields BS2 . . . . . . .86 B4
Backfields Ct BS2 . . . .86 B4
Backfields La BS2 . . . .86 B4
Back La
Keynsham BS31 . . . . . .76 A2
Pill BS20 . . . . .33 B1
Back Of Kingsdown Par
BS6 . . . . .86 A4
Back Rd BS3 . . . . .62 C4
Backwell Wlk BS13 . . .70 B4
Badenham Gr BS11 . . .34 B4
Baden Rd
Bristol, Kingswood
BS15 . . . . .60 C3
Bristol, Redfield BS5 . .57 B3
Badger Cl BS30 . . . . . .68 B3
Badgers Cl BS32 . . . . . .9 B3
Badger Sett BS5 . . . . .59 A3
Badgers Holt BS14 . . . .73 B2
Badger's La BS32 . . . . .7 A3
Badgers Rise BS10 . . .26 C4
Badgers Wlk BS14 . . .65 C2
Badminton BS16 . . . . .30 A1
Badminton Rd
Bristol, Downend
BS16 . . . . .42 A3
Bristol, Montpelier
BS2 . . . . .49 A1
Frampton Cotterell BS36,
BS37 . . . . .20 A2
Badminton Sch BS9 .36 C1
Badminton Wlk
BS16 . . . . .42 A3
Badock's Wood Prim
Sch BS10 . . . . .25 C1
Baglyn Ave BS15 . . . . .53 C3
Bagnell Cl BS14 . . . . . .74 A1
Bagnell Rd BS14 . . . . .74 A1
Bagworth Dr BS30 . . .68 B3
Bailey's Court Prim Sch
BS32 . . . . .17 A2
Baileys Court Rd
BS32 . . . . .17 A2
Baileys Ct BS32 . . . . . .17 A2
Baileys Mead Rd
BS16 . . . . .39 B1

Bakersfield BS30 . . . . .69 A3
Bakers Ground
BS34 . . . . .17 B1
Bakers Pk BS13 . . . . . . .71 A2
Balaclava Ind Est
BS16 . . . . .51 A3
Balaclava Rd BS16 . . .51 A3
Baldwin Chambers 6
BS1 . . . . .87 A2
Baldwin Lofts BS1 . . .87 A2
Baldwin St BS1 . . . . . .87 A2
Balfour Rd BS3 . . . . . .63 A3
Ballast La BS11 . . . . . .22 C2
Balmain St BS4 . . . . . .64 C4
Balmoral Cl BS34 . . . .28 B4
Balmoral Ct BS16 . . . .42 C1
Balmoral Ho BS1 . . . .85 C1
Balmoral Mans 3
BS7 . . . . .49 A2
Balmoral Rd
Bristol, Longwell Green
BS30 . . . . .68 B2
Bristol, Montpelier
BS7 . . . . .49 A2
Baltic Pl BS20 . . . . .45 C4
Bamfield BS14 . . . . . . .72 C2
Bampton Cl
Bristol, Emerson's
Green BS16 . . . . .43 B2
Bristol, Headley Park
BS13 . . . . .71 A3
Bampton Croft BS16 .43 B2
Bampton Dr BS16 . . . .30 B1
Banfield Cl BS11 . . . . .34 C4
Bangor Gr BS4 . . . . . . .58 B1
Bangrove Wlk BS11 . .34 A4
Banister Gr BS4 . . . . . .71 C3
Bank Leaze Prim Sch
BS11 . . . . .23 C2
Bank Pl BS20 . . . . .45 C4
Bank Rd
Avonmouth BS11 . . . .10 B3
Bristol BS15 . . . . .59 C4
Pilning BS35 . . . . .3 C2
Bankside BS16 . . . . . . .53 A4
Bankside Rd BS4 . . . . .65 C3
Bannerleigh La BS8 . .54 A2
Bannerleigh Rd BS8 .54 A2
Bannerman Rd BS5 . .57 B3
Bannerman Road Com
Sch BS5 . . . . .49 C1
Banner Rd BS6 . . . . . . .49 C1
Bantock Cl BS4 . . . . . . .71 C2
Bantry Rd BS4 . . . . . . .72 A4
Banwell Cl
Bristol BS13 . . . . .70 C4
Keynsham BS31 . . . . . .83 B2
Banwell Rd BS3 . . . . . .62 C3
Banyard Rd BS20 . . . .32 A1
BAPTIST MILLS 49 B2
Baptist St BS5 . . . . . . .49 B1
Baranwheel Ct BS5 . .58 B2
Barbour Gdns BS13 . .79 C3
Barbour Rd BS13 . . . . .79 C3
Barcroft Cl BS15 . . . . .59 B4
Barker Ct 5 BS5 . . . . . .57 B3
Barker Wlk BS5 . . . . . .49 B1
Barkleys Hill BS16 . . .39 B1
Barlands Ho BS10 . . . .25 A3
Barley Cl
Bristol BS16 . . . . .42 C2
Frampton Cotterell
BS36 . . . . .20 A3
Barley Close Com Prim
Sch BS16 . . . . .42 C2
Barley Croft BS9 . . . . .36 B1
Barleyfields BS2 . . . . .87 C2
Barnabas St 9 BS2 . .48 C1
Barnack Trad Est
BS3 . . . . .63 B1
Barnard Wlk BS31 . . .82 B4
Barn Cl BS16 . . . . .43 A2
Barnes Ct BS34 . . . . . .28 C3

Barnes St BS5 . . . . . . .57 C4
Barn Owl Way BS34 . .17 A1
Barnstaple Ct BS4 . . .72 A4
Barnstaple Rd BS4 . . .72 A4
Barnstaple Wlk BS4 . .72 B4
Barons Cl BS3 . . . . . . .62 B3
Barossa Pl BS1 . . . . . . .87 A1
Barrack's La BS11 . . . .33 C4
Barratt St BS5 . . . . . . .50 A1
Barrington Cl BS15 . .53 A2
Barrington Ct
Bristol BS4 . . . . .64 C4
11 Bristol, Knowle
BS2 . . . . .64 B4
Bristol, New Cheltenham
BS15 . . . . .52 C1
Barrow Hill Cres
BS11 . . . . .33 B3
Barrow Hill Rd BS11 .33 C3
Barrowmead Dr
BS11 . . . . .34 B3
Barrow Rd BS2 . . . . . .56 C3
Barrs Court Ave
BS30 . . . . .60 C1
Barrs Court Prim Sch
BS30 . . . . .60 B1
Barrs Court Rd
BS30 . . . . .60 C1
Barry Cl BS30 . . . . .69 B1
Barry Rd BS30 . . . . . . .69 B2
Barstaple Ho BS2 . . . .86 C3
Barter Cl BS15 . . . . . . .59 C4
Bartholomew Sq
BS7 . . . . .38 B3
Bartlett's Rd BS3 . . . .63 B2
Bartley Ct BS5 . . . . . . .57 C3
Bartley St BS3 . . . . . . .63 C4
Barton Cl
11 Bristol BS4 . . . . . .58 B2
Winterbourne BS36 . . .18 C1
Barton Ct BS5 . . . . . . .57 B2
Barton Gn BS5 . . . . . . .57 A3
BARTON HILL 57 B2
Barton Hill Prim Sch
BS5 . . . . .57 A2
Barton Hill Rd BS5 . . .57 A2
Barton Hill Trad Est 10
BS5 . . . . .57 A2
Barton Ho BS5 . . . . . . .57 B2
Bartonia Gr BS4 . . . . .65 C1
Barton Manor BS2 . . .56 C2
Barton Rd BS2 . . . . . . .87 C2
Barton St BS1 . . . . . . .86 A4
Barton The BS15 . . . . .67 B4
Barton Vale
6 Bristol BS2 . . . . . . .56 C2
Bristol BS2 . . . . .87 C2
Barwick Ho BS11 . . . .34 A3
Barwood Cl BS15 . . . .60 B4
Batches The BS3 . . . . .63 A2
Bates Cl BS5 . . . . .56 C4
Bath Bldgs BS6 . . . . . .48 C1
Bath Bridge Rdbt
BS1 . . . . .87 C1
Bath Hill BS31 . . . . . . .76 B1
Bath Rd
Bitton BS30 . . . . .77 C4
Bristol, Brislington
BS4 . . . . .66 B1
Bristol BS2, BS4 . . . . .87 C1
Bristol, Longwell Green
BS30 . . . . .68 B3
Bristol, North Common
BS30 . . . . .61 C2
Bristol, Totterdown
BS4 . . . . .65 A4
Bristol, Upper Knowle
BS4 . . . . .65 C2
Bristol, Willsbridge
BS30 . . . . .69 B1
Bath St
Bristol, Ashton Gate
BS3 . . . . .62 C4
Bristol BS1 . . . . .87 B2

Bath St continued
Bristol, Staple Hill
BS16 . . . . .52 C4
Bathurst Par BS1 . . . .87 A1
Bathwell Rd BS4 . . . . .64 C3
Batley Ct BS30 . . . . . . .69 C3
Battenburg Rd BS5 . .58 C4
Batten's La BS5 . . . . . .58 C2
Battens Rd BS5 . . . . . .59 A3
Battersby Way BS10 . .24 C2
Battersea Rd BS5 . . . .57 B4
Baugh Gdns BS16 . . . .30 C1
Baugh Rd BS16 . . . . . .30 C1
Baxter Cl BS15 . . . . . . .60 B4
Bay Gdns BS5 . . . . . . .50 A2
Bayham Rd BS4 . . . . . .64 C3
Bayleys Dr BS15 . . . . .59 B2
Baynham Ct 4
BS15 . . . . .59 A1
Baynton Ho 2 BS5 . . .57 A2
Baynton Mdw BS16 . .43 B2
Baynton Rd BS3 . . . . .62 C4
Bayswater Ave BS6 . .47 C3
Bayswater Rd BS7 . . .38 B3
Bay Tree Cl BS34 . . . . .15 A3
Bay Willow Dr BS6 . . .47 C2
Beach Ave BS35 . . . . . . .2 B3
Beachgrove Gdns
BS16 . . . . .52 A4
Beachgrove Rd
BS16 . . . . .51 C4
Beachley Wlk BS11 . .33 C3
Beach Rd BS35 . . . . . . .2 A3
Beacon La BS16 . . . . . .18 A2
Beaconlea BS15 . . . . .59 C2
Beacon Rise Prim Sch
BS15 . . . . .59 C2
Beaconsfield Cl 6
BS2 . . . . .57 A2
Beaconsfield Rd
Bristol, Clifton BS8 . . .47 B1
Bristol, Crew's Hole
BS5 . . . . .58 A3
Bristol, Kensington Park
BS4 . . . . .65 A3
Beaconsfield St 7
BS5 . . . . .57 A2
Beale Cl BS14 . . . . .74 A2
Beam St BS5 . . . . .57 B3
Bean Acre The BS11 . .33 C4
Bearbridge Rd BS13 . .78 B4
Bear Yard Mews 2
BS8 . . . . .85 A2
Beauchamp Rd BS7 . .48 B4
Beaufort Cl BS5 . . . . . .57 C3
Beaufort Cres BS34 . .28 C4
Beaufort Ct BS16 . . . .42 C4
Beaufort Ho 12 BS5 . .57 A2
Beaufort Hts BS5 . . . .58 A3
Beaufort Mews 11
BS8 . . . . .54 B3
Beaufort Pl
Bristol, Frenchay
BS16 . . . . .29 C1
Bristol, Upper Easton
BS5 . . . . .56 C4
Beaufort Rd
Bristol, Clifton BS8 . . .47 B1
Bristol, Horfield BS7 . .38 B2
Bristol, Kingswood
BS15 . . . . .52 A1
Bristol, Pile Marsh
BS5 . . . . .58 A3
Bristol, Staple Hill
BS16 . . . . .42 A1
Bristol, Vinney Green
BS16 . . . . .42 C4
Frampton Cotterell
BS36 . . . . .19 B4

Beaufort St
Bristol, Bedminster
BS3 . . . . .63 B2
4 Bristol, Upper Easton
BS5 . . . . .56 C4
Beaufort Way BS10 . .37 C4
Beauley Rd BS3 . . . . . .63 A4
Beaumont Cl BS30 . . .68 C3
Beaumont St BS5 . . . .56 C4
Beaumont Terr 6
BS5 . . . . .56 C4
Beaver Cl BS36 . . . . . .19 A3
Beazer Cl 4 BS16 . . . .52 B3
Beck Cl BS16 . . . . .43 B3
Beckford Gdns
BS14 . . . . .80 C3
Beck Ho BS34 . . . . .15 B4
Beckington Rd BS3 . . .64 B2
Beckington Wlk BS3 . .64 B2
Beckspool Rd BS16 . .30 A1
Bedford Cres BS7 . . . .38 B1
BEDMINSTER 63 B3
BEDMINSTER
DOWN 71 A4
Bedminster Down Rd
BS3, BS13 . . . . .63 A1
Bedminster Down Sch
BS13 . . . . .70 B3
Bedminster Par BS3 .63 C4
Bedminster Pl 9
BS3 . . . . .63 C4
Bedminster Rd BS3 . .63 C3
Bedminster Sta BS3 .63 C3
Beech Cl BS30 . . . . . . .60 C1
Beech Croft BS14 . . . .73 A1
Beechcroft Wlk BS7 . .38 C4
Beech Ct BS14 . . . . . . .72 C1
Beechen Dr BS16 . . . .51 C3
Beeches Gr BS4 . . . . . .65 C2
Beeches The
Bristol, Bradley Stoke
BS32 . . . . .16 B4
Bristol BS9 . . . . .46 B4
Bristol, Frenchay
BS16 . . . . .29 C1
Bristol, Oldland Common
BS30 . . . . .69 B2
Bristol, St Anne's
BS4 . . . . .58 A1
Beechfield Gr BS9 . . .35 B4
Beech Ho BS16 . . . . . .39 B1
Beechmount Ct
BS14 . . . . .73 A4
Beechmount Gr
BS14 . . . . .73 A4
Beech Rd BS7 . . . . .38 A1
Beechwood Ave
BS15 . . . . .59 C1
Beechwood Cl BS14 .73 B3
Beechwood Ho
BS16 . . . . .51 B4
Beechwood Rd
Bristol BS16 . . . . .51 C4
Easton-in-G BS20 . . . .44 C4
Beehive Trad Est
BS5 . . . . .58 A3
Beesmoor Rd BS36 . .19 C2
Begbrook Dr BS16 . . .40 B3
Begbrook La BS16 . . .40 A3
Begbrook Pk BS16 . . .40 C3
Begbrook Prim Sch
BS16 . . . . .40 B2
Beggarswell Cl BS2 . .86 C4
Belfast Wlk BS4 . . . . . .72 A4
Belfields La BS16 . . . .30 A1
Belfry BS30 . . . . .61 A2
Belfry Ave BS5 . . . . . . .58 C4
Belgrave Hill 5 BS8 . .47 B2
Belgrave Ho BS8 . . . . .84 A3
Belgrave Pl BS8 . . . . . .84 A3
Belgrave Rd BS8 . . . . .84 A4
Bellamy Ave BS13 . . .79 B4
Bellamy Cl BS15 . . . . .58 C1
Belland Dr BS14 . . . . .80 B4

Bell Ave BS1.........87 A1
Bell Barn Rd BS9 ....35 C2
Bell Cl BS10 ....38 A3
Belle Ct **7** BS2 .....64 B4
Bellevue BS8 ....85 B2
Bellevue Cl BS15 ....60 A3
Bellevue Cotts
　Bristol, Brandon Hill
　BS8 ....85 B2
　5 Bristol, Eastfield
　BS9 ....36 C3
Bellevue Cres BS8 ..85 B2
Bellevue Ct
　Bristol, Brandon Hill
　BS8 ....85 B2
　6 Bristol, St George
　BS5 ....58 C4
Bellevue Pk BS5 .....65 C2
Bellevue Rd
　Bristol, Kingswood
　BS15 ....60 B3
　Bristol, St George
　BS5 ....58 C4
　6 Bristol, Windmill Hill
　BS2 ....64 B4
Belle Vue Rd BS5 ....50 A1
Bellevue Terr
　Bristol, Brislington
　BS4 ....65 C2
　Bristol BS8 ....85 B2
　Bristol, Windmill Hill
　BS2 ....64 B4
Bell Hill BS16........50 A4
Bell Hill Rd BS5......59 B4
Bellhouse Wlk BS11 .23 C1
Bell La BS1..........86 A3
Bell Rd BS36 ....20 A2
Belluton Rd BS4 .....64 C3
Belmont Dr BS34 ....16 C1
Belmont Pk BS7 .....27 A1
Belmont Rd
　Bristol, Arno's Vale
　BS4 ....65 B3
　Bristol, Montpelier
　BS6 ....48 C2
Belmont St BS5......49 C1
Beloe Rd BS7.........38 A1
Belroyal Ave BS4 ....66 B3
Belsher Dr BS15 .....60 C2
Belstone Wlk BS4....71 B4
Belton Rd BS5........57 A4
Belvedere Rd BS6 ...47 C3
Belvoir Rd BS6 ......48 C2
Bence Ct **8** BS15...59 A1
Benford Cl BS16 .....41 B2
Bennett Rd BS5......58 A3
Bennett Way BS1,
　BS8 ....54 B1
Bensaunt Gr BS10 ..26 B4
Bentley Cl BS14......80 B3
Benville Ave BS9.....35 B4
Berchel Ho **4** BS3 ..68 B4
Berenda Dr BS30 ....69 A3
Berkeley Ave
　Bristol, Bishopston
　BS7 ....48 B3
　Bristol BS8 ....84 C3
Berkeley Cl BS16 ....42 C4
Berkeley Cres BS8 ..84 B3
Berkeley Ct BS7 .....48 B3
Berkeley Ct Bsns Pk
　BS5 ....57 A3
Berkeley Gdns BS31 .82 C4
Berkeley Gn BS16...29 C1
Berkeley Gn Rd BS5..50 B2
Berkeley Gr BS5 .....50 A2
Berkeley Ho
　Bristol BS1 ....84 C3
　7 Bristol, Staple Hill
　BS16 ....41 C1
Berkeley Pl
　Bristol, Brandon Hill
　BS8 ....84 B3

Berkeley Pl continued
Bristol, Windmill Hill
　BS3 ....63 C2
Berkeley Rd
　Bristol, Bishopston
　BS7 ....48 B3
　Bristol, Kingswood
　BS15 ....59 C3
　Bristol, Mayfield Park
　BS16 ....51 C2
　Bristol, Staple Hill
　BS16 ....41 C1
　Bristol, Westbury Park
　BS6 ....47 C4
Berkeleys Mead
　BS34 ....17 B2
Berkeley Sq BS8 ....84 C3
Berkeley St BS5 .....50 A3
Berkeley Way BS16 ..43 A3
Berkshire Rd BS7....48 B3
Berlington Ct BS1 ...87 B1
Berners Cl BS4 ......71 C3
Berrow Wlk BS3 .....64 A2
Berry Croft **5** BS3 ..63 C4
Berry Hill Cl BS10....26 B1
Berry La BS7 ....38 B2
BERWICK.............12 B2
Berwick Cl BS10.....12 C4
Berwick Ct BS10.....11 C1
Berwick Dr BS10.....12 C1
Berwick La BS10.....12 B3
Berwick Rd BS5......49 C2
Beryl Gr BS14 ....73 B4
Beryl Rd BS3 ....63 A3
Bethel Rd BS5........58 B4
Betjeman Ct **2**
　BS30 ....60 C1
Betts Gn BS16 ....43 B3
Bevan Ct BS34.......27 A2
Beverley Ave BS16...31 A1
Beverley Cl BS5 .....59 B2
Beverley Ct BS7 .....38 B4
Beverley Gdns BS9...35 C3
Beverley Rd BS7......38 B4
Beverstone BS15 ....59 B4
Beverston Gdns
　BS11 ....23 C2
Bevington Cl BS4 ....7 C1
Bevington Wlk BS34 ..7 C1
Bexley Rd BS16......51 C3
Bibstone BS15.......60 C4
Bibury Ave BS34 ....15 C4
Bibury Cl BS9........37 C3
Bibury Cres
　Bristol, Hanham
　BS15 ....59 B1
　Bristol, Henleaze
　BS9 ....37 C3
Bickerton Cl BS10 ...25 A3
Bickford Cl BS30.....60 C2
Bickley Cl BS15......67 B2
Biddestone Rd BS7..26 C1
Bideford Cres BS4...72 B4
Bidwell Cl BS10......25 C3
Bifield Cl BS14.......74 B1
Bifield Gdns BS14...74 A1
Bifield Rd BS14......74 B1
Bigwood La BS1.....85 C2
Bilberry Cl BS9......35 B4
Bilbie Cl BS10........38 A3
Billand Cl BS13......78 A3
Bindon Dr BS10......26 B4
Binley Gr BS14.......73 C1
Binmead Gdns BS13 .79 A4
Birbeck Rd BS9......36 A1
Birchall Rd BS6......48 A4
Birch Cl BS34........14 C3
Birch Croft BS14.....80 C3
Birch Ct BS31........82 A4
Birchdale Rd BS14...72 C4
Birch Ho BS16........41 A1
Birchills Trad Est
　BS4 ....66 B1

Birch Rd
　Bristol, Kingswood
　BS15 ....52 C3
　Bristol, Southville
　BS3 ....63 A4
Birchwood Ct BS4 ..58 B2
Birchwood Rd BS4...66 B4
Birdale Cl BS10......24 C3
Birdwood BS15 ......59 C2
Birkdale BS30 ....61 A2
Birkin St **5** BS2 ....56 C2
Bishop La BS7 ....48 C4
Bishop Manor Rd
　BS10 ....37 C3
Bishop Rd
　Bristol, Bishopston
　BS7 ....48 B4
　Bristol, Emerson's Green
　BS16 ....43 B2
Bishop Road Prim Sch
　BS7 ....48 B4
Bishops Cl BS9 ......46 C3
Bishops Cove BS13 ..70 B1
Bishops Ct BS9 .....46 A3
Bishops Knoll BS9 ..46 A3
Bishop St BS2 ....86 B4
BISHOPSTON 48 A3
BISHOPSWORTH......70 C1
Bishopsworth CE Jun
　Sch BS13 ....70 B2
Bishopsworth Rd
　BS13 ....70 C3
Bishop Terr BS2 .....86 C4
Bishopthorpe Rd
　BS10 ....38 A3
Bishport Ave BS13 ..79 B3
Bishport Cl BS13.....79 A4
Bishport Gn BS13....79 B3
Bissex Mead BS16 ..43 A1
Bittlemead BS13.....80 B4
Bitton Sta★ BS30....69 A1
Blackacre BS14......81 B4
Blackberry La **5**
　BS16 ....40 A1
Blackberry Dr BS36..20 A2
Blackberry Hill
　BS16 ....40 A1
Blackberry Hill Hospl
　BS16 ....40 B1
Blackdown Ct BS14..73 A1
Blackfriars BS1......86 A3
BLACKHORSE.........42 C3
Blackhorse Ct BS16..42 C4
Blackhorse Ct BS15..59 B4
Blackhorse Hill BS35,
　BS10 ....13 C4
Blackhorse La BS16..42 C4
Blackhorse Pl BS16..42 C2
Blackhorse Prim Sch
　BS16 ....42 C4
Blackhorse Rd
　Bristol, Kingswood
　BS15 ....59 C4
　Bristol, Mangotsfield
　BS16 ....42 C3
Blackmoors La BS3 ..62 A4
Blacksmith Ho **6**
　BS5 ....57 C3
Blacksworth Rd BS5 .57 C3
Blackthorn Cl BS13 ..71 C1
Blackthorn Dr BS32 ..16 B3
Blackthorn Rd BS13 ..71 C1
Blackthorn Wlk
　BS15 ....52 C2
Blagdon Cl BS3......64 A2
Blagrove Cl BS13 ....79 B3
Blagrove Cres BS13 ..79 B3
Blaisdon Cl BS10 ....25 B1
Blaise Castle Mus★
　BS10 ....24 C2
Blaisedell View
　BS10 ....24 B3
Blaise Hamlet BS11 ..24 B2

Blaise Prim Sch
　BS10 ....25 A2
Blaise Wlk BS9 ......35 B2
Blakeney Rd
　Bristol BS34 ....7 C1
　Bristol, Horfield BS7. .38 C3
Blake Rd BS7.........39 A2
Blandford Cl **2** BS9 .37 A2
Blandmour Way
　BS10 ....26 B2
Blenheim Ct
　10 Bristol, Kingsdown
　BS1 ....86 A4
　Bristol, Patchway
　BS32 ....9 B3
Blenheim Dr BS34 ...27 C4
Blenheim Rd BS6....47 C3
Blenheim St BS5.....49 B1
Blenman Cl BS16 ....40 C3
Blethwin Cl BS10 ....25 A1
Bloomfield Rd BS4...65 C4
Bloomfield Road Link
　BS4 ....65 B4
Bloy St BS5...........50 A1
Bluebell Cl BS9......35 A2
Bluebells The BS32 ..17 A3
Blue Falcon Rd
　BS15 ....52 C1
Bodey Cl BS30.......60 C1
Bodmin Wlk BS4.....72 B4
Boiling Wells La
　BS2 ....49 B3
Bolton Rd BS7.......48 C3
Bond St BS1..........86 B4
Bonnington Wlk
　BS7 ....39 A3
Bonville Bsns Ctr
　BS4 ....66 B2
Bonville Rd BS4 .....66 B2
Boon Villas BS11....34 A3
Booth Rd BS3 ....63 B4
Boot La BS3 ....63 C4
Bordesley Rd BS14 ..80 C3
Borleyton Wlk BS13..78 B4
Borver Gr BS13......79 A4
Boscombe Cres
　BS16 ....42 B3
Boston Rd BS7 ......38 B4
Botham Dr BS4......66 B1
Boucher Pl **2** BS2..49 B2
Boulters Rd BS13....79 B4
Boulton's La **6**
　BS15 ....59 C4
Boulton's Rd **5**
　BS15 ....59 C4
Boundary Rd
　Avonmouth BS11 .....22 B3
　Frampton Cotterell
　BS36 ....20 B3
Bourchier Gdns
　BS13 ....79 A3
Bourne Cl
　Bristol BS15 ....59 A4
　Winterbourne BS36 ...18 C3
Bourne La BS5 ......49 C2
Bourne Rd BS15 ....58 C4
Bourneville Rd BS5 ..57 C4
Boursland Cl BS32...9 B2
Bourton Ave BS34 ...16 A4
Bourton Cl BS34 ....16 A4
Bourton Wlk BS13 ..70 C4
Bouverie St BS5......57 A4
Boverton Rd BS34 ...24 C4
Bow Cotts BS20.....45 B4
Bowden Cl BS9......35 B4
Bowden Pl BS16.....42 B3
Bowden Rd BS5 .....50 C1
BOWER ASHTON.....62 A4
Bower Ashton Terr
　BS3 ....62 B4
Bower Ct BS13 ......62 C2
Bowerleaze BS9.....35 B1
Bower Rd BS3.......62 C3

Bower Wlk BS3......64 A3
Bowland Ct BS32 ....9 B1
Bowmead **7** BS4 ...65 C1
Bowood BS16 ....30 A1
Bowring Cl BS15.....79 B3
Bowsland BS32.......9 C2
Bowsland Green Prim
　Sch BS32............9 C2
Bowsland Way BS32 ..9 C2
Bowstreet La BS35...13 B3
Box Wlk BS31........82 A4
Boyce Dr BS2........49 B2
Boyce's Ave BS8....84 C3
Brabazon Rd BS34...27 C2
Bracewell Gdns
　BS10 ....26 A4
Bracey Dr BS16......41 B2
Brackenbury Dr
　BS34 ....17 A1
Brackendene BS32...9 A1
Bracton Dr BS14....72 C1
Bradeston Gr BS16 ..40 C3
Bradhurst St **8** BS5 .57 A2
Bradley Ave
　Bristol BS11 ....34 A3
　Winterbourne BS36 ...18 C1
Bradley Cres BS11 ...34 A2
Bradley Ct BS16 .....41 B1
Bradley Pavilions
　BS32 ....9 A2
Bradley Rd
　Bristol BS34 ....8 A1
　Portbury BS20 ....32 A1
BRADLEY STOKE....17 A4
Bradley Stoke Com Sch
　BS32 ....16 C3
Bradley Stoke Way
　BS32 ....16 C3
Bradstone Rd BS36 ..18 B1
Bradwell Gr BS10....37 B4
Braemar Ave BS7....27 A1
Braemar Cres BS7 ...27 A1
Braemor Ct BS9 .....36 C4
Bragg's La BS2.......86 C3
Braikenridge Rd
　BS4 ....65 C4
Brainsfield BS9......36 B2
Brake Cl
　Bristol, Bradley Stoke
　BS32 ....16 C3
　Bristol, Warmley Hill
　BS15 ....60 B3
Brake The BS36......20 A1
Brakewell Gdns
　BS14 ....80 C4
Bramble Dr BS9 .....46 B3
Bramble La BS9 .....46 B3
Brambles The
　Bristol BS13 ....79 B4
　Keynsham BS31 .....82 B3
Brambling Wlk
　BS16 ....40 B2
Bramley Cl BS20.....45 B4
Bramley Ct **6** BS30..68 B4
Branche Gr BS13 ....79 B3
Brandon Cotts BS1 ..85 C2
BRANDON HILL.....85 B2
Brandon Ho BS8.....85 B2
Brandon St BS1......85 C2
Brandon Steep BS1 ..85 B2
Brangwyn Gr BS7....39 A2
Branksome Cres
　BS34 ....27 C3
Branksome Dr
　Bristol BS34 ....27 C3
　Winterbourne BS36 ...18 C2
Branksome Rd BS3 ..63 C2
Branscombe Ct
　BS9 ....46 A4
Branwhite Cl BS7....39 A3

Bratton Rd BS4 ......71 C3
Braunton Rd BS3 ....63 B3
Braydon Ave BS32 ...16 B3
Brayne Ct BS30 ....68 B3
Breaches Gate BS32 .17 A2
Breaches The BS20 ..33 A1
Breach Rd BS3 ....62 C3
Brean Down Ave
BS9 ....37 A1
Brean Gdns BS3 ......64 A2
Brecknock Rd BS4 ...64 C3
Brecon Cl BS9 ....37 A2
Brecon Cl BS16 ....28 B1
Brecon Rd BS9 ....37 A2
Bredon Cl BS15 ....60 B3
Bredon Nook Rd
BS10 ....37 B3
Brendon Cl BS30 .....69 B4
Brendon Rd BS3 ......63 C3
Brenner St BS5 ....49 C2
Brent Rd BS7 ....38 B1
BRENTRY 25 C2
Brentry Ave BS5 .....57 A3
Brentry La BS10 ......25 C3
Brentry Lo BS10 ......25 B3
Brentry Prim Sch
BS10 ....25 C4
Brentry Rd BS16 ......51 A3
Brereton Way BS30 ..69 B4
Brewerton Cl BS10...26 A3
Brewery St BS3 ....62 C4
Brewhouse The BS1 ..87 B2
Briar St BS20 ....45 B4
Briarfield Ave BS15 ..59 B1
Briarside Ho BS10 ...26 B3
Briarside Rd BS10 ...26 B3
Briar Way BS16 ......52 A3
Briar Wlk BS16 ....52 A3
Briarwood BS9 ....36 B2
Briarwood Sch
BS16 ....51 C3
Briavels Gr BS6.......49 A2
Brick St BS2.............86 C3
Bridewell St BS1 .....86 A3
Bridge Cl BS14 ....81 B4
Bridge Farm Cl
BS14 ....80 C3
Bridge Farm Prim Sch
BS14 ....80 C4
Bridge Farm Wlk
BS16 ....53 C3
Bridge Ho BS1........87 B2
Bridgeleap Rd BS16..42 B4
Bridge Rd
Bristol, Eastville
BS5 ....49 C3
Bristol, Lower Soundwell
BS15 ....53 B4
Leigh Woods BS8 ....54 A2
Bridge Road Ind Est
BS15 ....53 B3
Bridges Ct 2 BS16 .51 C4
Bridges Dr 3 BS16 ..41 B2
Bridge St
Bristol BS1 ....87 A2
Bristol, Eastville BS5 ..50 B2
Bridge Valley Rd
BS8 ....54 A4
Bridge Way BS36 ....19 C4
Bridge Wlk BS7......38 C4
Bridgman Gr BS34 ...27 C3
Briercliffe Rd BS9 ...35 C3
Brierly Furlong
BS34 ....28 B3
Briery Leaze Rd
BS14 ....80 C4
Brighton Cres BS3 ...63 A2
Brighton Mews BS8..84 B4
Brighton Pk 16 BS5 ..57 A4
Brighton Pl BS15 ....52 B1

Brighton Rd
Bristol, Patchway
BS34 ....15 A4
Bristol, Redland BS6...48 A1
Brighton St
12 Bristol BS2 ....48 C1
7 Bristol BS2 ....86 B4
Brighton Terr 9
BS3 ....63 A2
Bright St
Bristol, Kingswood
BS15 ....59 C4
Bristol, Russell Town
BS5 ....57 A3
Brigstocke Rd BS2...86 B4
Brimbles The BS7 ....27 C2
Brinkworthy Rd
BS16 ....40 A2
Brinmead Wlk BS13..78 B3
Brins Cl BS34..........29 A4
Brinsmead Cres
BS20 ....45 C4
Briscoes Ave BS13 ..79 C4
BRISLINGTON 72 A4
Brislington Ent Coll
BS4 ....74 B4
Brislington Hill BS4..66 A2
Brislington Ret Pk
BS4 ....66 A1
Brislington Trad Est
BS4 ....66 B2
BRISTOL...............87 C2
Bristol & Anchor Ho
BS5 ....57 C4
Bristol and Exeter
Mews BS1 ....87 C1
Bristol Bsns Pk
BS16 ....28 C1
Bristol Cathedral Sch
BS1 ....85 C2
Bristol Dental Hospl
BS1 ....86 A3
Bristol Eye Hospl
BS1 ....86 A3
Bristol Gate 1 BS8 ..54 B1
Bristol Gateway Sch
The BS2...............49 B2
Bristol General Hospl
BS1 ....87 A1
Bristol Gram Sch
BS8 ....84 C3
Bristol Harbour Rly★
BS1 ....85 C1
Bristol Hill BS4 ......65 C2
Bristol Hippodrome
The★ BS1.............85 C2
Bristol Homeopathic
Hospl BS6...........84 C4
Bristol Old Vic (Theatre
Royal) closed for
refurbishment
BS1 ....87 A1
Bristol Old Vic Theatre
Sch BS8 ....47 B1
Bristol Parkway N
BS34 ....17 B1
Bristol Parkway Sta
BS34 ....28 C4
Bristol Rd
Bristol BS16 ....30 A2
Keynsham BS31 .....76 A2
Whitchurch BS14 ....81 C3
Winterbourne BS16 ..30 B4
Bristol Royal Hospl for
Children BS1.........86 A3
Bristol Royal Infmy
BS2 ....86 A4
Bristol Southend
BS3 ....63 C2
Bristol Steiner Waldorf
Sch BS6...............47 C2
Bristol Temple Meads
Sta BS1 ....87 C1

Bristol Vale Trad Est
BS3 ....63 A1
Bristol Zoo Gdns★
BS8 ....47 A1
Bristow Broadway
BS11 ....22 A1
Bristowe Ho BS16 ...41 A1
Bristowe Lodge
BS16 ....52 A4
Britannia Bldgs BS8 .85 A1
Britannia Cl 4
BS16 ....31 A1
Britannia Cres BS34 .16 B1
Britannia Ct 1
BS16 ....41 C1
Britannia Ho BS34 ...27 A2
Britannia Rd
Bristol, Kingswood
BS15 ....59 B4
Bristol, Lower Easton
BS5 ....50 A1
Bristol, Patchway
BS34 ....14 C3
British Empire &
Commonwealth Mus
The★ BS1.............87 C1
British Rd BS3........63 B3
Brittan Pl BS20 ......44 A3
Britten Ct 10 BS30 ..68 B4
Britton Gdns BS15 ...52 A1
Britton Ho BS15 .....61 A4
Brixham Rd BS3 ......63 B1
Brixton Rd BS5 ......57 A4
Brixton Road Mews 22
BS5 ....57 A4
Broadbury Rd BS4 ..72 A4
Broad Croft BS32 .....9 A2
Broadfield Ave
BS15 ....52 A1
Broadfield Ct BS15...59 B4
Broadfield Rd
Bristol BS4 ....65 A1
Bristol BS4 ....72 C4
Broad La BS36 ....20 B1
Broadlands Ave
BS31 ....75 C2
Broadlands Dr BS11 .23 B1
Broadlands Sch
BS31 ....75 C2
Broadleas BS13.......71 B3
Broadleaze BS11 .....34 A3
Broadleys Ave BS9...37 B3
Broadmead
Bristol BS1 ....86 B3
Keynsham BS31 .....77 A1
Broadmead La BS31 .76 C2
Broadmead Lane Ind
Est BS31 ....77 A3
Broadoak Hill BS41 ..78 B2
Broad Oak Rd BS13 ..78 B4
Broad Oaks BS8 .....54 A2
Broadoak Wlk BS16..51 C4
Broad Plain BS2......87 C2
Broad Quay BS1 .....87 A2
Broad Rd BS15 ....52 A1
Broad St
Bristol BS1 ....86 A3
Bristol, Staple Hill
BS16 ....53 A4
Broadstone Wlk
BS13 ....71 C1
Broadwalk Sh Ctr
BS4 ....65 A2
Broadway Ave BS9...37 C2
Broadway Rd
Bristol, Bishopston
BS7 ....48 B3
Bristol, Bishopsworth
BS13 ....70 B1
Broadways Br BS16 ..40 B3
Broad Weir BS1.......86 B3
Broad Wlk BS4 ......64 C2
Brockeridge Inf Sch
BS36 ....20 A3

Brockhurst Gdns
BS15 ....58 C4
Brockhurst Rd BS15 .58 C4
Brockley Cl BS34 ....16 A3
Brockley Wlk BS13...70 C4
Brockridge La BS36..20 A3
Brocks 4 BS4 ....65 C1
Brocks Rd BS13......79 B3
Brockworth Cres
BS16 ....30 A2
Bromfield Wlk BS16 .43 A3
Bromley Dr BS16 ....41 C4
Bromley Farm BS16..30 B1
BROMLEY HEATH ...30 B1
Bromley Heath Ave
BS16 ....41 C4
Bromley Heath Jun &
Inf Schs BS16........42 A4
Bromley Heath Rd
BS16 ....41 C4
Bromley Heath Rdbt
BS16 ....30 B1
Bromley Rd BS7......38 B1
Brompton Cl BS15...60 C4
Broncksea Rd BS7...27 A1
Bronte Wlk BS7......38 C4
Brookcote Dr BS34 ..16 B2
Brookdale Rd BS13 ..71 A2
Brookfield Ave BS7...48 B3
Brookfield La 2
BS6 ....48 B2
Brookfield Rd
3 Bristol, Montpelier
BS6 ....48 B2
Bristol, Patchway
BS34 ....15 C4
Brookfield Wlk
BS30 ....69 B3
Brook Gate BS3......62 A1
Brook Hill BS6........49 A1
Brook Ho BS34 ......16 A1
Brook La
Bristol, Montpelier
BS6 ....49 A1
Bristol, Stapleton
BS16 ....40 A2
Brookland Rd BS6...37 C1
Brooklea BS30........69 A3
Brookleaze BS9 ......35 B1
Brook Lintons BS4...65 C3
Brooklyn Rd BS13....71 A4
Brook Office Pk
BS16 ....31 C2
Brook Rd
Bristol, Hillfields
BS16 ....51 C4
Bristol, Mangotsfield
BS16 ....42 B2
Bristol, Montpelier
BS6 ....49 A1
Bristol, Southville
BS3 ....63 C4
Bristol, Speedwell
BS5 ....51 A1
Bristol, Warmley
BS15 ....61 A4
Brookridge Ct 6
BS16 ....52 B4
Brookridge Ho BS10.25 A3
Brookside BS20.......45 C3
Brookside Dr BS36...19 C4
Brookside Rd BS4 ...66 A2
Brook St BS5.........57 B3
Brookthorpe Ave
BS11 ....23 B1
Brookview Wlk
BS13 ....71 A3
Brook Way BS32 .....16 B4
BROOMHILL 40 A2
BROOM HILL 66 B3
Broom Hill BS16 .....40 A1
Broomhill Inf Sch
BS4 ....66 B3

Broomhill Jun Sch
BS4 ....66 B3
Broomhill Rd BS4....66 C2
Brooms The BS16 ....31 B1
Brotherswood Ct
BS32 ....9 B4
Broughton Ho BS1...87 B1
Browne Ct 4 BS6....84 B1
Browning Ct BS7 ....39 A4
Broxholme Wlk
BS11 ....34 B4
Bruce Ave BS5.......50 A1
Bruce Rd BS5 ....50 A1
Brunel Cl BS30 ......61 B3
Brunel Lock Rd BS1..54 B1
Brunel Pl BS13.......70 C4
Brunel Way BS1,BS3 .62 B4
Brunswick Pl 10
BS1 ....54 B1
Brunswick Sq BS2 ...86 B4
Brunswick St
Bristol BS2 ....86 B4
Bristol, Redfield BS5..57 B3
Bruton Cl BS5 ....58 B4
Bruton Pl BS8 ....84 B3
Bryansons Cl BS16...39 C2
Bryants Cl BS16 .....30 A1
Bryant's Hill BS5 ....59 A2
Brynland Ave BS7....48 A4
Brynland Ct BS7 .....38 A1
Buckingham Dr BS34.16 B1
Buckingham Gdns
BS16 ....42 A2
Buckingham Ho
BS34 ....27 A2
Buckingham Lodge 1
BS31 ....76 B2
Buckingham Pl
Bristol BS8 ....84 A3
Bristol, Mangotsfield
BS16 ....42 A2
Buckingham Rd
BS4 ....54 B2
Buckingham St BS3..63 B2
Buckingham Vale
BS8 ....84 A4
Bucklewell Cl BS11 ..34 B2
Bude Ave BS5 ....58 C4
Bude Rd BS34 ....27 C4
Bullens Cl BS32......69 B2
Buller Rd BS4 ....65 B2
Bull La
Bristol BS5 ....58 B2
Pill BS20 ....45 B4
Burbank Cl BS10 ....68 C3
Burchells Ave BS15 ..51 C1
BURCHELLS
GREEN 51 C1
Burchells Green Cl
BS15 ....51 C1
Burchells Green Rd
BS15 ....51 C1
Burcombe Cl BS36...20 B2
Burcott Rd BS11 .....10 B1
Burden Cl BS32.......17 A2
Burford Ave BS34....16 A4
Burford Gr BS11 .....34 B1
Burgess Green Cl
BS4 ....58 A3
Burghill Rd BS10 ....25 B1
Burghley Ct BS16 ...18 C1
Burghley Rd BS6.....48 C2
Burgis Rd BS14 ......73 C2
Burley Ave BS16 ....42 B1
Burley Crest BS16 ...42 B1
Burley Gr BS16 ......42 B1
Burlington Ct 9
BS6 ....47 C2
Burlington Rd BS6...47 C2
Burnbush Cl BS14 ...74 A2
Burnbush Prim Sch
BS14 ....73 C1

Burnell Dr BS2 . . . . . .86 C4
Burneside Cl BS10 . . .26 A2
Burnett Bsns Pk
  BS31 . . . . .83 C1
Burney Way BS30 . . . .68 C3
Burnham Cl BS15 . . . .53 A1
Burnham Dr BS15 . . . .53 A1
Burnham Rd BS11 . . .33 C2
Burrington Wlk
  BS13 . . . . .70 C4
Burrough Way BS36 .18 C2
Burton Cl BS1 . . . . . . .87 B1
Burton Ct
  Bristol BS8 . . . . .84 B3
  2 Bristol, Upper Eastville
  BS16 . . . . .50 C3
Burwalls Rd BS8 . . . . .54 A2
Burycourt Cl BS11 . . .23 B1
Bury Hill BS36 . . . . . . .31 A3
Bury Hill View BS16 . .30 C1
Bush Ave BS34 . . . . . . .16 B1
Bush Ct 10 BS2 . . . . . .64 B4
Bush Ind Est BS5 . . . .57 C4
Bushy Ho BS2 . . . . . . .64 B3
Bushy Pk BS2 . . . . . . .64 B3
Business Pk The
  BS13 . . . . .80 A3
Butcombe Wlk BS14 .73 A1
Butler Ho BS5 . . . . . . .58 B4
Butlers Cl BS5 . . . . . . .58 B3
Butlers Wlk 3 BS5 . .58 B2
Butterfield Cl
  Bristol BS10 . . . . .38 A3
  Frampton Cotterell
  BS36 . . . . .19 C2
Butterfield Rd BS10 . .38 A3
Butterworth Ct BS4 . .71 C3
Button Cl BS14 . . . . . .72 C2
Buxton Wlk BS7 . . . . .38 C4
Bye Mead BS16 . . . . . .43 A4
Byron Pl
  Bristol BS8 . . . . .84 B3
  Bristol, Staple Hill
  BS16 . . . . .52 C4
Byron St
  Bristol, Moorfields
  BS5 . . . . .57 B3
  5 Bristol, St Pauls
  BS2 . . . . .49 B1
Byzantine Ct BS1 . . . .87 A1

C

Cabot Cl BS15 . . . . . . .59 B3
Cabot Ct BS7 . . . . .27 A1
Cabot Pk BS11 . . . . . .10 B2
Cabot Prim Sch BS2 . 86 C4
Cabot Twr ★ BS8 . . . .85 B2
Cabot Way
  Bristol BS8 . . . . .54 B1
  Pill BS20 . . . . .45 C3
Cadbury Gdns BS30 . .61 A2
CADBURY HEATH 61 A1
Cadbury Heath Prim
  Sch BS30 . . . . .60 B2
Cadbury Heath Rd
  BS30 . . . . .61 A1
Cadbury Rd BS31 . . . .83 B2
Caddick Cl BS15 . . . . .53 A2
Cade Cl
  Bristol, Kingswood
  BS15 . . . . .60 B2
  Bristol, Stoke Gifford
  BS34 . . . . .16 C1
Cadmium Rd BS11 . . .22 A4
Cadogan Rd BS14 . . . .72 C4
Caen Rd BS3 . . . . .63 C3
Caernarvon Rd
  BS31 . . . . .82 A4
Caine Rd BS7 . . . . .38 B3
Cairns Cl BS15 . . . . . .60 A2
Cairn Gdns BS36 . . . . .30 C4
Cairns' Cres 12 BS2 . .49 A1

Cairns Ct BS6 . . . . . . .48 A4
Cairns Rd BS6 . . . . . . .48 A4
Caitlin Ct BS14 . . . . . .73 C2
Cala Trad Est BS3 . . . .62 B3
Calcott Rd BS4 . . . . . .64 C3
Caldbeck Cl BS10 . . . .26 B2
Calder Cl BS31 . . . . . .83 B4
Caldicot Cl
  Bristol, Lawrence
  Weston BS11 . . . . .24 A2
  Bristol, Willsbridge
  BS30 . . . . .69 A2
Caledonia Mews
  BS8 . . . . .54 B2
Caledonian Rd BS1 . .85 B1
Caledonia Pl BS8 . . . .54 B3
California Rd BS30 . . .69 A3
Callicroft Prim Sch
  BS10 . . . . .15 A4
Callicroft Rd BS34 . . .15 B3
Callington Rd BS4 . . .65 C1
Callowhill Ct BS1 . . . .86 B3
Camberley Dr BS36 . .19 A4
Camberley Rd BS4 . . .71 C4
Camborne Rd BS7 . . .38 C3
Cambridge Cres
  BS9 . . . . .36 C3
Cambridge Pk BS6 . . .47 C3
Cambridge Rd BS7 . .48 C4
Cambridge St
  8 Bristol, Redfield
  BS5 . . . . .57 B3
  Bristol, Windmill Hill
  BS3 . . . . .64 B4
Camden Rd BS3 . . . . .85 B1
Camden Terr BS8 . . . .85 A2
Camelford Rd BS5 . . .50 B1
Cameron Wlk BS7 . . .39 B2
Cameroons Cl BS31 . .82 C4
Camerton Rd BS5 . . . .50 B1
Campbell Ct BS11 . . . .23 A1
Campbell Farm
  BS11 . . . . .23 A1
Campbell Farm Dr
  BS11 . . . . .23 A1
Campbell St BS2 . . . . .48 C1
Campian Wlk BS4 . . . .71 C2
Campion Dr BS32 . . . .9 B2
Camp Rd BS8 . . . . .54 B3
Camp View BS36 . . . . .30 C4
Camwal Ind Est BS2 .56 C1
Camwal Rd BS2 . . . . . .56 C1
Canada Way BS1 . . . .85 B1
Canberra Gr BS34 . . .27 C4
Candy Ct BS4 . . . . .57 C1
Canford La BS9 . . . . . .36 A4
Canford Rd BS9 . . . . . .36 B4
Cannans Cl BS36 . . . . .18 C3
CANNON'S MARSH .85 C1
Cannon St
  Bristol BS1 . . . . .86 A4
  Bristol, Southville
  BS3 . . . . .63 B4
Canons Rd BS1 . . . . . .85 C2
Canon's Rd BS1 . . . . . .85 C1
Canon St BS5 . . . . .57 B4
Canons Way BS1 . . . . .85 C1
Canon's Wlk BS15 . . .53 A2
Canowie Rd BS6 . . . . .47 C3
Cantell Gr BS14 . . . . . .74 B1
Canterbury Cl BS16 . .40 C2
Canterbury St 5
  BS5 . . . . .57 A2
Cantock's Cl BS8 . . . .84 C3
Canvey Cl BS10 . . . . . .38 A3
Canynge Ho 2 BS1 . .87 B1
Canynge Rd BS8 . . . . .54 B4
Canynge Sq BS8 . . . . .54 B4
Canynge St BS1 . . . . . .87 B2
Capel Cl BS15 . . . . . . .61 A4
Capel Rd BS11 . . . . . . .23 C1
Capgrave Cl BS4 . . . . .66 C3
Capgrave Cres BS4 . .66 C3
Capital Edge BS8 . . . .85 B1

Capricorn Pl BS8 . . . .85 B2
Caraway Gdns BS5 . . .50 A2
Cardigan Mews BS9 .37 A1
Cardigan Rd BS9 . . . . .37 A2
Cardill Cl BS13 . . . . . .70 C4
Carfax Ct BS6 . . . . . . .47 B3
Carisbrooke Lodge
  BS6 . . . . .47 B3
Carisbrooke Rd BS4 .71 C3
Carlow Rd BS4 . . . . . . .72 A4
Carlton Ct
  1 Bristol, Ashley Down
  BS7 . . . . .49 A4
  3 Bristol, Eastfield
  BS9 . . . . .36 C3
Carlton Ho 2 BS9 . . . .36 C3
Carlton Pk BS5 . . . . . .57 B4
Carlyle Rd BS5 . . . . . .50 A1
Carmarthen Gr
  BS30 . . . . .69 A1
Carmarthen Rd BS9 . .36 C1
Carnarvon Rd BS6 . . .48 B2
Carolina Ho BS2 . . . . .86 A4
Caroline Cl BS31 . . . . .82 A4
Carpenters La BS31 . .76 A1
Carpenter's Shop La
  BS16 . . . . .42 A2
Carr Ho 3 BS2 . . . . . . .49 A1
Carriage Dr BS10 . . . .25 C2
Carrick Ho 8 BS8 . . . .54 B2
Carrington Rd BS3 . . .62 C3
Carroll Ct BS16 . . . . . .28 C1
Carsons Rd BS16 . . . .53 C2
Carters Bldgs 12
  BS8 . . . . .54 B3
Carter Wlk BS32 . . . . .16 B4
Cartledge Rd 6
  BS5 . . . . .50 A1
Cary Ct 2 BS2 . . . . . . .49 A1
Cashmore Ho 9
  BS5 . . . . .57 A3
Caslon Ct BS1 . . . . . . .87 B1
Cassell Rd BS16 . . . . .41 B1
Cassey Bottom La
  BS5 . . . . .58 C3
Casson Dr BS16 . . . . . .40 A4
Castle Cl BS10 . . . . . . .24 C2
Castle Ct
  Bristol, Arno's Vale
  BS4 . . . . .65 B4
  Bristol BS34 . . . . .29 B4
Castle Farm Rd
  BS15 . . . . .67 B2
Castlegate Ho BS4 . . .66 A3
Castle Prim Sch
  BS31 . . . . .82 B4
Castle Rd
  Bristol, Kingswood
  BS15 . . . . .52 B2
  Bristol, Oldland Common
  BS30 . . . . .69 C3
Castle St BS1 . . . . .86 B3
CATBRAIN 13 C2
Catbrain Hill BS10 . . .13 C2
Catbrain La BS10 . . . .13 C2
Cater Rd BS13 . . . . . . .71 A2
Cathedral Church of
  The Holy & Undivided
  Trinity ★ BS1 . . . . .85 B2
Cathedral Wlk BS1 . . .85 C1
Catherine Ct 14 BS6 .48 C1
Catherine Mead St
  BS3 . . . . .63 C4
Catherine St BS11 . . .33 B4
Cato St BS5 . . . . .49 C2
Cattistock Dr BS5 . . . .58 C2
Cattle Market Rd
  BS1 . . . . .87 C1
Cattybrook Rd BS16 . .43 C1
Cattybrook Rd N
  BS16 . . . . .43 C2
Cattybrook St
  7 Bristol BS5 . . . . .57 A3
  23 Bristol BS5 . . . . . . .57 A4

Causeway The BS36 . .20 B3
Causley Dr BS30 . . . . .60 C1
Cavan Wlk BS4 . . . . . .63 C1
Cave Cl BS16 . . . . .41 C2
Cave Ct BS2 . . . . .86 B4
Cave Dr BS16 . . . . .41 C2
Cave Gr BS16 . . . . .43 A3
Cavendish Gdns
  BS9 . . . . .46 A4
Cavendish Rd
  Bristol, Henleaze
  BS9 . . . . .36 C1
  Bristol, Patchway
  BS34 . . . . .15 A4
Caves Cotts BS16 . . . .42 A3
Cave St BS2 . . . . .86 B4
Cecil Ave BS5 . . . . .51 A1
Cecil Rd
  Bristol, Clifton BS8 . . . .54 B4
  Bristol, Kingswood
  BS15 . . . . .59 C4
Cedar Cl
  Bristol, Oldland
  BS30 . . . . .69 A4
  Bristol, Patchway
  BS34 . . . . .15 A3
Cedar Ct
  Bristol BS9 . . . . .46 A4
  Bristol, Combe Dingle
  BS9 . . . . .35 C3
  Bristol, Mangotsfield
  BS16 . . . . .42 A2
  Bristol, Westbury on T
  BS9 . . . . .36 B4
Cedar Dr BS31 . . . . . . .82 B4
Cedar Gr BS9 . . . . .35 C1
Cedar Hall BS16 . . . . .41 B4
Cedar Pk BS9 . . . . .35 C1
Cedar Row BS11 . . . . .34 B2
Cedars The BS9 . . . . . .46 B3
Cedars Way BS36 . . . .18 B1
Celia Terr BS4 . . . . . . .58 B2
Cemetery Rd BS4 . . . .64 C3
Cennick Ave BS15 . . . .52 C1
Centaurus Rd BS34 . .14 B3
Central Ave
  Bristol BS15 . . . . .59 B1
  Severn Beach BS10 . . . .4 B3
Central Pk BS14 . . . . . .73 A3
Central Trad Est
  BS4 . . . . .65 A4
Central Way BS10 . . . .38 A4
Centre The BS31 . . . . .76 B1
Ceres Cl BS30 . . . . . . .68 B2
Cerimon Gate BS34 . .16 C1
Cerney La BS11 . . . . . .34 A1
Chadleigh Gr BS4 . . . .71 C3
Chakeshill Cl BS10 . . .26 A3
Chakeshill Dr BS10 . .26 A4
Chalcombe Cl BS34 . .16 A4
Chalcroft Ho 2 BS3 . .62 C4
Chalcroft Wlk BS13 . .78 A4
Chalet The BS10 . . . . .25 A3
Chalfield Cl BS31 . . . .83 B2
Chalks Rd BS5 . . . . . . .57 C4
Challender Ave
  BS10 . . . . .25 A2
Challoner Ct BS1 . . . .87 A1
Champion Rd BS15 . .53 B2
Champneys Ave
  BS10 . . . . .25 A3
Champs Sur Marne
  BS32 . . . . .16 C4
Chancel Cl BS9 . . . . . .46 B3
Chancery St BS5 . . . . .57 A3
Chandag Inf Sch
  BS31 . . . . .83 B4
Chandag Jun Sch
  BS31 . . . . .83 B4
Chandag Rd BS31 . . . .83 B4
Chandos BS6 . . . . .48 A2
Chandos Rd
  Bristol BS6 . . . . .48 A1
  Keynsham BS31 . . . . . .76 A3

Chandos Trad Est
  BS2 . . . . .56 C1
Channell's Hill BS9 . .36 C4
Channon's Hill BS16 .51 A4
Chantry Ct BS1 . . . . . .85 C2
Chantry Gr BS11 . . . . .24 A2
Chantry La BS16 . . . . .31 A1
Chantry Rd BS8 . . . . . .47 C1
Chapei Way BS10 . . . .37 C4
Chapel Barton 7
  BS3 . . . . .63 A2
Chapel Cl BS15 . . . . . .61 A4
Chapel Ct
  Bristol, Brentry
  BS10 . . . . .26 B3
  Bristol, St Philip's Marsh
  BS2 . . . . .56 C1
Chapel Gdns BS10 . . .25 B1
Chapel Green La
  BS6 . . . . .47 C2
Chapel La
  Bristol, Clay Hill
  BS5 . . . . .50 C2
  Bristol, Fishponds
  BS16 . . . . .51 B4
  Bristol, Frenchay
  BS16 . . . . .41 B3
  Bristol, Lawrence Weston
  BS11 . . . . .24 A2
  Bristol, Warmley
  BS15 . . . . .61 A4
Chapel Rd
  Bristol, Bishopsworth
  BS13 . . . . .70 C2
  Bristol, Hanham
  BS15 . . . . .59 B1
  2 Bristol, Lower Easton
  BS5 . . . . .49 C1
Chapel Row BS20 . . . .45 B4
Chapel St BS2 . . . . . . .56 C1
Chapel Way BS4 . . . . .58 A2
Chaplin Rd BS5 . . . . . .49 C1
Chapter St BS2 . . . . . .86 B4
Chapter Wlk BS6 . . . .47 C3
Charbon Gate BS34 . .17 A1
Charborough Ct
  Bristol BS9 . . . . .27 A2
  Bristol BS34 . . . . .27 B2
Charborough Rd
  BS34 . . . . .27 A2
Charborough Road
  Prim Sch BS34 . . . . . . .27 A2
Charbury Wlk BS11 . .34 A1
Chard Ct BS14 . . . . . . .73 A2
Chardstock Ave BS9 .35 C4
Charfield 4 BS15 . . . .60 C4
Charfield Rd BS10 . . .26 B1
Chargrove 2 BS30 . . .61 A2
Charis Ave BS10 . . . . .37 B3
Charlecombe Ct
  BS9 . . . . .36 B2
Charlecombe Rd
  BS9 . . . . .36 B2
Charles Ave BS34 . . . .28 C4
Charles Ct 1 BS8 . . . .85 A2
Charles England Ho
  BS34 . . . . .15 A3
Charles Pl BS8 . . . . . . .85 A2
Charles Rd BS34 . . . . .27 C3
Charles St BS1 . . . . . . .86 A4
Charles Wesley Ct
  BS5 . . . . .58 C2
Charleton Ho 8
  BS2 . . . . .86 C3
Charlotte St S BS1 . . .85 C2
Charlotte St BS1 . . . . .84 C2
Charlton Ave BS34 . . .27 A2
Charlton Ct BS34 . . . . .8 A1
Charlton Gdns BS10 . .26 B4
Charlton La BS10 . . . . .25 B3

Charlton Leaze
BS10 . . . . .13 B2
Charlton Mead Ct
BS10 . . . . .26 B4
Charlton Mead Dr
BS10 . . . . .26 B3
Charlton Pk BS31 . . .75 C1
Charlton Pl BS10 . . . .26 B4
Charlton Rd
Bristol, Brentry
BS10 . . . . .26 A3
Bristol, Kingswood
BS15 . . . . .51 C1
Keynsham BS31,
BS14 . . . . .82 A3
Charlton Rd **17** BS5. . .57 A3
Charminster Rd
BS16 . . . . .51 C3
Charmouth Ct BS3 . . .63 C1
Charnell Rd BS16 . . . .52 C4
Charnhill Brow
BS16 . . . . .53 B4
Charnhill Cres BS16 .53 A4
Charnhill Dr BS16. . . .53 A4
Charnhill Ridge
BS16 . . . . .53 B4
Charnwood BS16 . . . .53 B4
Charnwood Rd
BS14 . . . . .81 A4
Charter Ho BS1 . . . . .85 B2
Charterhouse Rd
BS5 . . . . .57 C4
Charter Wlk BS14. . . .72 C2
Chartley BS9 . . . . . . .46 B2
Chasefield La **1**
BS16 . . . . .51 C4
Chase Rd BS15 . . . . . .52 B2
Chase The BS16. . . . . .52 A3
Chatford Ho BS8. . . . .54 B4
Chatsworth Rd
Bristol, Arno's Vale
BS4 . . . . .65 B4
Bristol, Hillfields
BS16 . . . . .51 C3
Chattenden Ho BS9. .47 A3
Chatterton Gn BS14. .80 B3
Chatterton Ho **5**
BS1 . . . . .87 B1
Chatterton Sq BS1 . . .87 C1
Chatterton St BS1 . . .87 C1
Chaundey Gr BS13 . . .71 A1
Chavenage BS15 . . . . .53 B1
Cheapside BS2 . . . . . .86 C4
Cheapside St **8**
BS3 . . . . .64 B4
Cheddar Gr BS13 . . . .70 C4
Cheddar Grove Prim
Sch BS13 . . . . .70 C4
Chedworth BS15. . . . .53 A3
Chedworth Rd BS7 . . .38 C2
Cheese La BS2 . . . . . .87 B2
Chelford Gr BS34 . . . .15 C4
Chelmer Gr BS31 . . . .83 A4
Chelmsford Wlk
BS4 . . . . .58 B1
Chelsea Cl BS31 . . . . .76 C1
Chelsea Pk BS5. . . . . .57 B4
Chelsea Rd BS5. . . . . .49 C1
Chelston Rd BS4 . . . .71 C3
Cheltenham Cres **2**
BS6 . . . . .48 B1
Cheltenham La BS6. .48 B2
Cheltenham Rd BS6 .48 C1
Chelvy Cl BS13 . . . . . .79 C3
Chelwood Rd BS11 . . .33 C3
Chepstow Pk BS16. . . .31 A1
Chepstow Rd BS4. . . .71 C4
Chepstow Wlk BS31 . .33 C2
Chequers Cl BS30. . . .69 B3
Chequers Ct BS34 . . . .17 B2

Cherington BS15 . . . . .59 A1
Cherington Rd BS10 . .37 C3
Cheriton Pl
Bristol, Eastfield
BS9 . . . . .37 A3
Bristol, Warmley
BS30 . . . . .61 B2
Cherry Ct **12** BS1 . . .86 A4
Cherry Garden La
BS30 . . . . .69 A2
Cherry Garden Prim
Sch BS30 . . . . .69 B2
Cherry Garden Rd
BS30 . . . . .69 B1
Cherry Gdns BS30 . . .69 B1
Cherry Gr BS16 . . . . .42 C2
Cherry La **4** BS1 . . .86 B4
Cherry Orchard La **4**
BS5 . . . . .58 B4
Cherry Tree Cl
Bristol BS16 . . . . .52 A2
Keynsham BS31 . . . . .82 A4
Cherrytree Cres
BS16 . . . . .52 A2
Cherrytree Rd BS16. .52 A2
Cherry Wood BS30 . . .69 A2
Chertsey Rd BS6. . . . .47 C1
Cherwell Rd BS31. . . .83 B4
Chesham Way BS15. .52 B1
Chessel Cl BS32 . . . . . .9 A2
Chessel Ct **6** BS3 . . .63 A2
Chessell Ave BS35 . . . .3 A3
Chessel Mews **8**
BS3 . . . . .63 B3
Chessel St BS3 . . . . . .63 A3
Chessington Ave
BS14 . . . . .73 A1
Chester Ct **4** BS5 . . .57 B3
Chesterfield Ave
BS6 . . . . .48 C2
Chesterfield Bldgs
BS8 . . . . .84 B3
Chesterfield Ho
BS10 . . . . .25 A1
Chesterfield Hospl
BS8 . . . . .85 A2
Chesterfield Rd
Bristol, Mangotsfield
BS16 . . . . .42 A1
Bristol, Montpelier
BS6 . . . . .48 C2
CHESTER PARK. 51 C2
Chester Park Jun & Inf
Schs BS16 . . . . .51 B3
Chester Park Rd
BS16 . . . . .51 C2
Chester Pk BS5. . . . . .50 C1
Chester Rd BS5. . . . . .50 C1
Chesters BS30 . . . . . .68 C4
Chester St BS5 . . . . . .49 C2
Chesterton Ho **6**
BS2 . . . . .86 B4
Chestnut Cl BS14 . . . .74 B1
Chestnut Ct
Bristol BS13 . . . . .70 C3
Bristol, Hillhouse
BS16 . . . . .42 C1
Chestnut Ho BS13 . . .79 C3
Chestnut Rd
Bristol, Lower
Soundwell BS15 . . . . .53 A3
Bristol, Mangotsfield
BS16 . . . . .41 C2
Chestnut Way BS15 . .53 A3
Chestnut Wlk BS13 . .70 C2
Chetwode Cl BS10. . . .26 B3
Chetwood Ho BS5. . . .57 B2
Chevening Cl BS34. . . .28 B4
Cheviot Way BS30 . . .61 B1
Chew Cotts BS31 . . . .76 B1
Chewton Cl BS16 . . . .51 C3
CHEWTON
KEYNSHAM. 82 C2
Chewton Rd BS31. . . .83 A2

Cheyne Rd BS9 . . . . . . .35 C2
Chichester Ho BS4. . .58 B2
Chiltern Cl
Bristol BS14 . . . . .81 A4
Bristol, Warmley
BS30 . . . . .61 B1
Chilton Rd BS4 . . . . . .72 C4
Chimney Steps BS2 . .87 C2
Chine The BS16. . . . . .39 C1
Chine View BS16 . . . .42 B4
Chiphouse Rd BS15. .53 A3
Chipperfield Dr
BS15 . . . . .53 A1
Chippings The BS16. .39 C1
Chisbury St BS5 . . . . .50 A3
Chittening Ind Est
BS11 . . . . .10 B3
Chittening Rd BS11. .10 C3
Chock La BS9 . . . . . . .36 C3
Christchurch Ave
BS16 . . . . .41 C1
Christ Church CE Inf
Sch BS16 . . . . .41 C1
Christ Church CE Jun
Sch BS16 . . . . .41 C1
Christ Church CE Prim
Sch BS8 . . . . .84 A3
Christ Church Hanham
CE Prim Sch BS15 . .67 A4
Christchurch La
BS16 . . . . .41 C1
Christchurch Rd
BS8 . . . . .84 A3
Christina Terr BS8 . . .85 A1
Christmas St **7** BS1 .86 A3
Christmas Steps **3**
BS1 . . . . .86 A3
Christmas Tree
BS34 . . . . .14 B2
Chubb Cl BS30. . . . . . .60 B1
Church Ave
Bristol BS9 . . . . .46 C4
3 Bristol, Upper Easton
BS5 . . . . .49 C1
Bristol, Warmley
BS30 . . . . .61 C3
Church Cl
Bristol BS10 . . . . .24 C2
Frampton Cotterell
BS36 . . . . .19 C4
Church Ct **8** BS16. . .52 B3
Churchdown Wlk
BS11 . . . . .34 A1
Church Dr BS5 . . . . . .58 A4
Church Farm Rd
BS16 . . . . .43 B2
Church Hill BS4 . . . . .66 A2
Church Hill Ho BS4 . .66 A2
Church Ho BS7 . . . . . .38 B4
Churchill Cl BS30 . . . .60 C1
Churchill Dr BS9. . . . .35 C3
Churchill Rd BS4 . . . .65 B4
Church La
Bristol, Bromley Heath
BS16 . . . . .31 A1
Bristol BS1 . . . . .87 B2
Bristol, Clifton Wood
BS8 . . . . .85 B2
Bristol, Dundry Hill
BS14 . . . . .81 A3
Bristol, Henbury
BS10 . . . . .24 C2
Bristol, Southville
BS3 . . . . .63 C3
Frampton Cotterell
BS36 . . . . .20 A2
Hambrook BS16 . . . . .30 C2
Portbury BS20 . . . . . .44 A3
Winterbourne BS36 . .18 A2
Churchlands Rd **8**
BS3 . . . . .63 A2
Church Leaze BS11 . .33 C3
Church Mdws BS14. .81 B4
Church Par BS4 . . . . .66 A2

Church Path Rd
BS20 . . . . .45 B4
Church Pl BS20 . . . . . .45 B4
Church Rd
Bristol, Bedminster
BS3 . . . . .63 B3
Bristol, Bishopsworth
BS13 . . . . .70 C2
Bristol BS9 . . . . .46 B3
Bristol, Filton BS34. . .27 B3
Bristol, Frenchay
BS16 . . . . .41 B3
Bristol, Hanham
BS15 . . . . .59 A1
Bristol, Horfield BS7. .38 A1
Bristol, Kingswood
BS15 . . . . .60 A4
Bristol, Moorfields
BS5 . . . . .57 C4
Bristol, Stoke Gifford
BS34 . . . . .28 C4
Bristol, Upper Soundwell
BS16 . . . . .52 C3
Bristol, Westbury on Trym
BS9 . . . . .36 C3
Easter Compton BS35 . .6 B1
Easton-in-G BS20 . . . .44 C4
Frampton Cotterell
BS36 . . . . .20 A4
Pilning BS35 . . . . .2 C3
Severn Beach BS35 . . . .2 B2
Whitchurch BS14 . . . .81 B4
Winterbourne BS36 . .30 C4
Churchside BS16 . . . .41 A3
Church St
Bristol BS1 . . . . .87 B2
Bristol, Lower Easton
BS5 . . . . .49 C1
Bristol, Russell Town
BS5 . . . . .57 A2
Church View
Almondsbury BS32. . . .8 A4
6 Bristol BS15 . . . . .60 A4
Bristol, Filton BS34. . .27 B3
Bristol, Staple Hill
BS16 . . . . .41 C1
Churchward Cl
BS15 . . . . .59 A1
Churchways BS14. . . .81 B4
Churchways Ave
BS7 . . . . .38 A2
Churchways Cres
BS7 . . . . .38 A2
Church Wlk BS20 . . . .45 B4
Churston Cl BS14 . . . .80 C3
Cicil Rd **1** BS15 . . . .59 C4
Circuit 32 BS5. . . . . . .57 A4
Circular Rd BS9 . . . . .46 C2
City Academy Bristol
The BS5 . . . . .57 B4
City Bsns Pk BS5 . . . .56 C4
City Mus & Art Gal★
BS8 . . . . .84 C3
City of Bristol Coll
BS1 . . . . .85 C2
City of Bristol Coll,
Ashley Down Ctr
BS7 . . . . .49 A4
City of Bristol Coll,
Bedminster Ctr
BS3 . . . . .64 C2
City of Bristol Coll,
Downend Ctr
BS16 . . . . .42 C4
City of Bristol College
Lawrence Weston Ctr
BS11 . . . . .23 C1
City of Bristol Coll
(Folly La Ctr) BS2 . . .56 C2
City of Bristol Coll
(Hartcliffe Ctr)
BS13 . . . . .79 C2

City of Bristol Coll
(Kingswood Ctr)
BS15 . . . . .60 A4
City of Bristol Coll,
Parkway Transport
Tech Ctr BS34 . . . . . .28 B3
City of Bristol Coll,
Soundwell Ctr
BS16 . . . . .52 C2
City Rd BS2. . . . . .86 B4
City View BS4. . . . . . .64 C3
Clamp The BS30 . . . . .69 B3
Clanage Rd BS3 . . . . .62 A4
Clapton Wlk BS9 . . . .35 B1
Clare Ave BS7 . . . . . . .48 A3
Claremont Ave BS7 . .48 B3
Claremont Ct BS9. . . .37 B1
Claremont Rd BS7 . . .48 B3
Claremont Specl Sch
BS9 . . . . .37 B1
Claremont St BS5. . . .49 B1
Claremont Terr **10**
BS5 . . . . .57 C3
Clarence Ave BS16. . .42 A1
Clarence Ct **3** BS15 .51 C1
Clarence Gdns BS16 .42 A1
Clarence Ho **2**
BS15 . . . . .51 C1
Clarence Pl BS2 . . . . .84 C4
Clarence Rd
Bristol BS1 . . . . .87 B1
Bristol, Kingswood
BS15 . . . . .51 C1
Bristol, Newton BS2. .56 C3
Bristol, Staple Hill
BS16 . . . . .42 A1
Clarendon Mews
BS16 . . . . .41 A4
Clarendon Rd BS6 . . .48 A3
Clare Rd
Bristol, Cotham
BS6 . . . . .48 B1
Bristol, Kingswood
BS15 . . . . .52 A2
Bristol, Lower Easton
BS5 . . . . .49 C2
Clare St
Bristol BS1 . . . . .87 A2
Bristol, Moorfields
BS5 . . . . .57 B4
Clark Dr BS16 . . . . . . .40 B3
Clarke St BS3. . . . . . .63 C4
Clark St BS5. . . . . . . .56 C4
Clatworthy Dr BS14. .72 C3
Clavell Rd BS10. . . . . .25 A2
Claverham Rd BS16. .40 C1
Clay Bottom BS5 . . . .50 C2
Claydon Gn BS14 . . . .80 B3
Clayfield Rd BS4. . . . .66 A3
CLAY HILL. 50 C2
Clay Hill BS5 . . . . . . .50 C2
Clay La
Bitton BS30. . . . . .77 C4
Bristol, Little Stoke
BS34 . . . . .16 A3
Bristol, Willsbridge
BS30 . . . . .69 C1
Claymore Cres **1**
BS15 . . . . .51 C1
Claypiece Rd BS13 . . .78 C4
Clay Pit Rd BS6 . . . . .47 B3
Claypool Rd BS15. . . .60 A3
Clayton St
Avonmouth BS11 . . . .21 B1
21 Bristol BS5 . . . . . .57 A4
Cleave St BS2 . . . . . . .49 C2
Cleeve Ave BS16. . . . .42 A3
Cleeve Ct BS16 . . . . . .41 C3
Cleeve Gdns BS16 . . .41 C3
Cleeve Gr BS31 . . . . . .75 C1
Cleeve Hill BS16. . . . .41 C3
Cleeve Hill Extension
BS16 . . . . .42 A2
Cleeve Lawns BS16 . .41 C3

Cleeve Lodge Cl
 BS16 . . . . .42 A2
Cleeve Lodge Rd
 BS16 . . . . .42 A2
Cleeve Park Rd
 BS16 . . . . .42 A3
Cleeve Rd
 Bristol BS4 . . . . .65 A3
 Bristol, Frenchay
 BS16 . . . . .41 B4
 Bristol, Mangotsfield
 BS16 . . . . .42 A2
Cleeves Ct BS30 . . . . . .68 B2
Cleeve Wood Pk
 BS16 . . . . .41 B4
Cleeve Wood Rd
 BS16 . . . . .41 C3
Clement St BS2 . . . . . .86 C4
Clermont Cl BS34 . . . .15 A4
Cleve Ct
 3 Bristol, Clifton Wood
 BS8 . . . . .54 B2
 Bristol, Filton BS34 . . . .27 C4
Clevedale BS16 . . . . . .41 C3
Clevedale Ct BS16 . . . .41 C3
Clevedon Rd BS7 . . . .48 B4
Clevedon Terr BS6 . .86 A4
Cleve House Sch
 BS4 . . . . .65 A3
Cleve Rd BS34 . . . . . . .27 B4
Clevewood Ho BS16 .41 B3
Clewson Rise BS14 . .80 B3
Cliff Court Dr BS16 . .41 A3
Clifford Gdns BS11 . .34 A2
Clifford Rd BS16 . . . .52 A4
Clift House Rd BS3 . .62 C4
Clift House Spur
 BS3 . . . . .62 B4
CLIFTON 84 A4
Clifton Arc BS8 . . . . . .84 A3
Clifton Cl 1 BS8 . . . .54 B3
Clifton Coll BS8 . . . .84 A4
Clifton College Prep
 Sch BS8 . . . . .54 B3
Clifton Down BS8 . . .54 B3
Clifton Down Rd
 BS8 . . . . .84 A3
Clifton Down Sh Ctr 11
 BS8 . . . . .47 C1
Clifton Down Sta
 BS8 . . . . .47 C1
Clifton High Gr BS9 .36 A1
Clifton High Sch
 BS8 . . . . .84 A4
Clifton Hill BS8 . . . . .85 A2
Clifton Metro 10
 BS8 . . . . .47 C1
Clifton Park Rd BS8 .54 B4
Clifton Pk BS8 . . . . . .84 A3
Clifton Pl BS5 . . . . . .56 C4
Clifton Rd BS8 . . . . . .85 A2
Clifton St
 Bristol, Bedminster
 BS3 . . . . .63 B3
 Bristol, Upper Easton
 BS5 . . . . .56 C4
Clifton Suspension
 Bridge * BS8 . . . . . .54 A1
Clifton Vale BS8 . . . .85 A2
Clifton Vale Cl BS8 . .85 A2
Clifton View
 Bristol, Bedminster
 Down BS13 . . . . .62 C1
 1 Bristol, Windmill Hill
 BS3 . . . . .64 B4
CLIFTON WOOD 85 A2
Cliftonwood Cres
 BS8 . . . . .85 B2
Clifton Wood Ct
 BS8 . . . . .85 B2
Clifton Wood Rd
 BS8 . . . . .85 B3
Cliftonwood Terr
 BS8 . . . . .85 A2

Clift Pl BS1 . . . . .87 A1
Clift Rd BS3 . . . . .62 C4
Clinton Rd BS3 . . . . . .63 B2
Clive Rd BS14 . . . . . . .73 B4
Cloisters BS8 . . . . .54 B4
Cloisters Ct BS36 . . . .18 C2
Cloisters Rd BS36 . . . .19 A2
Cloisters The BS6 . . . .48 A3
Clonmel Rd BS4 . . . . .63 C1
Close The
 Bristol BS16 . . . . .29 A1
 Bristol, Henbury
 BS10 . . . . .13 B1
 Bristol, Little Stoke
 BS34 . . . . .16 A2
 Bristol, Patchway
 BS32 . . . . .9 A1
 Bristol, Upper Soundwell
 BS16 . . . . .52 B3
 Frampton Cotterell
 BS36 . . . . .20 A2
Clothier Rd BS4 . . . .66 B2
Clouds Hill Ave BS5 . .58 A4
Clouds Hill Rd BS5 . .58 B4
Clovelly Cl BS5 . . . . . .58 B4
Clovelly Rd BS5 . . . . .58 B4
Cloverdale Dr BS30 . .68 C3
Clover Ground BS9 . .37 A3
Cloverlea Rd BS30 . . .61 B1
Clover Leaze BS32 . .16 B2
Clyde Ave BS31 . . . . .83 A4
Clyde Ct 2 BS3 . . . . . .63 B3
Clyde Gdns BS5 . . . . .59 A2
Clyde Gr BS34 . . . . . .27 A2
Clyde La BS6 . . . . .48 A2
Clyde Mews 3 BS6 . .48 A2
Clyde Rd
 Bristol, Redland
 BS6 . . . . .47 C2
 Bristol, Totterdown
 BS4 . . . . .64 C3
 Frampton Cotterell
 BS36 . . . . .19 C4
Clydesdale Cl BS14 . .72 C2
Clyde Terr
 Bristol, Bedminster
 BS3 . . . . .63 B3
 Bristol, Totterdown
 BS4 . . . . .64 C3
Coach House La
 BS5 . . . . .58 A4
Coaley Rd BS11 . . . . . .33 C1
COALPIT HEATH 20 B2
Coalsack La BS36 . . . .31 C3
Coalville Rd BS36 . . . .20 B3
Coape Rd BS14 . . . . . .74 B1
Coates Wlk BS4 . . . . .71 C2
Cobblestone Mews
 BS8 . . . . .84 A4
Cobden Ctr The
 BS16 . . . . .31 C2
Cobden St BS5 . . . . . .57 B3
Coberley BS15 . . . . . .59 B2
Cobhorn Dr BS13 . . . .78 B4
Cobourg Rd BS6 . . . . .49 A2
Cock Rd BS15 . . . . . . .60 B2
Codrington Pl BS8 . . .84 A3
Codrington Rd BS7 . .48 B3
Cody Ct 2 BS15 . . . . .59 A1
Cogan Rd BS16 . . . . . .52 C3
Cogsall Rd BS14 . . . . .74 B2
Colburn Ct BS7 . . . . .38 B3
Colchester Cres
 BS4 . . . . .71 C3
Coldharbour La
 BS16 . . . . .40 A4
Coldharbour Rd
 BS6 . . . . .47 C4
Coldpark Gdns BS13 .70 A1
Coldpark Rd BS13 . . .70 A1
Coldrick Cl BS14 . . . .80 B3
Colebrook Rd BS15 . .59 B4
Coleford Rd BS10 . . . .26 B1
Colemead BS13 . . . . . .71 A1

Cole Rd BS2 . . . . .57 A2
Coleridge Ct 10 BS3 .63 B3
Coleridge Ho BS34 . . .8 B1
Coleridge Rd BS5 . . . .50 A3
Coleshill Dr BS13 . . . .71 A1
Collard Ho 2 BS16 . .51 A4
Coledge Ave BS16 . . . .40 C1
College Ct
 Bristol BS8 . . . . .84 A4
 Bristol, Fishponds
 BS16 . . . . .40 C1
College Fields BS8 . .54 B4
College Gn BS1 . . . . .85 C2
College Mews BS9 . . .36 C3
College Park Dr
 BS10 . . . . .25 A1
College Rd
 Bristol, Clifton BS8 . . .54 B4
 Bristol, Fishponds
 BS16 . . . . .40 C1
 Bristol, Westbury on Trym
 BS9 . . . . .36 C3
College Sq BS1 . . . . . .85 C2
College St BS1 . . . . . .85 C2
College Way BS34 . . .27 B4
Collett Cl BS15 . . . . . .59 A1
Collett Ho BS36 . . . . .30 B4
Colliers Break BS16 . .43 A1
Colliers Gdns BS16 . .41 A1
Collingwood Ave
 BS15 . . . . .52 C1
Collingwood Rd 4
 BS6 . . . . .47 C1
Collin Rd BS4 . . . . . . .65 C4
Collins Ave BS34 . . . .16 A2
Collins Dr BS35 . . . . . . .5 A3
Collinson Rd BS13 . . .71 A1
Collins St BS11 . . . . . .33 A4
Colliter Cres BS3 . . . .63 A2
Colne Gn BS31 . . . . . .83 B4
Colston Ave BS1 . . . . .86 A3
Colston Cl
 Bristol BS16 . . . . .52 B3
 Winterbourne BS36 . . .30 C4
Colston Ct BS7 . . . . . .48 B3
Colston Dale BS16 . . .50 C4
Colston Fort 2 BS2 . .86 A4
Colston Hall * BS1 . .86 A3
Colston Hill BS16 . . .50 B4
Colston Mews BS6 . .48 C1
Colston Par BS1 . . . . .87 B1
Colston Rd BS5 . . . . . .50 A1
Colston's Almshouses
 1 BS1 . . . . .86 A3
Colstons Girls' Sch
 BS8 . . . . .48 C1
Colston's Lower Sch
 BS16 . . . . .39 C1
Colston's Prim Sch
 BS6 . . . . .48 B1
Colston's Sch BS16 . .50 A4
Colston St
 Bristol BS1 . . . . .86 A3
 Bristol, Upper Soundwell
 BS16 . . . . .52 B3
Colston Yd BS1 . . . . . .86 A3
Colthurst Dr BS15 . . .60 A1
Colthurst Mews BS2 .65 A4
Colwyn Rd 2 BS5 . . . .50 A1
Colyton Ct BS3 . . . . . .63 C1
Combfactory La 13
 BS5 . . . . .57 A4
Comb Paddock BS9 . .47 C4
Commercial Rd BS1 .87 A1
Common (East) The
 BS32 . . . . .9 A1
Commonfield Rd
 BS11 . . . . .23 C1
Common La BS20 . . . .45 A2
Common Mead La
 BS16 . . . . .29 B1
Common Rd
 Bristol BS15 . . . . .67 A3

Common Rd continued
 Winterbourne BS36 . . .19 A3
Common The
 Bristol, Frenchay
 BS16 . . . . .41 A3
 Bristol, Patchway
 BS32 . . . . .9 A1
Compton Dr BS9 . . . . .35 B3
Compton Gn BS31 . . .82 C4
COMPTON
 GREENFIELD 13 A4
Compton Lodge 3
 BS6 . . . . .47 C1
Compton St BS5 . . . . .57 B3
Comyn Wlk BS16 . . . .40 C1
Concorde Dr BS10 . . .25 C1
Concorde Ho BS34 . . .27 A2
Concorde Rd BS34 . . .14 C3
Condor Ho BS7 . . . . . .39 B3
Condover Rd BS4 . . . .66 C3
Conduit Pl 2 BS2 . . . .49 B1
Conduit Rd BS2 . . . . .49 B1
Cone The BS10, BS34 .14 A2
Coneygree BS13 . . . . .70 B2
Congleton Rd BS5 . . .57 C4
CONHAM 58 C1
Conham Hill BS15 . . .58 C1
Conham Ho BS15 . . . .58 C1
Conham Rd BS4, BS5,
 BS15 . . . . .58 B1
Conifer Cl BS16 . . . . . .41 C2
Coniston Ave BS9 . . . .36 A2
Coniston Cl BS30 . . . .61 C2
Coniston Prim Sch
 BS34 . . . . .8 A1
Coniston Rd BS34 . . . .8 A1
Connaught Prim Sch
 BS4 . . . . .72 A4
Connaught Rd BS4 . .72 A4
Constable Cl BS31 . . .76 B2
Constable Rd BS7 . . .39 A2
Constantine Ave
 BS34 . . . . .16 C1
Constitution Hill
 BS8 . . . . .85 B2
Contemporis BS8 . . . .84 A3
Convent Cl BS10 . . . . .24 B3
Conway Gn BS31 . . . .83 B3
Conway Rd BS4 . . . . .65 B4
Conygre Gr BS34 . . . .28 A3
Conygre Rd BS34 . . . .27 C3
Cook Cl BS30 . . . . .69 B4
Cooke's Dr BS35 . . . . .6 B1
Cooks Cl BS32 . . . . .9 B3
Cook's Folly Rd BS9 .46 B3
Cooksley Rd BS5 . . . .57 B4
Cook St BS11 . . . . .33 B4
Cookworthy Cl 2
 BS5 . . . . .57 A2
Coombe Bridge Ave
 BS9 . . . . .35 C2
Coombe Brook La
 BS15 . . . . .50 C2
Coombe Cl BS10 . . . . .24 B3
Coombe Dale BS9 . . .35 B2
COOMBE DINGLE . . .35 B4
Coombe Gdns BS9 . . .36 A2
Coombe Ho 4 BS15 . .60 A4
Coombe La
 Bristol BS9 . . . . .36 A2
 Easton-in-G BS8 . . . . . .44 C2
Coombe Rd BS5 . . . . .50 A2
Coombes Way BS30 . .69 C4
Coombe Way BS10 . . .25 A1
Coomb Rocke BS9 . . .35 C2
Cooperage La BS3 . . .85 B1
Cooperage Rd BS5 . . .57 C3
Co-operation Rd
 BS5 . . . . .50 A1
Cooper Rd BS9 . . . . . .36 B3
Coots The BS14 . . . . . .74 A2
Copeland Dr BS14 . . .73 A1
Copley Ct BS15 . . . . . .60 A1
Copley Gdns BS7 . . . .39 A2

Coppice The
 Bristol, Bradley Stoke
 BS32 . . . . .16 C3
 Bristol, Highridge
 BS13 . . . . .78 A4
Copse Rd BS4 . . . . . . .65 A3
Copthorne Cl BS14 . .73 A1
Corbet Cl BS11 . . . . . .24 A2
Corbett Ho 11 BS5 . . .57 B3
Cordwell Wlk BS10 . .37 C3
Corey Cl 6 BS2 . . . . . .49 A1
Corfe Cres BS31 . . . . .82 C4
Corfe Pl BS30 . . . . . . .69 A1
Corfe Rd BS4 . . . . .71 C3
Coriander Dr BS34 . . .17 B3
Coriander Wlk BS5 . .50 A2
Corinthian Ct 9
 BS1 . . . . .87 B1
Corinum Cl BS16 . . . .43 B2
Corker's Hill 9 BS5 . .58 B2
Cornfield Cl BS32 . . . .9 A1
Cornhill Dr BS14 . . . .72 C3
Cornish Gr BS14 . . . . .74 A2
Cornish Rd BS14 . . . . .74 A2
Cornish Wlk BS14 . . .74 A2
Cornleaze BS13 . . . . . .70 C1
Corn St BS1 . . . . .86 A3
Cornwallis Ave BS8 . .85 A2
Cornwallis Cres BS8 .54 B2
Cornwallis Gr BS8 . . .85 A2
Cornwallis Ho BS8 . .85 A2
Cornwall Rd BS7 . . . .48 B4
Coronation Ave
 Bristol BS16 . . . . .51 B4
 Keynsham BS31 . . . . . .82 B4
Coronation Cl BS30 . .60 C1
Coronation Pl BS1 . . .87 A2
Coronation Rd
 Bristol BS3 . . . . .85 B1
 Bristol, Cadbury Heath
 BS30 . . . . .61 A1
 Bristol, Mangotsfield
 BS16 . . . . .42 A1
 Bristol, Warmley
 BS15 . . . . .60 C3
Corsley Wlk BS4 . . . .72 B4
Corston Wlk BS11 . . .33 C3
Cossham Memorial
 Hospl BS16 . . . . .52 A2
Cossham Rd BS5 . . . .57 C3
Cossham St BS16 . . . .43 A1
Cossham Wlk BS5 . . .51 B1
Cossington Rd BS4 . .72 B4
Cossins Rd BS6 . . . . . .47 C3
Costiland Dr BS13 . . .70 B2
Cote Bank Ho BS9 . . .37 A3
Cote Dr BS9 . . . . .47 B4
Cote House La BS9 . .36 C1
Cote La BS9 . . . . .36 C1
Cote Lea Pk BS9 . . . . .37 A3
Cote Paddock BS9 . . .47 A4
Cote Pk BS9 . . . . .36 A2
Cote Rd BS9 . . . . .47 B4
COTHAM 49 A3
Cotham Brow BS6 . . .48 B1
Cotham Gdns 15
 BS6 . . . . .47 C1
Cotham Gr BS6 . . . . . .48 B1
Cotham Gram Sch
 (Charnwood Annex)
 BS6 . . . . .48 A1
Cotham Hill BS6 . . . .84 C4
Cotham Lawn Ho
 BS6 . . . . .84 C4
Cotham Lawn Rd
 Bristol BS6 . . . . .48 A1
 Bristol BS6 . . . . .84 C4
Cotham Pk BS6 . . . . . .48 A1
Cotham Pk N BS6 . . .48 A1
Cotham Pl BS6 . . . . . .84 C4
Cotham Rd BS6 . . . . . .84 C4

Cotham Rd S BS6....**86** A4
Cotham Sch BS6....**84** C4
Cotham Side BS6....**48** B1
Cotham Vale BS6....**48** A1
Cotman Rd BS7....**39** A2
Cotrith Gr BS10....**24** C3
Cotswold Ct BS16....**28** C1
Cotswold Ed Ctr The
BS34....**27** A2
Cotswold Rd BS3....**63** C3
Cotswold View
Bristol, Filton BS34....**27** B3
Bristol, Kingswood
BS15....**52** B2
Cottage Gdns BS5....**58** C3
Cottage Pl BS2....**49** B3
Cottington Ct BS15....**60** A1
Cottisford Rd BS5....**49** C4
Cottle Gdns BS14....**74** B2
Cottle Rd BS14....**74** B2
Cotton Mill La BS5....**57** B2
Cottonwood Dr
BS30....**68** C3
Cottrell Ave BS15....**52** A2
Cottrell Rd BS5....**50** A3
Coulson BS 2 BS7....**49** A4
Coulson's Cl BS14....**80** C3
Coulson's Rd BS14....**80** C3
Coulson Wlk BS15....**52** A2
Counterpool Rd
BS15....**59** B3
Counterslip BS1....**87** B2
Counterslip Gdns
BS14....**73** B2
Countess Wlk BS16....**39** C2
County St BS4....**64** C4
County Way BS34....**29** B4
Court Cl BS7....**38** A3
Courtenay Cres BS4....**71** C3
Courtenay Rd BS31....**83** C2
Court Farm Rd
Bristol BS14....**80** B3
Bristol, Longwell Green
BS30....**68** A2
Courtfield Gr BS16....**51** B4
Court Hay BS20....**44** C4
Courtlands
Bristol BS32....**9** A1
Keynsham BS31....**76** A1
Courtlands La BS3....**62** A4
Courtney Prim Sch
BS15....**60** B3
Courtney Rd BS15....**60** A3
Courtney Way BS15....**60** C3
Court Rd
Bristol, Horfield
BS7....**38** B2
Bristol, Kingswood
BS15....**59** C3
Bristol, Oldland Common
BS30....**69** B3
Frampton Cotterell
BS36....**19** A4
Courtside Mews
BS6....**48** A1
Cousins Cl BS10....**24** B3
Cousins La BS5....**58** B4
Cousins Mews BS5....**58** B4
Cousins Way BS16....**43** C4
Couzens Pl BS34....**17** A1
Coventry Wlk BS34....**58** B2
Cowdray Rd BS4....**71** C3
Cowhorn Hill BS30....**69** B4
Cowler Wlk BS13....**78** B4
Cowling Dr BS14....**73** C1
Cowling Rd BS14....**73** C1
Cowper Rd BS6....**48** A1
Cowper St BS5....**57** B3
Cox Ct BS30....**68** B4
Crabtree Wlk BS5....**50** B2

Cradock Cl BS30....**69** A4
Craftes Ct BS5....**50** C1
Cranberry Wlk BS9....**35** B4
Cranbourne Rd
BS34....**15** A3
Cranbrook Rd BS6....**48** A3
Crandell Cl BS10....**25** A4
Crane Cl BS15....**61** A4
Cranford Ct **1** BS9....**37** A2
Cranham Cl BS15....**53** A2
Cranham Dr BS34....**9** A1
Cranham Rd BS10....**37** B4
Cranleigh Gdns BS9....**46** C4
Cranleigh Rd BS14....**73** A1
Cranmoor Gn BS35....**3** B2
Cranmore Ave BS31....**76** A3
Cranmore Cres
BS10....**26** B1
Cranside Ave BS6....**48** A4
Cransley Cres BS9....**37** B3
Crantock Ave BS13....**71** A4
Cranwell Gr BS14....**72** C1
Crates Cl BS15....**60** A4
Craven Cl BS30....**60** B1
Craven Way BS30....**60** B1
Craydon Gr BS14....**81** C4
Craydon Rd BS14....**73** C1
Craydon Wlk BS14....**73** C1
Create Ctr ★ BS1....**54** B1
Crediton Cres BS14....**64** B1
Crescent Rd BS16....**41** B2
Crescent The
Bristol BS16....**29** A1
Bristol, Frenchay
BS16....**29** A1
Bristol, Henleaze BS9....**37** B2
Bristol, Sea Mills BS9....**35** B2
Bristol, Upper Soundwell
BS16....**52** B3
Crest The BS4....**65** B2
Creswicke Ave BS15....**59** B1
Creswicke Ho **12**
BS1....**86** A3
Creswicke Rd BS4....**72** A3
CREW'S HOLE....**58** A3
Crew's Hole Rd BS5....**58** A3
CRIBBS
CAUSEWAY....**14** B2
Cribbs Causeway Ctr
BS34....**13** B2
Cribbs Causeway Ret
Pk BS10....**13** B2
Cribbs Cswy BS10....**13** B2
Cricket La BS10....**36** C4
Cricklade Rd BS7....**48** C4
Cripps Rd BS3....**63** B3
Crispin Way BS15....**53** A2
Crockerne CE Prim Sch
BS20....**45** B4
Crockerne Dr BS20....**45** B3
Crockerne Ho BS20....**45** C4
Croft Ave BS16....**50** A4
Croft Cl BS36....**37** C4
Crofters Wlk BS32....**16** B4
Crofton Ave BS7....**38** B2
Crofton Fields BS36....**18** C2
Crofton Mews BS15....**60** A3
CROFTS END....**51** A1
Crofts End Ind Est
BS5....**50** C1
Crofts End Rd BS5....**50** C1
Croft The
Bristol, Mangotsfield
BS16....**42** B1
Bristol, Oldland Common
BS30....**69** B3
Croft View BS9....**37** B2
Crokeswood Wlk
BS11....**23** B1
Crome Rd BS7....**39** A3
Cromer Rd BS5....**50** A2
Cromwell Ct BS15....**60** A1

Cromwell Rd
Bristol, Montpelier
BS6....**48** C2
Bristol, St George
BS5....**58** C4
Cromwells Hide
BS16....**40** A1
Cromwell St BS3....**63** B3
Cromwell View BS6....**48** C2
Croomes Hill BS16....**19** A3
Cropthorne Rd BS7....**27** B1
Cropthorne Road S
BS7....**38** C4
Crosby Row BS8....**85** A2
Crosscombe Dr
BS13....**79** B3
Cross Combe Wlk
BS13....**79** A3
Cross Elms La BS9....**36** A1
Crossfield Rd BS16....**52** C3
Cross Hands Rd BS35....**3** B3
Cross Lanes BS20....**45** B4
Crossleaze Rd BS15....**67** B3
Crossley Cl BS36....**19** A3
Crossley Farm Bsns Ctr
BS36....**18** C3
Crossman Ave BS36....**18** C1
Cross St
Bristol BS15....**52** B1
Keynsham BS31....**76** B3
Cross Tree Gr BS32....**16** B4
Crossways Rd BS4....**64** C1
Cross Wlk BS14....**72** C2
Crow La
Bristol BS1....**87** A2
Bristol, Henbury
BS10....**25** A2
Crowley Way BS11....**21** C1
Crowndale Rd BS4....**64** C3
Crown Gdns BS30....**61** A3
Crown Hill BS5....**58** B4
Crown Hill Wlk BS5....**51** A1
Crown Ho BS1....**87** A2
Crown Ind Est BS30....**61** B3
Crown La BS16....**52** B3
Crownleaze BS16....**52** B3
Crown Rd
Bristol, Upper
Soundwell BS15....**52** B2
Bristol, Warmley
BS30....**61** B2
Crown Way BS30....**61** B3
Crows Gr BS32....**9** B3
Crowther Pk BS7....**49** B4
Crowther Rd BS7....**49** B4
Crowther St **4** BS3....**63** B4
Croydon Ho **1** BS5....**57** A4
Croydon St BS5....**57** A4
Crunnis The BS32....**16** C2
Crusader Ho **4** BS1....**87** A2
Crusty La BS20....**33** B1
Crystal Way BS32....**16** C4
Cuckoo La BS36....**37** A1
Cuffington Ave BS4....**65** C4
Culvers Cl BS31....**76** A2
Culvers Rd BS31....**76** A2
Culver St BS1....**85** C2
Culvert The BS32....**16** B4
Culverwell Rd BS13....**78** C4
Cumberland Basin Rd
BS8....**54** B1
Cumberland Cl BS1....**85** A1
Cumberland Gr **5**
BS6....**49** A2
Cumberland Pl **6**
BS8....**54** B2
Cumberland Rd BS1....**85** B1
Cumberland St BS2....**86** B4
Cunningham Gdns
BS16....**41** A1
Cunnington Cl BS30....**69** A1
Curland Gr BS14....**73** A1
Curlew Cl BS16....**40** B2
Curtis La BS34....**29** B4

Custom Cl BS14....**72** C3
Custom Ho BS1....**87** A1
Cutler Rd BS13....**70** B2
Cutters Row BS3....**64** A4
Cylde Pk BS6....**47** C2
Cynder Way BS16....**31** B1
Cypress Ct BS9....**46** B3
Cypress Gdns BS8....**54** A2
Cypress Gr BS9....**37** B2
Cyrus Ct BS16....**43** A3

D

Daines Ct **4** BS16....**50** C3
Dairycroft BS2....**86** B4
Daisy Rd BS5....**50** A2
Dakin Cl BS4....**64** A1
Dakota Dr BS14....**80** C4
Dalby Ave BS3....**63** C4
Dale St BS5....**58** B4
Dalkeith Ave BS15....**52** A1
Dalrymple Rd **10**
BS2....**48** C1
Dalston Rd BS3....**63** A4
Dalton Sq BS2....**86** B4
Dampier Rd BS3....**62** C3
Danbury Cres BS10....**26** A1
Danbury Wlk BS10....**26** A1
Danby Ho BS7....**38** C1
Dancey Mead BS13....**70** B2
Dangerfield Ave
BS13....**70** B2
Dapps Hill BS31....**76** B1
Darley Cl BS10....**24** B3
Darnley Ave BS7....**38** B2
Dartmoor St BS3....**63** A3
Dartmouth Wlk
BS31....**82** B4
Daubeny Cl BS16....**41** A1
Daubeny Ct BS1....**87** A1
Davenport Cl BS30....**68** C2
Daventry Rd BS4....**64** B1
Davey St BS2....**49** A1
Davey Terr **8** BS2....**49** A1
David's Rd BS14....**73** B2
David St BS2....**86** C3
David Thomas Ho
BS6....**48** C2
Davies Dr BS4....**58** B1
Davin Cres BS20....**45** B3
Davis Cl BS30....**60** B1
Davis St BS11....**33** A4
Davron Ct BS3....**64** A4
Dawes Ct **2** BS8....**54** B2
Dawley Cl BS36....**18** C3
Dawlish Rd BS3....**63** C2
Dawn Rise BS15....**53** B1
Daws Ct BS16....**51** C4
Day's Rd BS2....**56** C4
Days Road Commercial
Ctr BS2....**56** C3
Deacon Cl BS36....**18** C1
Dean Cl BS15....**67** A4
Dean Cres
8 Bristol BS3....**63** B4
1 Bristol BS3....**63** B4
Deanery Cl BS15....**61** A4
Deanery Rd
Bristol BS1....**85** C2
Bristol, Warmley
BS15....**61** A4
Deanery Rd Rdbt
BS15....**61** A4
Dean La BS3....**63** B4
Deanna Ct BS16....**42** A2
Dean Rd BS11....**10** A1
Dean's Cl BS11....**85** C2
Dean's Dr BS5....**51** B2
Deans Mead BS11....**34** C4
Dean St
Bristol BS2....**86** B4
Bristol, Southville
BS3....**63** B4
Debecca's La BS20....**45** A4

De Clifford Rd BS11....**24** A2
Deep Coombe Rd
BS3....**62** C2
Deep Pit Rd BS5....**51** A2
Deep St BS1....**86** A3
Deerhurst BS15....**52** C3
Deering Cl BS11....**23** C1
Deerswood BS15....**52** C3
Delabere Ave BS16....**41** A1
De La Warre Ct **11**
BS4....**58** B2
Delius Gr BS4....**71** C3
Dell The
Bristol, Bradley Stoke
BS32....**16** C3
Bristol, Oldland Common
BS30....**61** B1
Bristol, Westbury on T
BS9....**36** B1
Delvin Rd BS10....**37** B4
Denbigh St BS2....**49** A1
Dene Cl BS31....**83** A3
Dene Rd BS14....**81** B4
Denleigh Cl BS14....**80** C4
Denmark Ave BS1....**85** C2
Denmark Pl BS7....**48** C3
Denmark St BS1....**85** C2
Dennor Pk BS14....**73** A3
Denny Isle Dr BS35....**2** B2
Denston Wlk BS13....**70** C3
Denton Patch BS16....**43** A3
Dentwood Gr BS9....**35** A4
Derby Rd BS7....**48** C3
Derby St BS5....**57** C3
Derham Rd BS13....**70** C1
Dermot St **11** BS2....**49** A1
Derricke Rd BS14....**74** B2
Derrick Rd BS15....**59** C4
Derry Rd BS3....**63** A2
Derwent Cl BS34....**15** B4
Derwent Gr BS31....**76** C1
Derwent Rd BS5....**51** A1
Devaney Cl BS4....**58** B1
Deverel Gr BS31....**83** B4
De Verose Ct BS15....**68** A4
Devon Gr BS5....**57** B4
Devon Rd BS5....**50** A1
Devon Road Trad Est
1 BS5....**50** A1
Devonshire Bldgs
BS3....**64** A4
Devonshire Rd BS6....**47** C4
Dewfalls Dr BS32....**9** B1
Dial La BS16....**41** C2
Diamond Rd BS5....**58** B3
Diamond St BS3....**63** B3
Diamonite Ind Pk
BS16....**51** B3
Diana Gdns BS32....**16** C4
Dibden Cl BS16....**42** C4
Dibden La BS16....**43** A3
Dibden Rd BS16....**42** C3
Dickens Cl BS7....**38** C4
Dickinsons Fields
BS3....**63** C2
Didsbury Cl BS10....**35** A1
Dighton Ct **3** BS2....**86** B4
Dighton Gate BS34....**16** C1
Dighton St BS2....**86** B4
Dillon Ct **10** BS5....**57** C3
Dingle Cl BS9....**35** B2
Dingle Ct BS13....**70** B3
Dingle Rd BS9....**35** C3
Dingle The
Bristol BS9....**35** C3
Winterbourne BS36....**31** A3
Dingle View BS9....**35** B3
Dinglewood Cl BS9....**35** C3
DINGS THE....**56** C2
Dings Wlk BS2....**56** C2
Dirac Rd BS7....**49** A4
District Ctr BS32....**16** A4
Dixon Bsns Ctr BS4....**66** B2
Dixon Rd BS4....**66** B2

Dock Gate La BS8....85 A1
Dodisham Wlk BS16 .41 A2
Dolman Cl BS10 .....25 A3
Dominion Rd BS16...51 A3
Donald Rd BS13 .....70 B3
Donal Early Way
  BS7................38 A4
Doncaster Rd BS10 ..37 B4
Donegal Rd BS4 .....63 C1
Dongola Ave BS7....48 C4
Dongola Rd BS7.....48 C4
Don John Ho BS5....58 A4
Donnington Wlk
  BS31...............82 B4
Doone Rd BS7........38 B4
Dorcas Ave BS34.....17 A1
Dorchester Rd BS7 ..38 C3
Dorester Cl BS10 ....26 A4
Dorian Cl BS7 ....38 A3
Dorian Rd BS7.......38 A3
Dorian Way BS7 .....38 A4
Dormer Cl BS36 .....20 B2
Dormer Rd BS5......49 C3
Dorset Gr 10 BS2 ...49 B2
Dorset Rd
  Bristol, Kingswood
  BS15...............52 B1
  Bristol, Westbury on Trym
  BS9................37 A2
Dorset St 6 BS3....63 A3
Doudney Ct BS3 .....64 A4
Douglas Rd
  Bristol, Horfield
  BS7................38 B3
  Bristol, Kingswood
  BS15...............59 C3
Douglas Road Ind Pk
  BS15...............59 C3
Doulton Way BS14...73 A1
Dove La
  Bristol BS2 ....86 C4
  Bristol, Russell Town
  BS5................57 B3
Dovercourt Rd BS7..38 C2
Dover Pl BS8 ....44 B3
Dover Place Cotts
  BS8................84 B3
Dove St S BS2.......86 A4
Dove St BS2.........86 A4
Doveswell Gr BS13..78 C4
Dovey Ct BS16.......61 B1
Dowdeswell Cl
  BS10...............25 A3
Dower Ho The BS16..40 A3
Dowland Gr BS14....71 C2
Dowling Rd BS13 ....79 C2
DOWNEND 42 A4
Downend Comp Sch
  BS16...............42 A4
Downend Park Rd
  BS16...............41 C1
Downend Pk BS7 ....38 B1
Downend Rd
  Bristol, Fishponds
  BS16...............41 B1
  Bristol, Horfield BS7..38 B1
  Bristol, Kingswood
  BS15...............52 B1
Down Farm Ho
  BS36...............18 B2
Downfield
  Bristol BS9 ....35 B3
  Keynsham BS31 .....75 C1
Downfield Dr BS36...19 C4
Downfield Lodge
  BS8................47 B1
Downfield Rd BS8 ...47 B1
Downleaze
  Bristol, Downend
  BS16...............41 C4
  Stoke Bishop BS9 ....47 A3
Downleaze Rd BS9...47 A3
Downman Rd BS7 ....38 C1
Down Rd BS36.......31 A4

Downs Cote Ave
  BS9................36 B2
Downs Cote Dr BS9 .36 B2
Downs Cote Gdns
  BS9................36 C2
Downs Cote Pk BS9 .36 C2
Downs Cote View
  BS9................36 C2
Downs Ct BS9 ....37 A2
Downside Cl BS30 ...60 B1
Downside Rd BS8....47 B1
Downs Pk E BS6.....47 B4
Downs Pk W BS6 ....47 B4
Downs Rd BS9.......36 C2
Downsview Ct BS8...47 B1
Downton Rd BS4 ....63 C1
Down View BS7......49 A3
Dowry Pl 3 BS8.....54 B1
Dowry Rd BS8 ....85 A2
Dowry Sq BS8 ....85 A2
Dragon Ct BS5.......50 C1
Dragonfly Cl BS15 ..59 C3
Dragon Rd BS36.....18 B1
Dragons Hill Cl
  BS31...............76 B1
Dragons Hill Ct
  BS31...............76 B1
Dragons Hill Gdns
  BS31...............76 B1
Dragonswell Rd
  BS10...............25 B2
Dragon Wlk BS5.....51 A1
Drake Rd BS3........62 C3
Dram La BS5.........58 C2
Dramway Rdbt BS16 .43 C2
Draper Ct 3 BS5....57 B3
Draycot Pl BS1 ......87 A1
Draycott Rd BS7.....38 B1
Draydon Rd BS4.....71 C4
Drayton Cl BS14 ....73 A4
Drayton Rd BS9 .....35 B4
Drive The
  Bristol BS14 ....73 B2
  Bristol, Henleaze
  BS9................37 A1
  Keynsham BS31 .....76 A2
Druetts Cl BS10......38 A2
Druid Cl BS9 ....36 A1
Druid Hill BS9 ....36 A1
Druid Rd BS9........46 B4
Druid Stoke Ave
  BS9................35 C1
Druid Woods BS9....35 B1
Drummond Ct BS30..68 B4
Drummond Rd
  Bristol, Fishponds
  BS16...............51 A3
  Bristol, St Pauls BS2..48 C1
Dr White's Cl BS1....87 B1
Dryleaze BS31.......76 A3
Dryleaze Rd BS16...40 B2
Dubbers La BS5......50 C2
Dublin Cres BS9 .....37 A2
Duchess Rd BS8 .....47 B1
Duchess Way BS16...39 C2
Ducie Ct BS16.......52 C4
Ducie Rd
  Bristol, Russell Town
  BS5................57 A3
  Bristol, Staple Hill
  BS16...............42 A1
Ducie Rd Bsns Pk 9
  BS5................57 A3
Duckmoor Rd BS3...62 C3
Duckmoor Road Ind Est
  BS3................62 C4
Dudley Cl BS31......82 C4
Dudley Ct 3 BS30 ..68 B4
Dudley Gr BS7.......38 C4
Dugar Wlk BS6 ......48 A3
Dulverton Rd BS7...48 B4
Dumaine Ave BS34..16 C1
Duncan Ho BS8......84 A3
Duncombe La BS15..51 C2

Duncombe Rd BS15..51 C1
Dundas Cl BS10......24 C2
Dundonald Rd BS6...47 C3
Dundridge Gdns
  BS5................58 C2
Dundridge La BS5 ...58 C2
Dundry Cl BS15......59 C2
DUNDRY HILL.......81 A3
Dundry View BS4 ....64 C1
Dunford Rd BS3 .....63 C3
Dunkeld Ave BS34...27 A2
Dunkerry Rd BS3 ....63 C3
Dunkirk Rd BS16....51 A3
Dunmail Rd BS10....26 A2
Dunmore St 8 BS2..64 B4
Dunmurry BS9.......46 B3
Dunster Gdns BS30..69 A2
Dunster Rd
  Bristol BS4 ....72 B4
  Keynsham BS31.....82 C4
Durban Rd BS34.....15 A4
Durbin Wlk BS5......56 C4
Durdham Ct BS6.....47 B3
Durdham Pk BS6.....47 B3
Durham Gr BS31.....82 B4
Durham Rd 11 BS2...49 B2
Durleigh Cl BS13 ....70 C3
Durley Hill BS31 .....75 B3
Durley La BS31.......75 C3
Durnford Ave BS3....62 C4
Durnford St BS3......62 C4
Dursley Rd BS11.....34 A1
Durville Rd BS13.....71 A2
Durweston Wlk
  BS14...............73 B4
Dutton Cl BS14......73 C2
Dutton Rd BS14......73 C2
Dutton Wlk BS14 ....73 C2
Dyers Cl BS13........79 C4
DYER'S COMMON...5 A3
Dylan Thomas Ct 4
  BS30...............60 C1
Dyrham BS16........30 A1
Dyrham Cl
  Bristol, Henleaze
  BS9................37 C2
  Bristol, Kingswood
  BS15...............60 B4
Dyrham Par BS34...16 A4
Dyrham Rd BS15....60 B4

E

Eagle Dr BS34.......14 C1
Eagle Rd BS4.......65 C2
Eagles Wood BS32....9 B3
Eagles Wood Bsns Pk
  BS32................9 A3
Earl Russell Way
  BS5................57 A3
Earlsmead BS16 .....50 C4
Earl St BS1..........86 A4
Earlstone Cl BS30...68 C4
Earlstone Cres BS30.68 C4
Easedale Cl BS10....26 B2
Eastbourne Rd 9
  BS5................57 A4
Eastbury Rd BS16...51 B4
Eastcote Pk BS14....73 A1
East Croft BS9.......37 B3
EAST DUNDRY......78 C1
East Dundry La
  BS41...............78 C1
East Dundry Rd BS13,
  BS14...............80 B2
EASTER COMPTON ..6 B2
EASTFIELD.........37 A3
Eastfield BS9........37 A3
Eastfield Rd
  Bristol, Eastville
  BS9................37 A3
  Bristol, Montpelier
  BS6................48 B2

Eastfield Rd continued
  Bristol, Westbury on Trym
  BS9................36 C3
Eastfield Terr BS9....37 A2
Eastgate Office Ctr
  BS5................49 C3
Eastgate Ret Pk
  BS5................49 C3
East Gr BS6.........49 A1
East Hill BS9 ....37 A3
Eastlake Cl BS7......39 A3
Eastleigh Cl BS16....52 C4
Eastleigh Rd
  Bristol, Brentry
  BS10...............26 B1
  Bristol, Staple Hill
  BS16...............52 C3
Eastlyn Rd BS13.....71 A4
Eastmead Ct BS9....46 C4
Eastmead La BS9....46 C4
Eastnor Rd BS14.....80 C3
Easton Bsns Ctr BS5 .57 B4
Easton CE Prim Sch
  BS5................56 C4
EASTON-IN-
GORDANO.........44 C4
Easton Rd
  Bristol, Newton
  BS5................56 C3
  Bristol, Upper Easton
  BS5................57 A4
  Pill BS20 ....45 B4
Easton Way BS5.....56 C4
Eastover Cl BS9.....36 C4
East Par BS9 ....35 B2
East Park Dr BS5 ....50 A2
Eastpark Trad Est
  BS5................50 B1
East Pk BS5 ....50 A2
East Priory Cl BS9 ...36 C3
East Ridge Dr BS13 .70 B1
East Shrubbery 3
  BS6................47 C2
East St
  Avonmouth BS11 ....21 B1
  Bristol, Southville
  BS3................63 C4
East View BS16 .....42 B2
EASTVILLE.........50 A3
Eastwood Cres BS4 .66 B3
Eastwood Rd BS4...66 B3
Eaton Cl
  Bristol BS14 ....74 A1
  Bristol, Fishponds
  BS16...............51 C4
Eaton Cres BS8 .....84 A4
Eaton St 14 BS3 ....63 B3
Ebenezer La BS9 ....36 A1
Ebenezer St BS5.....57 C3
Eccleston Ho 1
  BS5................57 A2
Eclipse Ct 1 BS16..52 A4
Eclipse Office Pk 2
  BS16...............52 A4
Eden Gr BS7.........27 B2
Edgecombe Cl BS15 .53 A1
Edgecumbe Rd BS6..48 B2
Edgefield Cl BS14...80 B3
Edgefield Rd BS14...80 B3
Edgeware Rd
  Bristol, Southville
  BS3................63 B4
  Bristol, Staple Hill
  BS16...............52 B4
Edgewood Cl
  Bristol BS14 ....73 A4
  Bristol, Longwell Green
  BS30...............68 C3
Edinburgh Rd BS31..82 C4
Edington Gr BS10...25 B2
Edmund Cl BS16....41 C2
Edna Ave BS4.......66 A3
Edward Bird Ho
  BS7................39 A2

Edward Ct BS31 .....83 A4
Edward Rd
  Bristol, Kingswood
  BS15...............60 A4
  Bristol, Totterdown
  BS4................65 A4
Edwards Ct 17 BS5..57 C3
Edward St
  Bristol, Eastville
  BS5................50 B2
  Bristol, Moorfields
  BS5................57 B3
Effingham Rd BS6 ...48 C2
Egerton Brow BS7...48 B4
Egerton Ct BS7 .....48 C4
Egerton St BS7 .....48 B4
Eglin Croft BS13.....79 A4
Eighth Ave
  Bristol BS14 ....72 C3
  Bristol, Filton BS7...27 C1
Eirene Terr BS20.....45 C4
Elberton BS15 ....60 C4
Elberton Rd BS9.....35 B3
Elbridge Ho 3 BS2 .86 C3
Elbury Ave BS15 ....52 A2
Elderberry Wlk
  BS10...............26 A3
Elderwood Dr BS30..68 C3
Elderwood Rd BS14 .73 A3
Eldon Terr BS3.......63 C3
Eldonwall Trad Est
  BS4................57 B1
Eldon Way BS4 .....57 B1
Eldred Cl BS9........35 C1
Eleventh Ave BS7...27 C1
Elfin Rd BS16........40 C1
Elgar Cl BS4.........71 C2
Elgin Ave BS7 ....27 A1
Elgin Pk BS6 ....47 C2
Elgin Rd BS16 ......51 C2
Eliot Cl BS7 ....27 B1
Elizabeth Cres BS34 .28 C4
Elizabeths Mews 12
  BS4................58 B2
Elizabeth Way BS16..53 C3
Elkstone Wlk BS30...69 B2
Ella Cl BS16 ....41 B2
Ellacombe Rd BS30..68 B2
Ellan Hay Rd BS34...17 B2
Ellbridge Cl BS9 .....35 C1
Ellenborough Ho
  BS8................85 A2
Ellesmere Rd 1
  BS4................65 C1
Ellfield Cl BS13......70 B2
Ellicks Cl BS32.......9 C3
Ellicott Rd BS7 ......38 B1
Ellinghurst Cl BS10 ..25 B2
Elliott Ave BS16.....30 A1
Elliott Ho BS7 ....49 B3
Ellis Ave BS13.......70 C4
Elliston La BS6......48 A2
Elliston Rd BS6......48 A2
Ellsbridge Cl BS31...77 A1
Ellsbridge Ho Norton
  Radstock Coll
  BS31...............77 A1
Ellsworth Rd BS10...25 A2
Ellyott Ct 5 BS16...50 C4
Elm Cl
  Bristol BS34 ....16 B3
  Bristol, Lawrence Weston
  BS11...............23 A1
Elmcroft Cres BS7 ..49 B4
Elm Ct
  Bristol BS14 ....72 C2
  Bristol, Redland BS6..47 C2
  Keynsham BS31.....82 A4
Elmdale Gdns 4
  BS16...............51 B4

Elmdale Rd
Bristol, Bedminster
BS3 . . . . .63 A2
Bristol BS8 . . . . .84 B3
Elmfield BS15 . . . . . .60 A2
Elmfield Cl BS15 . . . .60 A2
Elmfield Rd BS9 . . . . .36 C4
Elmfield Sch for Deaf
Children BS10 . . . . .37 A4
Elmgrove Ave 10
BS5 . . . . .57 A4
Elmgrove Pk 1 BS6 .48 B1
Elmgrove Rd
Bristol, Fishponds
BS16 . . . . .50 C3
Bristol, Redland BS6 .48 B1
Elm Hayes BS13 . . . .70 B2
Elmhurst Ave BS5 . . .50 B3
Elming Down Cl
BS32 . . . . .16 B2
Elm La BS6 . . . . .47 C2
Elmlea Ave BS9 . . . . .36 B1
Elmlea Jun & Inf Schs
BS9 . . . . .36 B1
Elmleigh Ave BS16 . .43 A1
Elmleigh Cl BS16 . . . .43 A1
Elmleigh Rd BS16 . . .43 A1
Elmore BS15 . . . . . . .53 A2
Elmore Rd
Bristol BS34 . . . . .8 A1
Bristol, Horfield BS7 . .38 C2
Elm Park Prim Sch
BS36 . . . . .18 C2
Elm Pk BS34 . . . . . . .27 B2
Elm Rd
Bristol, Horfield
BS7 . . . . .38 A1
Bristol, Kingswood
BS15 . . . . .60 A2
Elms Gr BS34 . . . . .8 C1
Elms The
Bristol, Frenchay
BS16 . . . . .30 A1
Bristol, Henbury
BS10 . . . . .25 A2
Elmtree Ave BS16 . . .42 C3
Elmtree Cl BS15 . . . . .52 B1
Elmtree Dr BS13 . . . .70 B1
Elmtree Way BS15 . .52 B1
Elsbert Dr BS13 . . . . .70 A2
Elstree Rd BS5 . . . . . .50 C1
Elton Ho
Bristol, Clifton BS8 . . .84 A3
2 Bristol, Newton
BS2 . . . . .86 C3
Elton La BS7 . . . . . . .48 B2
Elton Mans 5 BS7 . .48 B2
Elton Rd
Bristol, Bishopston
BS7 . . . . .48 B2
Bristol BS8 . . . . .84 C3
Bristol, Kingswood
BS15 . . . . .52 A1
Elton St BS2 . . . . . . .86 C4
Elvard Cl BS13 . . . . . .78 C4
Elvard Rd BS13 . . . . .78 C4
Elvaston Rd BS3 . . . .64 A3
Ely Gr BS9 . . . . .35 A3
Embassy Rd BS5 . . . .50 C1
Embassy Wlk BS5 . . .50 C1
Embleton Rd BS10 . . .26 A2
EMERSON'S GREEN 43 B2
Emersons Green La
BS16 . . . . .43 A3
Emersons Green Prim
Sch BS16 . . . . .43 A3
Emerson Sq BS7 . . . .38 C4
Emerson Way BS16 . .43 B3
Emery Rd BS4 . . . . . .66 B1
Emet Gr BS16 . . . . . . .43 A2
Emet La BS16 . . . . . . .43 A2

Eminence BS1 . . . . . .87 B1
Emlyn Rd BS5 . . . . . .50 A2
Emma-Chris Way
BS34 . . . . .28 A2
Emmanuel Ct BS8 . . .84 A4
Emmett Wood BS14 . .81 A3
Empire Cres BS15 . . .68 A4
Emra Cl BS5 . . . . .51 A1
Emra Ho 10 BS5 . . . .56 C4
Enfield Rd BS16 . . . . .51 A1
England's Cres BS36 .18 C3
Englishcombe Rd
BS13 . . . . .79 B3
Ennerdale Rd BS10 . .26 B2
Enterprise Trade Ctr
BS4 . . . . .72 A3
Epney Cl BS31 . . . . . . .8 A1
Epsom Cl BS16 . . . . . .31 A1
Epworth Rd BS10 . . . .25 B3
Equinox BS32 . . . . .9 A3
Erin Wlk BS4 . . . . . . .71 C4
Ermine Way BS11 . . . .33 B3
Ermleet Rd 1 BS6 . . .48 A2
Ernest Barker Cl 15
BS5 . . . . .57 A3
Ernestville Rd BS16 . .51 A3
Ervine Terr BS2 . . . . .86 C4
Essery Rd BS5 . . . . . .50 A2
Esson Rd BS15 . . . . . .51 C1
Estcourt Gdns BS16 . .39 C1
Etloe Rd BS6 . . . . .47 B4
Eton Rd BS4 . . . . .65 C3
Ettricke Dr BS16 . . . .41 A1
Eugene Flats 7
BS2 . . . . .86 A4
Eugene St
Bristol, Kingsdown
BS2 . . . . .86 A4
Bristol, St Pauls BS2,
BS5 . . . . .86 C4
Evans Cl BS4 . . . . . . .58 B1
Evans Rd BS6 . . . . . . .47 C2
Evelyn Rd BS10 . . . . .37 B3
Evenlode Gdns BS11 34 B1
Evenlode Way BS31 . .81 A4
Evercreech Rd BS14 .81 A4
Eve Rd BS5 . . . . .49 C1
Everest Ave BS16 . . . .50 C4
Everest Rd BS16 . . . . .50 C4
Ewell Rd BS14 . . . . . .73 A2
Exchange Ave BS1 . . .87 A2
Exchange Ct 8
BS15 . . . . .59 C4
Exeter Bldgs BS6 . . . .47 C2
Exeter Rd BS4 . . . . . .63 A4
Exley Cl BS30 . . . . . . .61 C1
Exmoor St BS3 . . . . . .63 A3
Exmouth Rd BS4 . . . . .64 B1
Explore La BS1 . . . . . .85 C2
Exton Cl BS14 . . . . . . .73 A1
Eyer's La BS2 . . . . . . .86 C3

F

Faber Gr BS13 . . . . . . .79 B4
Fabian Dr BS34 . . . . . .16 C1
Factory Rd BS36 . . . . .19 A3
Failand Cres BS9 . . . .35 B1
Failand La
Easton-in-G BS8 . . . . .44 C1
Portbury BS20 . . . . . .44 B2
Failand Wlk BS9 . . . . .35 B2
Fairacre Cl BS7 . . . . . .39 A1
Fairacres Cl BS31 . . . .76 B1
Fairfield High Sch
Bristol BS5, BS7 . . . . .49 B3
Bristol BS6 . . . . .49 A2
Fairfield Pl BS3 . . . . . .63 A4
Fairfield Rd
Bristol, Montpelier
BS6 . . . . .49 A2
Bristol, Southville
BS3 . . . . .63 A4

Fairfoot Rd BS4 . . . . . .64 C3
Fairford Cl BS15 . . . . .53 A2
Fairford Cres BS34 . . .16 A4
Fairford Rd BS11 . . . . .33 C3
Fair Furlong BS13 . . . .78 C4
Fair Furlong Prim Sch
BS13 . . . . .79 A4
Fairhaven Rd BS6 . . . .48 A4
Fairlawn BS16 . . . . . . .52 B4
Fair Lawn BS30 . . . . . .69 A4
Fairlawn Ave BS34 . . .27 B3
Fairlawn Rd BS6 . . . . .49 A2
Fairlyn Dr BS15 . . . . . .53 A3
Fairoaks BS30 . . . . . . .68 C3
Fairview Ct BS15 . . . . .59 C2
Fair View Dr BS6 . . . . .48 A2
Fairview Ho BS9 . . . . . .36 B4
Fairview Rd BS15 . . . .60 B4
Fairway BS4 . . . . .65 C1
Fairway Cl BS30 . . . . .69 A4
Fairway Ind Ctr
BS34 . . . . .27 A3
Falcon Cl
Bristol, Patchway
BS34 . . . . .14 C4
Bristol, Westbury on T
BS9 . . . . .36 B4
Falcon Cres BS5 . . . . .50 A2
Falcondale Rd BS9 . . .36 B3
Falcondale Wlk BS9 . .36 C4
Falcon Dr BS34 . . . . . .14 C4
Falcon Wlk BS34 . . . . . .7 C1
Falfield Rd BS4 . . . . . .65 B3
Falfield Wlk BS10 . . . .37 B4
Falkland Rd 4 BS6 . . .49 A2
Fallodon Ct BS9 . . . . . .37 A1
Fallodon Way BS9 . . . .37 A1
Fallowfield BS30 . . . . .61 C1
Falmouth Rd BS7 . . . .48 C4
Fane Cl BS35 . . . . .25 B3
Fanshawe Rd BS14 . . .72 C3
Faraday Rd 2 BS8 . . .54 B1
Farendell Rd BS16 . . .31 C1
Far Handstones
BS30 . . . . .68 C4
Farington Rd BS10 . . .37 C3
Farleigh Rd BS31 . . . .82 B4
Farleigh Wlk BS13 . . .70 C4
Farley Cl BS34 . . . . . . .16 A3
Farm Cl BS16 . . . . .43 A2
Farm Ct BS16 . . . . .42 A3
Farmer Rd BS13 . . . . .78 A4
Farm La BS35 . . . . .5 C2
Farm Rd BS16 . . . . . . .42 A3
Farmwell Cl BS13 . . . .71 A1
Farnaby Cl BS4 . . . . . .71 B3
Farndale BS5 . . . . .58 C2
Farne Cl BS9 . . . . .37 A1
Farrant Cl BS4 . . . . . . .71 B3
Farringford Ho BS5 . . .50 B2
Farr's La BS1 . . . . .87 A2
Farr St BS11 . . . . .33 A4
Fawkes Cl BS15 . . . . . .61 A4
Featherstone Rd 4
BS16 . . . . .51 A4
Feeder Rd BS2 . . . . . .56 C1
Felix Rd BS5 . . . . .57 A4
Felstead Rd BS10 . . . .26 C1
Feltham Ct BS34 . . . . .27 A2
Felton Gr BS13 . . . . . .70 C4
Fenbrook Cl BS16 . . . .29 C1
Fennel Dr BS34 . . . . . .17 B3
Fennell Gr BS10 . . . . . .25 B2
Fenton Cl BS7 . . . . . . .48 B4
Fenton Rd BS7 . . . . . . .48 B4
Fermaine Ave BS4 . . . .66 B3
Fernbank Ct 2 BS6 . . .48 A2
Fernbank Rd BS6 . . . .48 A2
Fernbrook Cl BS16 . . .29 C1
Fern Cl BS10 . . . . .25 C3
Ferndale Ave BS30 . . .68 C3
Ferndale Rd BS34 . . . .27 B2
Ferndene BS32 . . . . . . .9 A2

Ferndown Cl BS11 . . . .34 C3
Ferndown Grange
BS9 . . . . .37 A2
Fern Gr BS32 . . . . .16 B4
Fernhill Ct BS11 . . . . . .23 C1
Fernhill La BS11 . . . . .23 C1
Fernhurst Rd BS5 . . . .51 A1
Fernlea Gdns BS20 . . .45 A4
Fernleaze BS36 . . . . . .20 A2
Fernleigh Ct 1 BS6 . .47 C2
Fern Rd BS16 . . . . .41 C1
Fern St BS2 . . . . .49 C4
Fernsteed Rd BS13 . . .70 B2
Ferryman's Ct BS2 . . .87 B2
Ferry Rd BS15 . . . . . . .67 C1
Ferry St BS1 . . . . .87 B2
Ferry Steps Ind Est
BS2 . . . . .64 C3
Fiddes Rd BS6 . . . . . . .48 A4
Fiddlers Wood La
BS32 . . . . .16 C4
Field Farm Cl BS34 . .29 A4
Field La BS30 . . . . .68 B3
Field Marshal Slim Ct
24 BS2 . . . . .86 C3
Field Rd BS15 . . . . . . .51 C1
Field View 9 BS5 . . . .56 C4
Field View Dr BS16 . . .41 B2
Fiennes Cl BS16 . . . . . .52 C4
Fifth Ave
Bristol BS14 . . . . .73 A3
Bristol, Filton BS7 . . . .27 B1
Fifth Way BS11 . . . . . .22 C2
Filby Dr BS34 . . . . .16 A4
FILTON 27 C3
Filton Abbey Wood Sta
BS34 . . . . .38 C3
Filton Ave
Bristol, Filton BS34 . . .27 C3
Bristol, Horfield BS7,
BS34 . . . . .38 C3
Filton Avenue Jun & Inf
Schs BS7 . . . . .38 C3
Filton Coll BS34 . . . . . .28 A3
Filton Coll (WISE
Campus) BS34 . . . . . .28 B3
Filton Gr BS7 . . . . .38 B2
Filton High Sch
BS34 . . . . .28 B3
Filton Hill Prim Sch
BS34 . . . . .27 C4
Filton La BS34 . . . . . . .28 B2
Filton Rd
Bristol, Frenchay
BS16 . . . . .29 A2
Bristol, Harry Stoke
BS34 . . . . .28 B2
Bristol, Horfield BS7 . .38 B4
Filton Rdbt BS34 . . . . .27 B2
Filwood Broadway
BS4 . . . . .72 A4
Filwood Ct BS16 . . . . .51 C3
Filwood Dr BS15 . . . . .60 B4
Filwood Ho BS15 . . . . .60 B4
FILWOOD PARK 72 A4
Filwood Rd BS16 . . . . .51 B3
Fireclay Rd BS5 . . . . . .57 C2
Fire Engine La BS36 . .20 B3
Fire Station La BS11 . .21 C2
Firework Cl BS15 . . . . .61 A4
Firfield St BS4 . . . . . . .64 C4
Firs Ct BS31 . . . . .82 A4
First Ave
Bristol BS14 . . . . .72 C3
Bristol, St Anne's
BS4 . . . . .58 A1
Portbury BS20 . . . . . .32 A1
Firs The BS16 . . . . . . .42 A2
First Way BS11 . . . . . .22 A1
Fir Tree Cl BS34 . . . . .15 A3
Fir Tree La BS5 . . . . . .58 C3
Fisher Ave BS15 . . . . .53 B1
Fisher Rd BS15 . . . . . .53 B1
FISHPONDS 40 C1

Fishponds Rd BS5 . . .50 B3
Fishponds Trad Est
BS5 . . . . .50 C2
Fishpool Hill BS10 . . . .25 C4
Fitchett Wlk BS10 . . . .25 A3
Fitzgerald Rd BS3 . . . .64 B3
Fitzharding Ho 8
BS1 . . . . .86 A3
Fitzroy Rd BS16 . . . . . .51 C2
Fitzroy St BS4 . . . . . . .64 C4
Fitzroy Terr 7 BS6 . . .47 C2
Five Acre Dr BS16 . . . .40 C3
Flaxman BS7 . . . . .39 A2
FLAXPITS 18 C1
Flaxpits La BS36 . . . . .18 C1
Florence Brown Com
Sch BS4 . . . . .71 C4
Florence Pk BS6 . . . . .47 C4
Florence Rd BS16 . . . .52 C3
Flowers Hill BS4 . . . . .66 A1
Flowers Hill Cl BS4 . .66 A1
Flowers Hill Trad Est
BS4 . . . . .66 A1
Flowerwell Rd BS13 . .70 A1
Folliot Cl BS16 . . . . . . .40 C3
Folly Brook Rd BS16 .31 C1
Folly La BS2 . . . . .56 C2
Folly The BS16 . . . . . . .42 B3
Fontana Cl BS30 . . . . .69 A3
Fonthill Prim Sch
BS10 . . . . .26 C2
Fonthill Rd BS10 . . . . .26 B2
Fonthill Way BS30 . . . .69 B2
Fontmell Ct BS14 . . . . .73 C3
Fontwell Dr BS16 . . . . .31 A1
Footes La BS36 . . . . . .19 C3
Footshill Cl BS15 . . . . .59 B3
Footshill Dr BS15 . . . . .59 B3
Footshill Rd BS15 . . . .59 B3
Forde Cl BS30 . . . . . . .60 B1
Fordell Pl BS4 . . . . . . .64 C3
Ford La BS16 . . . . .43 A2
Ford St BS5 . . . . .57 B2
Forest Ave BS15 . . . . .51 C3
Forest Dr BS10 . . . . . .24 C3
Forest Edge BS15 . . . .67 B4
Forest Rd
Bristol, Fishponds
BS16 . . . . .51 C4
Bristol, Kingswood
BS15 . . . . .59 C3
Forest Wlk
Bristol, Fishponds
BS16 . . . . .51 C4
Bristol, Kingswood
BS15 . . . . .59 B3
Forge End BS20 . . . . . .44 A3
Fortfield Rd BS14 . . . .73 A1
Foss Ct 8 BS5 . . . . . . .58 B4
Fossedale Ave BS14 . .73 B2
Fosseway BS8 . . . . . . .85 A2
Fosseway The BS8 . . .84 A3
Foster's Almshouses 4
BS1 . . . . .86 A3
Foster St BS5 . . . . .49 C2
Foundry La BS5 . . . . . .51 A2
Foundry Yd BS5 . . . . . .51 A2
Fountain Ct BS32 . . . . . .9 A3
Fountaine Ct 3
BS5 . . . . .50 A2
Fountains Dr BS30 . . . .60 B2
Four Acre Ave BS16 . .42 A4
Four Acre Cres
BS16 . . . . .30 C1
Four Acre Rd BS16 . . .42 A4
Four Acres BS13 . . . . .78 A4
Four Acres Cl BS13 . .78 B4
Four Acres Prim Sch
BS13 . . . . .78 A4
Fourth Ave
Bristol BS14 . . . . .73 A3
Bristol, Filton BS7 . . . .27 B1
Fourth Way BS11 . . . .22 C2

Fox and Hounds La
BS31 . . . . .76 B1
Foxborough Gdns
BS32 . . . . 9 B2
Fox Cl BS4 . . . . .58 B1
Foxcombe Rd BS14 . .81 A4
Foxcote BS15 . . . . .60 B3
Foxcote Rd BS3 . . . . . .62 C3
Foxcroft Cl BS32 . . . . .17 A2
Foxcroft Rd BS5 . . . . .57 C4
Fox Ct BS30 . . . . .68 B3
Fox Den Rd BS34 . . . .28 B3
Foxe Rd BS36 . . . . .19 C4
Foxfield Ave BS32 . . . . 9 B3
Foxglove Cl BS16 . . . .40 A1
Fox Ho
Bristol, Broom Hill
BS4 . . . . .66 A3
Bristol, Victoria Park
BS8 . . . . .84 A3
Fox Rd BS5 . . . . .49 C1
Foye Ho BS8 . . . . .54 A2
Fraley Rd BS9 . . . . . . .36 C3
FRAMPTON
COTTERELL 19 C3
Frampton Cotterell CE
Prim Sch BS36 . . .19 B4
Frampton Cres
BS16 . . . . .52 A4
Frampton Ct
8 Bristol, Longwell
Green BS30 . . . . . . .68 B4
16 Bristol, Pile Marsh
BS5 . . . . .57 C3
FRAMPTON END 20 B4
Frances Greeves Ct
BS10 . . . . .25 A1
Frances Mews 12
BS3 . . . . .63 B4
Francis Cl BS35 . . . . . .58 B3
Francis Ho BS2 . . . . . .86 A4
Francis Pl BS30 . . . . . .68 B4
Francis Rd
Bristol, Bedminster
BS3 . . . . .63 B2
Bristol, Westbury on Trym
BS10 . . . . .37 B4
Francis Way BS30 . . . .61 C2
Francombe Gr BS10 . .38 A2
Francombe Ho BS1 . . .87 A1
Franklin Ct BS1 . . . . . .87 B1
Franklyn Ct 6 BS16 . .50 C3
Franklyn La 10 BS2 . . .49 A1
Franklyn St BS2 . . . . . .49 A1
Fraser St BS3 . . . . .63 C3
Frayne Rd BS3 . . . . . . .62 C4
Frederick Pl BS8 . . . . .84 B3
Fredrick St BS4 . . . . . .64 C4
Freeland Bldgs 1
BS5 . . . . .50 A2
Freeland Pl BS8 . . . . . .54 B2
Freeling Ho BS1 . . . . . .87 B1
Freemantle Gdns
BS5 . . . . .50 A3
Freemantle Ho BS2 . .86 A4
Freemantle Rd BS5 . . .50 A3
Freestone Rd BS2 . . . .56 C2
Fremantle La 9
BS6 . . . . .48 B1
Fremantle Rd BS6 . . . .48 B1
Fremantle Sq BS6 . . . .48 B1
FRENCHAY 41 A4
Frenchay CE Prim Sch
BS16 . . . . .41 A3
Frenchay Cl BS16 . . . .41 A3
Frenchay Hill BS16 . .41 B3
Frenchay Hospl
BS16 . . . . .41 A4
Frenchay Park Rd
BS16 . . . . .40 B2
Frenchay Rd BS16 . . .41 B2
Frenchay Village Mus★
BS16 . . . . .40 C4

Freshland Way
BS15 . . . . .59 A4
Friary BS1 . . . . .87 C1
Friary Grange Pk
BS36 . . . . .18 C2
Friary Rd BS7 . . . . .48 B4
Friendly Row BS2 . . . .33 B1
Friendship Rd BS4 . . .64 C2
Friezewood Rd BS3 . .62 C4
Fripp Cl BS5 . . . . .57 A2
Frobisher Rd BS3 . . . .62 C3
Frog La
Bristol BS1 . . . . .85 C2
Frampton Cotterell
BS36 . . . . .20 C3
Frogmore St BS1 . . . .85 C2
Frome Bank Gdns
BS36 . . . . .30 C3
Frome Glen BS36 . . . .30 C4
Frome Pl 1 BS16 . . . .40 A1
Fromeside Pk BS16 . .41 A3
Frome Terr BS16 . . . . .40 A1
Frome Valley Rd
BS16 . . . . .40 B2
Frome View BS36 . . . .19 C3
Frome Villas BS16 . . .41 B3
Frome Way BS36 . . . .18 C1
Froomshaw Rd
BS16 . . . . .40 C3
Frost & Reed Ho 3
BS5 . . . . .58 B4
Fry Ct 2 BS3 . . . . .63 B4
Fry's Cl BS16 . . . . .50 B4
Frys Hill BS15 . . . . . . .52 C2
Fry's Hill BS4 . . . . .65 C2
Frys House of Mercy 11
BS1 . . . . .87 B1
Fulford Rd BS13 . . . . .71 B1
Fulford Wlk BS13 . . . .71 A1
Furber Ct BS5 . . . . .59 A2
Furber Rd BS5 . . . . . . .59 A2
Furber Ridge BS5 . . . .59 A2
Furber Vale BS5 . . . . . .59 A2
Furlong The BS6 . . . . .37 C2
Furnwood BS5 . . . . . . .58 C2
Furze Rd BS16 . . . . . . .52 A3
Furzewood Rd BS15 .60 B4
Fussell Ct BS15 . . . . . .60 B4
Fylton Croft BS14 . . . .81 A3

G

Gable Cl BS35 . . . . 6 B2
Gable Rd 8 BS5 . . . . . .49 B1
Gadshill Dr BS34 . . . .16 C1
Gadshill Rd BS5 . . . . . .50 A2
Gages Cl BS15 . . . . . . .60 B3
Gages Rd BS15 . . . . . .60 B3
Gainsborough Mews
BS10 . . . . .25 C2
Gainsborough Rd
BS31 . . . . .76 B3
Gainsborough Sq
BS7 . . . . .39 A3
Gallagher Ret Pk
BS30 . . . . .68 A4
Gallivan Cl BS34 . . . . .15 C4
Galway Rd BS4 . . . . . .64 A1
Gander Cl BS13 . . . . . .71 A1
Garamond Ct BS1 . . . .87 B1
Garden Cl BS9 . . . . . . .35 B1
Garden Ct BS8 . . . . . . .84 A4
Gardens The
Bristol, Frenchay
BS16 . . . . .29 A1
3 Bristol, Upper
Soundwell BS16 . . .52 B3
Gardner Ave BS13 . . .70 B3
Garfield Ct BS5 . . . . . .58 B4
Garfield Rd BS5 . . . . . .58 C4
Garnet St BS3 . . . . . . .63 A3
Garnett Pl BS16 . . . . . .52 A3
Garonor Way BS20 . . .32 B1
Garrett Dr BS32 . . . . . .16 B3

Garth Rd BS13 . . . . . . .70 C4
Garton Ho 3 BS16 . . .41 C1
Garvey Ho 14 BS5 . . . .57 B3
Gasferry Rd BS1 . . . . . .85 B1
Gaskins The BS7 . . . . .38 C1
Gas La BS2 . . . . .56 C2
Gaston Ave BS31 . . . . .76 B2
Gastons The BS11 . . . .34 C4
Gatcombe Dr BS34 . . .28 C4
Gatcombe Rd BS13 . .71 A1
Gatehouse Ave
BS13 . . . . .70 C1
Gatehouse Cl BS13 . .70 C1
Gatehouse Ct BS13 . .71 A1
Gatehouse Ctr The
BS13 . . . . .71 A1
Gatehouse Way
BS13 . . . . .70 C1
Gatesby Mead BS34 . .16 C1
Gathorne Rd BS3 . . . .63 A4
Gatton Rd BS2 . . . . . . .49 B1
Gaunt's La BS1 . . . . . . .85 C2
Gay Elms Prim Sch
BS13 . . . . .78 C4
Gay Elms Rd BS13 . . .78 C4
Gayner Rd BS7 . . . . . . .27 B1
Gays Rd BS15 . . . . .67 A4
Gaywood Ho 7 BS3 . .63 A3
Gazzard Cl BS36 . . . . .18 C3
Gazzard Rd BS36 . . . .18 C3
GEE MOOR 60 B2
Gee Moors BS15 . . . . .60 B3
Gefle Cl BS1 . . . . .85 B1
Geoffrey Cl BS13 . . . .70 A2
George Cl 12 BS16 . . .50 C4
George & Dragon La 1
BS5 . . . . .57 C3
George Jones Rd
BS2 . . . . .56 C2
Georges Sq BS1 . . . . . .87 B2
George St BS5 . . . . . . .57 B4
Georgian House
(Mus)★ BS1 . . . . . . .85 C2
Gerald Rd BS3 . . . . . . .62 C3
Gerrard Cl BS4 . . . . . . .71 C3
Gerrish Ave
Bristol, Moorfields
BS5 . . . . .57 B4
Bristol, Staple Hill
BS16 . . . . .42 B1
Gibbet La BS14 . . . . . .81 C1
Gibbs Ct 15 BS5 . . . . .57 C3
Gibbsfold Rd BS13 . . .79 B4
Gibson Rd BS6 . . . . . . .48 B1
Giffard Ho BS34 . . . . . .16 B2
Gifford Cres BS34 . . . .16 A2
Gifford Ct BS34 . . . . . .28 B2
Gifford Rd BS10 . . . . . .25 A4
Giffords Pl BS13 . . . . .70 C3
Gilbert Rd
Bristol, Kingswood
BS15 . . . . .52 B1
Bristol, Moorfields
BS5 . . . . .57 B4
Gilda Cl BS14 . . . . .73 B1
Gilda Cres BS14 . . . . . .73 A2
Gilda Par BS14 . . . . . . .73 B1
Gilda Sq W BS14 . . . . .73 A1
Gillard Cl BS15 . . . . . . .59 A4
Gillard Rd BS15 . . . . . .59 A4
Gill Ave BS16 . . . . .41 A2
Gillebank Cl BS14 . . . .73 C1
Gillham Ho 4 BS7 . . .48 B2
Gillingham Hill 7
BS15 . . . . .59 A1
Gillray Cl BS7 . . . . .39 A2
Gilpin Cl BS15 . . . . . . .53 A1
Gilroy Cl BS30 . . . . . . .69 A3
Gilslake Ave BS10 . . . .25 C3
Gilton Ho BS4 . . . . . . .66 A2
Gingell's Gn 4 BS5 . .58 C4
Gipsy Patch La
BS34 . . . . .16 A2
Glades The BS5 . . . . . .50 C2

Gladstone Ct BS16 . . .52 C4
Gladstone Dr BS16 . . .52 C3
Gladstone La BS36 . . .20 A3
Gladstone Rd
Bristol BS14 . . . . . . .73 A2
2 Bristol, Kingswood
BS15 . . . . .52 B1
Gladstone St
Bristol, Bedminster
BS3 . . . . .63 A3
Bristol, Kingswood
BS16 . . . . .52 B3
13 Bristol, Pile Marsh
BS5 . . . . .57 C3
Glaisdale Rd BS16 . . .40 C1
Glanville Gdns BS15 .60 A3
Glass House La BS2 . .57 A1
Glastonbury Cl BS30 .60 B1
Glebelands BS34 . . . . .27 B3
Glebe Rd BS5 . . . . .58 A4
Glebes The BS5 . . . . . .58 A4
Glebe The BS35 . . . . . . 3 A3
Glebe Wlk BS31 . . . . . .82 A4
Gledemoor Dr BS36. .29 C3
Glena Ave BS4 . . . . . . .65 A2
Glenarm Rd BS4 . . . . .66 A2
Glenarm Wlk BS4 . . . .66 A2
Glenavon Ct BS9 . . . . .46 A4
Glenavon Pk BS9 . . . .46 A4
Glen Brook BS9 . . . . . .46 B4
Glenburn Rd BS15 . . .51 C1
Glencoyne Sq BS10 . .26 A2
Glendale
17 Bristol BS8 . . . . . .54 B4
Bristol, Downend
BS16 . . . . .42 A4
Bristol, Hillfields
BS16 . . . . .52 A3
Glendare St BS5 . . . . .57 B2
Glendevon Rd BS14 . .80 C3
Glendower Ho BS8 . . .54 B3
Glen Dr BS9 . . . . .35 C1
Gleneagles Dr BS10 . .26 A4
Gleneagles Rd BS30 .61 A2
Glenfrome Prim Sch
BS5 . . . . .49 C4
Glenfrome Rd BS2 . . .49 C3
Glen La BS4 . . . . .65 C2
Glen Park Gdns BS5 .58 C4
Glen Pk
Bristol, Eastville
BS5 . . . . .50 A2
Bristol, St George
BS5 . . . . .58 C4
Glenroy Ave BS15 . . . .51 C1
Glenside Cl BS16 . . . .41 B3
Glenside Hospl Mus★
BS16 . . . . .40 A1
Glenside Pk 3
BS16 . . . . .40 A1
Glen The
Bristol, Hanham
BS15 . . . . .67 A4
Bristol, Redland BS6. .47 C3
Glentworth Rd
Bristol BS8 . . . . .85 B2
Bristol, Redland BS6. .48 A2
Glenview Rd BS4 . . . .65 C2
Glenwood BS16 . . . . . .52 A3
Glenwood Dr BS30 . . .69 A4
Glenwood Rd BS10 . .37 B3
Glevum Cl BS16 . . . . . .43 B3
Gloster Ave BS5 . . . . . .50 B3
Gloucester Cl BS34 . .16 B1
Gloucester Ho 11
BS2 . . . . .86 C3
Gloucester La 18
BS2 . . . . .86 C3
Gloucester Pl 2
BS2 . . . . .86 A3
Gloucester Rd
Avonmouth BS11 . . .21 B1

Gloucester Rd continued
Bristol, Bishopston
BS7 . . . . .48 C4
Bristol, Patchway
BS34 . . . . .15 C3
Bristol, Staple Hill
BS16 . . . . .52 C3
Gloucester Rd N BS7,
BS34 . . . . .27 B3
Gloucester Row 6
BS8 . . . . .54 B3
Gloucestershire Cty
Cricket Club★
BS7 . . . . .49 A4
Gloucester St
5 Bristol BS2 . . . . . .86 B4
9 Bristol, Clifton
BS8 . . . . .54 B3
Bristol, Eastville BS5 .50 B3
Glyn Vale BS3 . . . . .64 A1
Goddard Way BS10 . . .25 B1
Godfrey Ct 7 BS30 . . .68 B4
Goffenton Dr BS16 . . .41 A2
GOLDEN HILL 37 C1
Golden Hill BS6 . . . . . .37 B1
Golden Lion Ct 1 BS2 .87 B2
Goldney Ave
Bristol BS8 . . . . .85 A2
Bristol, Warmley
BS30 . . . . .61 B3
Goldney Ct 7 BS16 . .50 C3
Goldney Rd BS8 . . . . . .54 A3
Goldsbury Wlk BS11 .23 B1
Golf Course La
BS34 . . . . .27 A3
Gooch Ct BS30 . . . . . .69 B3
Goodeve Pk BS9 . . . . .46 B3
Goodeve Rd BS9 . . . . .46 B3
Goodhind St BS5 . . . .56 C4
Goodneston Rd
BS16 . . . . .51 B3
Good Shepherd Cl
BS7 . . . . .48 A4
Goodwin Dr BS14 . . . .80 B4
Goodwood Gdns
BS16 . . . . .31 A1
Goolden St BS4 . . . . . .64 C3
Goose Acre BS32 . . . .17 A2
Goose Gn BS36 . . . . . .20 A4
Gooseland Cl BS14 . .80 B3
Gordano Way BS20 . . .32 B1
Gordon Ave BS5 . . . . .50 C1
Gordon Cl BS5 . . . . . . .50 C1
Gordon Rd
Bristol BS8 . . . . .84 B3
14 Bristol, St Pauls
BS2 . . . . .49 A1
Bristol, Whitehall
BS5 . . . . .50 B1
Gore Rd BS3 . . . . .62 C2
Gore's Marsh Rd
BS3 . . . . .62 C2
Gorham Cl BS11 . . . . .24 A2
Gorlangton Cl BS14 . .72 C3
Gorse Cover Rd BS35 . 2 B3
Gorse Hill BS16 . . . . . .52 A3
Gorse La BS8 . . . . .85 B2
Gosforth Cl BS10 . . . .25 C1
Gosforth Rd BS10 . . . .25 C1
Goslet Rd BS14 . . . . . .74 A1
Gotley Rd BS4 . . . . . . .65 C2
Gott Dr BS4 . . . . .57 C1
Goulston Rd BS13 . . .70 C1
Goulston Wlk BS13 . .70 C1
Goulter St BS5 . . . . . . .57 A2
Gourney Cl BS11 . . . . .23 C2
Gover Rd BS15 . . . . . . .67 B3
Govier Way BS35 . . . . . 5 A4
Grace Ct BS16 . . . . . . .41 C2

Grace Dr BS15.......60 C4
Gracefield Sch BS16 41 B1
Grace Park Rd BS4 ..65 C1
Grace Rd BS16 ......41 B1
Graeme CI BS16 .....51 B4
Graham Rd
3 Bristol, Bedminster
BS3 ....63 B3
Bristol, Downend
BS16 ....42 B2
21 Bristol, Upper Easton
BS5 ....49 C1
Grainger Ct BS11 ....34 A3
Grain Loft The **9**
BS1...............87 A2
Grampian CI BS30 ...69 B4
Granary The **8** BS1 .87 A2
Granby Ct **18** BS8 ..54 B2
Granby Hill BS8......54 B2
Grange Ave
Bristol, Hanham
BS15 ....59 C1
Bristol, Little Stoke
BS34 ....16 A2
Grange CI
Bristol, Patchway
BS32 ....9 A2
Bristol, Stoke Gifford
BS34 ....29 B4
Grange CI N BS9.....37 A2
Grange Court Rd
BS9 ....36 C2
Grange Ct
Bristol BS15 ....59 C1
Bristol, Henleaze
BS9 ....37 A2
Grange Dr BS16 .....41 B2
Grange Pk
Bristol, Frenchay
BS16 ....41 B4
Bristol, Westbury on Trym
BS9 ....37 A2
Grange Rd
Bristol, Bishopsworth
BS13 ....70 C1
Bristol BS8 ....84 A3
Grange Sch & Sports
Coll The BS30.......61 A3
Grange The
Bristol, Coombe Dingle
BS9 ....35 C3
Bristol, Sneyd Park
BS9 ....47 A3
Grangeville CI BS30..69 A3
Grangewood CI **4**
BS16 ....41 B2
Granny's La BS15 ....60 A2
Grantham Ct **1**
BS15 ....59 B4
Grantham Ho BS15 ..52 A1
Grantham La BS15...59 B4
Grantham Rd BS15...52 A1
Grantson CI BS4 .....66 A2
Granville CI BS15 ....67 A3
Granville St BS5 .....57 B2
Grasmere CI BS10 ...36 C4
Grass Meers Dr
BS14 ....80 C4
Grassmere Gdns
BS30...............61 C2
Gratitude Rd BS5.....50 A1
Graveney CI BS4.....65 C1
Gray CI BS10 ....24 C2
Grayle Rd BS10 ......25 B2
Grayling Ho BS9 .....36 B3
Great Ann St BS2 ....86 C3
Great Britain S.S. *
BS1...............85 B1

Great Brockeridge
BS9 ....36 B2
Great Dowles BS30 ..68 C4
Great George St
Bristol, Brandon Hill
BS1...............85 C2
Bristol, St Pauls BS2..86 C3
Great Hayles Rd
BS14 ....72 C2
Great Leaze BS30 ...68 C4
Great Mdw BS34....17 B2
Great Meadow Rd
BS32 ....17 A2
Great Park Rd BS32...9 A3
GREAT STOKE 17 A1
Great Stoke BS34....17 B1
Great Stoke Way
Bristol, Great Stoke
BS34 ....17 B1
Bristol, Harry Stoke
BS34 ....28 B3
Great Western Ct
BS34 ....29 A4
Great Western La
BS5 ....57 B2
Great Wood CI BS13 .79 B4
Green Acre Rd BS14 .80 C3
Greenacres BS9 .....36 A3
Greenacres Park
Homes BS36.........20 C1
Greenbank Ave E
BS5 ....50 A1
Greenbank Ave W
BS5 ....50 A1
Greenbank Rd
Bristol, Hanham
BS15 ....59 C1
Bristol, Lower Easton
BS5 ....50 B2
Bristol, Southville
BS3 ....62 C4
Greenbank View
Bristol, Kingswood
BS15 ....60 A3
Bristol, Lower Easton
BS5 ....50 B2
Green CI BS7 ....38 C4
Green Croft BS5 .....51 B1
Greendale Rd
Bristol, Lower Knowle
BS3 ....64 A2
Bristol, Redland BS6..47 C3
Green Dell CI BS10...24 B3
Greenditch Ave
BS13 ....71 B1
Greendown BS5 .....58 C3
Green Dragon Rd
BS36 ....18 B1
Greenfield Ave
BS10 ....37 C4
Greenfield Ct BS10 ..26 B1
Greenfield Prim Sch
BS4 ....71 B3
Greenfield Rd BS10..26 B1
Greenfinch Lodge
BS16 ....40 A2
Greenhaven **5** BS5..50 A1
Greenhill Gr BS3.....62 C2
Greenhill La BS11....24 A1
Green La
Avonmouth BS11 ....21 C1
Bristol BS11 ....33 A4
Easter Compton BS35 ..5 A1
Severn Beach BS35 ...2 C4
Winterbourne BS36 ...18 A3
Greenlands Way
BS10 ....25 A4
Greenleaze BS4 .....65 A1
Greenleaze Ave
BS16 ....30 B1
Greenleaze CI BS16..30 B1
Greenmore Rd BS4 ..65 A2
Greenore BS15 ......59 B3
Greenpark Rd BS10 ..26 C1

Greenridge CI BS13..78 A4
Green's Hill BS16 ....50 C3
Green Side BS16.....16 C3
Greenside CI BS10 ..24 B3
Greensplott Rd
BS11..............10 C3
Green St BS3 ....64 B4
Green The
Bristol, New
  Cheltenham BS15 ..52 C2
Bristol, Stoke Gifford
BS34 ....28 C4
Pill BS20 ....45 C4
Greenview BS30 .....68 C2
Greenway Bush La
BS3 ....63 A4
Greenway Dr BS10...37 C4
Greenway Ho **10**
BS6 ....47 C2
Greenway Pk BS10...37 C4
Greenway Rd BS6....47 C2
Greenways BS15.....53 B1
Greenway The BS16..52 A3
Greenwich Apartments
BS6 ....47 B4
Green Wlk BS4 ......64 C1
Greenwood CI BS7...38 A3
Greenwood Rd BS4 ..64 C1
Gregory Ct BS30 .....60 C2
Grenville Chapel **5**
BS8 ....54 B1
Grenville CI BS5 .....58 B4
Grenville Pl **7** BS1 ..54 B1
Grenville Rd BS6 ....48 C3
Greve Ct **5** BS30 ....48 B4
Greville Rd BS3 .....63 A4
Greville St BS3 ......63 A4
Greylands Rd BS13...70 B3
Greystoke Ave BS10..26 A1
Greystoke Gdns
BS10 ....36 C4
Greystones BS16.....30 C1
Griggfield Wlk BS14 .72 C3
Grimsbury Rd BS15 ..60 C3
Grindell Rd BS5 .....57 C3
Grinfield Ave BS13...79 B4
Grinfield Ct BS13 ....79 B4
Grittleton Rd BS7....38 A4
Grosvenor Ct **2**
BS6 ....47 C1
Grosvenor Rd
Bristol BS2 ....49 A1
Bristol BS2 ....86 C3
Grove Ave
Bristol BS1 ....87 A1
Bristol, Coombe Dingle
BS9 ....35 B3
3 Bristol, Fishponds
BS16 ....51 A4
Grove Bank BS16 ....30 A1
Grove CI BS9 ....36 A1
Grove Hall BS4 ......65 C2
Grove Ind Est The
BS34 ....15 C4
Grove Leaze BS11....33 C2
Grove Mews The
BS36 ....18 C3
Grove Park Ave BS4..65 C2
Grove Park Rd BS4 ..65 C2
Grove Park Terr
BS16 ....51 A4
Grove Pk
Bristol, Brislington
BS4 ....65 C2
Bristol, Redland BS6..48 A2
Grove Rd
Bristol, Coombe Dingle
BS9 ....35 C4
Bristol, Fishponds
BS16 ....51 A4
Bristol, Redland BS6..47 B2
Groves The BS13.....79 C4
Grove The
Bristol BS1 ....87 A1

Grove The continued
Bristol, Oldland BS30 ..68 C4
Bristol, Patchway
BS34 ....15 C3
Grove View BS16.....40 A2
Guardian Ct **8** BS8..54 B3
Guernsey Ave BS4...66 B4
Guest Ave BS16......43 A3
Guild Ct BS1.........87 B2
Guildford Rd BS4....58 A2
Guildhall The * BS1..86 A3
Guinea La
Bristol BS16 ....51 B4
Bristol, Fishponds
BS16 ....40 C1
Guinea St BS1.......87 A1
Gullimores Gdns
BS13 ....79 A4
Gullons CI BS13 .....70 C2
Gullon Wlk BS13.....70 B1
Gullybrook La **3**
BS5 ....57 A2
Gully The BS36.......19 A3
Gunning CI BS15.....59 C2
Gunter's Hill BS5.....58 C2
Guthrie Rd BS8 ......54 A4
Gwilliam St BS3 .....63 C3
Gwyn St BS2 ....48 C1

H

Haberfield Ho **1**
BS8 ....54 B2
Hadley Ct BS30 .....61 A2
Hadrian CI BS9 ......46 A4
Hadrians Wlk BS16 ..43 B2
Haig CI BS9 ....35 A3
Halbrow Cres BS16 ..41 B1
Haldon CI BS3 ......63 C1
Hale CI BS15 ....67 C4
Hales Horn CI BS32 ..16 B2
Half Acre CI BS14....80 C3
Halfacre La BS14 ....81 A4
Hallards CI BS11.....34 B4
HALLEN 12 A1
Hallen CI
Bristol, Emerson's
  Green BS16.........43 B2
Bristol, Henbury
BS10 ....24 B3
Hallen Dr BS9 ....35 B3
Hallen Ind Est BS10..11 B3
Hallen Rd BS10......24 B4
Halls Gdns BS34 ....29 B4
Halls Rd BS15 ....59 C4
Hall St BS3 ....63 B2
Halsbury Rd BS6.....47 C4
Halstock Ave BS16...51 A3
Halston Dr BS2......86 C4
Halswell Gdns BS13..79 A4
Halt End BS14 ......81 B3
Halwyn CI BS9.......35 C1
Hambledon Ho BS6..84 C4
HAMBROOK 30 A3
Hambrook La BS34 ..29 B3
Hambrook Prim Sch
BS16 ....30 B3
Ham Farm La BS16 ..43 A2
Ham Gn BS20.......45 C3
Hamilton Ct **11** BS1 ..86 A4
Hamilton Rd
Bristol, Southville
BS3 ....63 A4
Bristol, Upper Easton
BS5 ....57 A4
Ham La BS16 ....40 A2
Hammersmith Rd
BS5 ....57 C4
Hammond CI BS4....66 A1
Hammond Gdns
BS9 ....36 A3
Hampden Rd BS4 ...65 A3
Hampstead Rd BS4 ..65 B3
Hampton CI BS30....60 C1

Hampton Cnr BS11 ..34 A2
Hampton Ct BS6.....47 C1
Hampton La
17 Bristol BS6 ....47 C1
Bristol BS6 ....84 B4
Hampton Pk BS6 ....47 C1
Hampton Rd BS6 ....47 C1
Hampton St BS15....52 B1
Hams Rd BS31.......76 B3
Hanbury CI BS15.....59 C1
Hanbury Ct BS8 .....84 A4
Hanbury Rd BS8 ....84 A4
Handel Ave **2** BS5...57 C3
Handel Cossham Ct **3**
BS15 ....52 A1
Handel Rd BS31 .....76 A1
Handford Way BS30..69 A3
Hanford Ct BS14.....73 C3
HANHAM 67 B4
Hanham Abbots Jun
Sch BS15...........67 B4
Hanham Bsns Pk
BS15 ....59 A1
HANHAM GREEN...67 B3
Hanham High Sch
BS15 ....67 B4
Hanham Lodge
BS15 ....59 C3
Hanham Mills BS15 ..67 C1
Hanham Rd BS15....59 C3
Hannah More Prim Sch
BS2 ....87 C2
Hanover CI BS34.....27 B3
Hanover Ho BS2.....56 C3
Hanover PI BS1......85 B1
Hanover St
2 Bristol BS1 ....87 A2
Bristol, Russell Town
BS5 ....57 B3
Happerton La BS20 ..45 C2
Harbour Ho BS1.....85 A1
Harbours Edge BS8..85 B2
Harbour Way BS1....85 C1
Harbour Wlk BS1....85 C1
Harbury Rd BS9 .....37 B3
Harcombe Hill BS36 .30 C4
Harcombe Rd BS36 ..18 B1
Harcourt Ave BS5....58 C2
Harcourt Hill BS6....48 A3
Harcourt Rd BS6.....47 C3
Hardenhuish Rd
BS4 ....57 C1
Harden Rd BS14 ....74 A1
Harding PI BS31 .....77 A1
Hardings Row BS2...65 A4
Hardington Dr BS31 .83 B2
Hardwick CI
Bristol, Broom Hill
BS4 ....66 A3
Bristol, North Common
BS30 ....61 C1
Hardwick Rd BS20...33 B1
Hardy Ave BS3.......62 C4
Hardy Ct BS30.......60 B1
Hardy Rd BS3.......63 A2
Hareclive Prim Sch
BS13 ....79 B4
Hareclive Rd BS13 ..79 B4
Harefield CI BS15 ...67 B2
Harewood Ho BS6 ..47 B3
Harewood Rd BS5 ..51 B1
Harford CI BS9 ......35 B3
Harford Dr BS16.....30 A1
Harlech Way BS30...69 A2
Harleston St **1** BS5...56 C4
Harley Ct **3** BS8....54 B3
Harley Mews **2** BS8 .54 B3
Harley PI **4** BS8.....54 B3
Harmer CI BS10 .....25 A3
Harnhill CI BS13 .....79 A4
Harolds Way BS15 ...59 B2
Harptree Ct BS30 .68 C4
Harptree Gr BS3.....63 A2
Harriets Yd BS31.....76 B1

Harrington Ave
BS14 . . . .**74** A2
Harrington Gr BS14. .**74** A2
Harrington Rd BS14. .**74** A2
Harrington Wlk
BS14 . . . .**74** A2
Harris Barton BS36 . .**19** C3
Harris Ct BS30. . . . . . .**68** B4
Harris Gr BS13. . . . . .**79** A3
Harrison Cl BS16 . . . .**43** A2
Harrowdene Rd BS4 .**65** A3
Harrow Rd BS4 . . . . . .**65** C3
HARRY STOKE **28** C2
Harry Stoke Rd
BS34 . . . .**28** C2
HARTCLIFFE **79** B4
Hartcliffe Engineering
Com Coll BS13 . . . . .**80** A4
Hartcliffe Rd BS4 . . . .**72** A4
Hartcliffe Way BS3, BS4,
BS13 . . . .**71** B3
Hartcliffe Wlk BS4 . . .**72** B4
Hartfield Ave BS6. . . .**84** C4
Hartgill Cl BS13. . . . . .**79** A3
Hartington Pk BS6. . . .**48** A2
Hartland Rd BS5. . . . . .**57** B2
Harvest Cl BS32 . . . . . .**9** B1
Harvey's La **6** BS5. . .**58** B4
Harwood Ho **14** BS5. .**57** A3
Harwood Sq BS7 . . . . .**38** A1
Haskins Ct **4** BS30 . .**68** C4
Haslemere Ind Est
BS11. . . . .**22** A2
Hassell Dr BS2 . . . . . .**56** C3
Hastings Cl BS3 . . . . . .**63** B1
Hastings Rd BS3 . . . . .**63** B1
Hatchet La BS34 . . . . .**28** C4
Hatchet Rd BS34. . . . .**16** C1
Hathaway Ho **13**
BS2 . . . .**86** A4
Hatherley Rd BS7. . . .**48** C4
Hathway Wlk BS5. . . .**56** C4
Haven The BS15 . . . . .**52** C1
Haverstock Rd BS4 . . .**64** C3
Haviland Ho **7** BS2. .**86** C3
Hawburn Cl BS4 . . . . .**65** C2
Haweswater BS10 . . . .**25** C2
Haweswater Cl
BS30. . . . .**61** C2
Hawkesbury Rd
BS16 . . . .**50** C3
Hawkesley Dr BS34 . .**16** B2
Hawkfield Bsns Pk
BS14 . . . .**71** C1
Hawkfield Cl BS14 . . .**71** C1
Hawkfield Rd BS13 . . .**71** C1
Hawkfield Way
BS14 . . . .**71** C1
Hawkins Cl BS30. . . . .**61** B1
Hawkins Cres BS32 . .**16** C4
Hawkins St BS2. . . . . .**86** C3
Hawkley Dr BS32 . . . . .**9** B3
Hawksmoor Cl BS14 .**72** C2
Hawksmoor La
BS16 . . . .**40** A4
Hawksworth Dr
BS15 . . . .**59** A1
Hawthorn Cl BS34 . . .**14** C3
Hawthorne Gdns
BS16 . . . .**53** A4
Hawthorne Rise
BS10 . . . .**26** A3
Hawthorne St BS4 . . .**64** C4
Hawthornes The
BS16 . . . .**53** A4
Hawthorns La BS31 . .**76** A1
Hawthorn Way BS34 .**16** C1
Haycombe BS14 . . . . .**72** B2
Haycroft Rd BS34. . . .**27** B3
Haydock Cl BS16 . . . . .**31** A1
Haydon Cl **12** BS8. . . .**47** B2
Haydon Gdns BS7. . . .**39** A1
Hayeley Dr BS32 . . . . .**16** C2

Hayes Cl BS2 . . . .**56** C3
Hayes Ct BS34 . . . .**15** B3
Hayleigh Ho BS13. . . .**79** B4
Haymarket The BS1. . .**86** A3
Haymarket Wlk **9**
BS1 . . . .**86** A4
Haynes Ho **3** BS16 . .**52** B4
Haynes La BS16 . . . . . .**51** C1
Hayter Ct BS10 . . . .**26** B3
Haythorne Ct BS16 . . .**42** B1
Haythorne Ct **8**
BS16 . . . .**50** C3
Haytor Ho BS9 . . . .**35** C2
Hayward Ind Est **1**
BS16 . . . .**52** B3
Hayward Rd
Bristol, Russell Town
BS5 . . . .**57** A3
Bristol, Staple Hill
BS16 . . . .**52** B3
Hazel Ave BS6 . . . .**47** C2
Hazelbury Dr BS30. . . .**61** C3
Hazelbury Rd BS14 . . .**73** B3
Hazel Cote Rd BS14 . .**81** A4
Hazeldene Rd BS34 . . .**15** B3
Hazel Gr BS7 . . . .**38** C4
Hazelgrove BS36 . . . . .**18** C1
Hazelton Rd BS7. . . . .**48** B3
Hazelwood Ct BS9 . . .**46** B3
Hazelwood Rd BS9 . . .**46** B3
Headford Ave BS5 . . . .**59** A3
Headford Rd BS4 . . . . .**63** C1
Headington Cl BS15 . .**67** C4
Headley Cl BS13. . . . . .**71** A2
Headley La BS13. . . . . .**71** A3
HEADLEY PARK **71** A2
Headley Park Ave
BS13 . . . .**71** A3
Headley Park Prim Sch
BS13 . . . .**71** A3
Headley Park Rd
BS13 . . . .**70** C3
Headley Rd BS13 . . . . .**70** C2
Headley Wlk BS13 . . . .**71** A3
Heart Meers BS14 . . . .**73** A1
Heath Cl BS36 . . . .**18** C2
Heathcote Dr BS36 . . .**20** B3
Heathcote La BS36 . . .**20** B3
Heathcote Rd
Bristol, Chester Park
BS16 . . . .**51** C2
Bristol, Staple Hill
BS16 . . . .**42** A1
Heathcote Wlk
BS16 . . . .**52** A2
Heath Ct BS16 . . . .**41** C3
Heather Ave BS36. . . .**19** C2
Heather Cl BS15 . . . . . .**59** A4
Heatherdene BS14. . . .**72** B3
Heathfield Cl BS31. . . .**75** B1
Heathfield Cres
BS14 . . . .**81** A4
Heathfields BS16 . . . .**41** C4
Heath Gdns
Bristol BS16 . . . .**41** C4
Frampton Cotterell
BS36 . . . .**20** A1
Heath House La BS7,
BS16 . . . .**39** B1
Heath House Priory
Hospl BS16 . . . .**49** C4
Heath Rd
Bristol, Downend
BS16 . . . .**41** C4
Bristol, Eastville BS5 . .**49** C3
Bristol, Hanham
BS15 . . . .**67** A4
Heath Rise BS30. . . . . .**61** A1
Heath St BS5 . . . .**50** A3
Heath The BS9. . . . . . .**46** C3
Heath Wlk BS16 . . . . . .**41** C3
Heber St BS5. . . . .**57** B3
Hebron Ct BS3. . . . . . .**63** B3
Hebron Rd BS3. . . . . . .**63** B3

Hedgemead Cl BS16 .**39** C1
Hedgemead View
BS16 . . . .**40** A1
Hedgerows **2** BS16 . . .**9** B1
Hedgers Cl BS3. . . . . . .**62** C2
Hedwick Ave BS5 . . . .**58** A3
Hedwick St BS5 . . . . . .**58** A3
Heggard Cl BS13. . . . . .**70** C1
Hellier Wlk BS13. . . . . .**79** B3
Hemmings Par **4**
BS5 . . . .**57** A3
Hemplow Cl BS14. . . . .**73** C3
Hempton La BS32. . . . . .**8** C2
Henacre Rd BS11. . . . . .**34** B4
HENBURY **24** C2
Henbury Court Prim
Sch BS10. . . . .**25** A3
Henbury Ct BS10 . . . . .**24** C3
Henbury Gdns BS10. . .**24** C2
Henbury Hill
Bristol BS9 . . . .**25** A1
Bristol BS9 . . . .**36** B4
Henbury Rd
Bristol BS9 . . . .**36** B4
Bristol, Hanham
BS15 . . . .**59** A1
Bristol, Henbury
BS10 . . . .**25** A2
Bristol, Westbury on Trym
BS9 . . . .**36** C3
Henbury Sch BS10. . . .**24** C3
Hencliffe Rd BS14 . . . .**73** C3
Hencliffe Way BS15. . .**67** A3
Henderson Ho **1**
BS2 . . . .**86** B4
Henderson Rd BS15. . .**59** A1
Hendre Rd BS3 . . . .**62** C2
Henfield Cres BS30 . . .**69** A3
Hengaston St BS3 . . . .**63** A2
HENGROVE **73** A2
Hengrove Ave BS14 . . .**73** A4
Hengrove Com Arts
Coll BS14. . . . .**73** A3
Hengrove La BS14 . . . .**73** A4
Hengrove Rd BS4 . . . . .**64** C2
Hengrove Way BS14 . .**72** A2
HENLEAZE **37** B2
Henleaze Ave BS9 . . . .**36** C1
Henleaze Gdns BS9 . . .**36** C1
Henleaze Jun & Inf
Schs BS9 . . . .**37** B1
Henleaze Park Dr
BS9 . . . .**37** B2
Henleaze Pk BS9 . . . . .**37** B1
Henleaze Rd BS9 . . . . .**37** A2
Henleaze Terr BS9 . . . .**37** A1
Henley Gr BS9 . . . .**37** A1
Henley Grove Ct
BS9 . . . .**37** A1
Hennessy Cl BS14. . . . .**80** B3
Henrietta St
Bristol BS2 . . . .**86** A4
5 Bristol, Lower Easton
BS5 . . . .**49** C1
Henry St BS3 . . . .**64** B4
Henry Williamson Ct **1**
BS30 . . . .**60** C1
Henshaw Cl BS15. . . . .**52** A2
Henshaw Rd BS15 . . . .**52** A2
Henshaw Wlk BS15 . . .**52** A2
Hensman's Hill BS8. . .**85** A2
Hepburn Rd BS2. . . . . .**86** B4
Herald Cl BS9 . . . .**35** C1
Herapath St BS5. . . . . .**57** B2
Herbert Cres BS5. . . . .**50** B3
Herbert St
Bristol, Moorfields
BS5 . . . .**57** B4
Bristol, Southville
BS3 . . . .**63** C4
Hercules Cl BS34 . . . . .**16** B2
Hereford Rd BS2. . . . . .**49** B2
Hereford St BS3 . . . . . .**63** C3
Herkomer Cl BS7 . . . . .**39** A3

Hermitage Cl BS11. . . .**34** A3
Hermitage Rd BS16 . . .**42** A1
Heron Rd BS5 . . . .**49** C1
Herridge Cl BS13 . . . . .**79** A4
Herridge Rd BS13. . . . .**79** A4
Hersey Gdns BS13 . . . .**78** A3
Hesding Cl BS15. . . . . .**67** B3
Hestercombe Rd
BS13 . . . .**71** A2
Hewland Ct BS11 . . . . .**24** A2
Heyford Ave BS5. . . . . .**49** C4
Heyron Wlk BS13 . . . . .**79** A4
Heywood Rd BS20 . . . .**45** B4
Heywood Terr BS20 . . .**45** B4
Hicking Ct **6** BS15. . . .**52** B1
Hicks Ave BS16. . . . . . .**43** A4
HICKS COMMON **19** A1
Hicks Common Rd
BS36 . . . .**18** C1
Hicks Ct
Bristol, Crofts End
BS5 . . . .**58** B4
Bristol, Stone Hill
BS30 . . . .**68** B4
HICKS GATE **75** A4
Hide Mkt BS2. . . . .**86** C3
Higham St **4** BS2 . . . .**64** B4
Highbury Rd
Bristol, Bedminster
BS3 . . . .**63** B2
Bristol, Horfield BS7. . .**38** B3
Highbury Villas BS2 . .**84** C4
High Cnr BS10. . . . .**25** A1
Highcroft **3** BS30 . . . .**61** B2
Highcroft Jun Sch
BS36 . . . .**20** A4
Highdale Cl BS14. . . . . .**81** A4
High Elm BS15. . . . .**60** A2
Highett Dr BS5 . . . .**49** B1
Highfield Ave BS15 . . .**59** C1
Highfield Gdns BS30 . .**69** B2
Highfield Gr BS7. . . . . .**37** C1
Highfield Rd BS31. . . . .**81** C4
Highfields Cl BS34 . . . .**29** A3
High Gr BS9 . . . .**35** A3
Highgrove St BS4. . . . .**64** C3
High Kingsdown
BS2 . . . .**84** C4
High La BS36 . . . .**18** A4
Highland Cres **3**
BS8 . . . .**47** B2
Highland Pl **13** BS8 . . .**47** B2
Highland Sq **4** BS8. . .**47** B2
Highleaze Rd BS30. . . .**69** B4
Highmead Gdns
BS13 . . . .**78** A4
Highmore Ct BS7 . . . . .**39** A3
Highmore Gdns BS7 . .**39** B3
Highnam Cl BS34 . . . . . .**8** C1
High Pk BS14. . . . .**65** A1
High Point Ho **1**
BS15 . . . .**52** A1
HIGHRIDGE **70** B2
Highridge Cres
BS13 . . . .**70** B1
Highridge Gn BS13 . . . .**70** A2
Highridge Inf Sch
BS13 . . . .**70** B2
Highridge Pk BS13. . . .**70** B2
Highridge Rd
Bristol, Bedminster
BS3 . . . .**63** B2
Bristol, Withywood BS13,
BS41 . . . .**78** A3
Highridge Wlk BS13 . .**70** A3
High St
Bristol BS1 . . . .**87** A2
Bristol, Clifton BS8 . . .**47** B2
Bristol, Jefferies Hill
BS15 . . . .**59** B1
Bristol, Kingswood
BS15 . . . .**60** A4
Bristol, Lower Easton
BS5 . . . .**49** C1

Har–Hil **101**

High St continued
Bristol, Oldland Common
BS30. . . . .**69** C4
Bristol, Shirehampton
BS11. . . . .**34** A2
Bristol, Staple Hill
BS16 . . . .**52** B4
Bristol, Warmley
BS15 . . . .**61** A4
Bristol, Westbury on Trym
BS9 . . . .**36** C3
Keynsham BS31 . . . . . .**76** A2
Portbury BS20 . . . .**44** A3
Winterbourne BS36 . . .**18** B2
Highview Rd BS15 . . . .**53** A2
Highwood Bsns Pk
BS34 . . . .**14** C3
Highwood La BS10,
BS34 . . . .**14** B3
Highwood Pk Cvn Site
BS34 . . . .**14** C2
Highwood Rd BS34 . . .**15** A3
Highworth Rd BS4. . . .**57** C2
Hilhouse BS9 . . . .**35** B2
Hill Ave BS3 . . . .**64** A3
Hill Burn BS9 . . . .**37** B2
Hillburn Rd BS5 . . . . . .**58** C4
Hill Cl BS16. . . . .**43** A4
Hill Crest BS4 . . . .**65** A1
Hillcrest Prim Sch
BS4 . . . .**64** C3
Hillcroft Cl BS15. . . . . .**68** A4
Hill End Dr BS10 . . . . . .**24** B3
HILLFIELDS **51** C3
Hillfields Ave BS16 . . .**52** A3
Hillfields Prim Sch
BS16 . . . .**52** A2
Hill Gr BS9 . . . .**37** B2
Hillgrove St BS2 . . . . . .**86** B4
HILLHOUSE **42** C1
Hill House Rd BS16 . . .**42** B1
Hill Lawn BS4 . . . .**65** C3
Hill's Barton BS13 . . . .**62** C1
Hillsborough BS8. . . . .**85** A2
Hillsborough Rd
BS4 . . . .**65** B4
Hills Cl BS31. . . . .**76** C1
Hillsdon Rd BS9 . . . . . .**36** B4
Hillside
Bristol BS6 . . . .**84** C4
Bristol, Mangotsfield
BS16 . . . .**42** C1
Hillside Ave BS15 . . . .**59** A4
Hillside Cl BS36 . . . . . .**20** A3
Hillside Gdns BS15 . . .**59** A3
Hillside Ho **6** BS6 . . . .**48** B1
Hillside La BS36 . . . . . .**20** A3
Hillside Rd BS5 . . . .**58** C3
Hillside St BS4 . . . .**64** C4
Hill St
Bristol BS1 . . . .**85** C2
Bristol, Kingswood
BS15 . . . .**60** B4
Bristol, St George
BS5 . . . .**58** B4
Bristol, Windmill Hill
BS3 . . . .**64** B4
Hill The BS32 . . . .**8** C4
Hilltop Gdns
Bristol, St George
BS5 . . . .**58** C3
Bristol, Upper Soundwell
BS16 . . . .**52** B2
Hilltop Rd BS16. . . . . . .**52** B2
Hilltop View BS5. . . . . .**58** C3
Hill View
Bristol, Blackhorse
BS16 . . . .**42** C4
Bristol BS8 . . . .**85** B2
Bristol, Filton BS34. . . .**27** B3
Bristol, Henleaze BS9. . .**37** B2

Hill View *continued*
Bristol, Upper Southwell
BS16 . . . .**52** B2
Hill View CI BS30. . . .**69** B4
Hill View Ct BS16 . . . .**41** B1
Hill View Ho 2
BS15 . . . .**52** A1
Hill View Rd BS13 . . . .**70** C4
Hillyfield Rd BS13. . . .**70** C2
Hilton Ct 5 BS5 . . . . .**57** A4
Hinton Dr BS30 . . . . . .**61** B2
Hinton La 13 BS8 . . . .**54** B2
Hinton Rd
Bristol, Fishponds
BS16 . . . .**51** B4
Bristol, Lower Easton
BS5 . . . .**50** A1
Hither Bath Bridge
BS4 . . . .**65** B1
Hither Mead BS36 . . . .**19** C2
Hobbs La BS30 . . . . . .**53** C1
Hobb's La BS1. . . . . . .**85** C2
Hockeys La BS16. . . . .**51** B4
Hogarth Wlk BS7 . . . . .**39** B3
Hogues Wlk BS13 . . . . . .**8** A4
Holbeach Way BS14 .**80** C2
Holbrook Cres BS13 .**79** C4
Holcombe BS14 . . . . . .**72** C1
Holcombe Gr BS31. . . .**75** C1
Holdenhurst Rd
BS15 . . . .**52** A1
Holford Ct BS14 . . . . .**73** A1
Hollidge Gdns 3
BS3 . . . .**63** C4
Hollies The BS15. . . . .**60** B2
Hollister's Dr BS13 . .**79** C4
Holloway Rd BS35 . . . . .**5** A4
Hollow Rd
Almondsbury BS32. . . . .**8** B4
Bristol BS15 . . . .**60** A4
Hollway CI BS14 . . . . .**74** A1
Hollway Rd BS14 . . . . .**74** A1
Hollybrook Pk BS15. .**51** C2
Hollybush La
Bristol BS9 . . . .**36** A1
Bristol BS9 . . . .**47** A4
Holly CI BS5 . . . .**51** B2
Holly Cres BS15. . . . . .**52** C1
Holly Ct BS2. . . . .**84** C4
Holly Gn BS15 . . . .**53** B1
Holly Gr BS16. . . . .**51** A3
Hollyguest Rd BS15. .**60** A2
Holly Hill Rd BS15 . . .**53** A1
Holly Ho BS11 . . . .**24** A2
Hollyleigh Ave BS34 .**36** A3
Holly Lodge CI BS5 . .**51** B2
Holly Lodge Rd BS5. .**51** A2
Hollymead La BS9 . . . .**46** C4
Hollyridge BS14 . . . . .**73** B2
Holly Wlk BS31 . . . . . .**82** B4
Hollywood La BS10,
BS35 . . . .**13** B3
Hollywood Rd BS4 . . .**65** C2
Holmdale Rd BS34. . . .**28** A3
Holmes Ct BS9 . . . .**37** A1
Holmesdale Rd BS3. . .**64** A3
Holmes Gr BS9 . . . .**37** A1
Holmes Hill Rd BS5. . .**58** B4
Holmes St BS5 . . . .**57** A2
Holmoak Rd BS31 . . . .**82** A4
Holmwood BS15. . . . . .**59** B1
Holmwood CI BS36 . .**18** B2
Holmwood Gdns
BS9 . . . .**37** A4
Holroyd Ho BS3 . . . . . .**63** C3
Holsom Ct BS14 . . . . . .**74** B2
Holsom Rd BS14 . . . . .**74** B2
Holst Gdns BS4 . . . . . .**71** C4
Holton Rd BS7. . . . .**38** C2

Holybrook Trad Est
BS15 . . . .**51** C2
Holy Cross RC Prim
Sch BS3 . . . .**63** B4
Holy Family RC Prim
Sch BS34 . . . .**15** C4
Holymead Inf Sch
BS4 . . . .**65** C2
Holymead Jun Sch
BS4 . . . .**65** C3
Holyrood CI BS34. . . .**28** B4
Holy Trinity Prim Sch
BS32 . . . .**9** A2
Holy Well CI BS4. . . . .**58** A2
Homeavon Ho BS31. .**76** B1
Home CI BS10 . . . .**26** C2
Home Farm Way
BS35. . . . .**6** B1
Home Field CI BS16. .**43** A2
Homefield Dr BS16 . .**40** C1
Homeground BS16. . . .**43** A2
Home Ground
Bristol, Eastfield
BS9 . . . .**37** A3
Bristol, Shirehampton
BS11. . . . .**33** C3
Homeleaze Rd BS10 .**26** B3
Home Mead
Bristol, Cadbury Heath
BS30 . . . .**68** C4
Bristol, Filwood Park
BS4 . . . .**72** A3
Homemead Dr BS4 . .**65** C1
Homestead CI BS36. .**20** B3
Homestead Gdns
BS16 . . . .**41** A4
Homestead Rd BS34 .**27** B3
Homestead The
BS31. . . . .**83** A2
Honey Garston CI
BS13 . . . .**79** A4
Honey Garston Rd
BS13 . . . .**79** A4
Honey Hill Rd BS15 . .**60** B4
Honeymead BS14 . . . .**73** B2
Honeysuckle CI BS32 . .**9** C2
Honey Suckle La
BS16 . . . .**40** A1
Honey Way BS15. . . . .**60** B4
Honeywick CI BS3. . . .**63** B2
Honister Ho BS34. . . .**15** B4
Honiton Rd BS16 . . . . .**51** B3
Hooper Rd BS14 . . . . .**73** C1
Hopechapel Hill 11
BS8 . . . .**54** B2
Hope Ct BS1. . . . .**85** B1
Hope Rd BS3 . . . .**63** B2
Hope Sq BS8 . . . .**54** B2
Hopetoun Rd BS2. . . .**49** A3
Hopewell Gdns
BS11. . . . .**34** B3
HOPEWELL HILL . . .**52** B1
Hopkins Ct 13 BS6. . .**47** C1
Hopland CI BS30. . . . .**69** A3
Hopp's Rd BS15 . . . . . .**59** C3
Horesham Gr BS13. . .**71** B1
HORFIELD **38** B2
Horfield CE Prim Sch
BS10 . . . .**37** C3
Horfield Ct BS7. . . . . .**48** C4
Horfield Rd BS2 . . . . .**86** A4
Horley Rd BS2. . . . . . .**49** B2
Hornbeam Ho 5
BS16 . . . .**41** B2
Hornbeams The
BS16 . . . .**29** C1
Hornbeam Wlk
BS31. . . . .**81** A3
Horsecroft Gdns
BS30 . . . .**60** C2
Horsefair The BS1 . . .**86** B3
Horsepool Rd BS13 . .**78** A3
Horseshoe Ct BS36 . .**20** B3
Horseshoe Dr BS9 . . .**46** A4

Horse World * BS14 .**81** C3
Horton St BS2 . . . .**86** C3
Horwood Ct 3
BS30 . . . .**68** C4
Hosey Wlk BS13 . . . . .**70** C1
Host St BS1 . . . .**86** A3
Hottom Gdns BS7. . . .**38** C3
Hot Water La BS15. . .**53** B3
Hotwell Hts BS8 . . . . .**85** A2
Hotwell Rd BS8. . . . . .**85** B1
HOTWELLS **85** A1
Hotwells Ho BS8. . . . .**85** A1
Hotwells Prim Sch
BS8 . . . .**54** B2
Houlton St BS2 . . . . . .**86** C4
Howard Ave BS5 . . . . .**58** A4
Howard Rd
Bristol, Southville
BS3 . . . .**63** B4
Bristol, Staple Hill
BS16 . . . .**52** B4
Bristol, Westbury Park
BS6 . . . .**47** C4
Howard St BS5 . . . . . .**50** C1
Howard Wlk BS30. . . .**61** C3
Howecroft Ct BS9. . . .**46** C4
Howecroft Gdns
BS9 . . . .**46** C4
Howells Mead BS16. .**43** A3
Howes CI BS30 . . . . . .**60** C2
Howett Rd 16 BS5 . . .**57** B3
Howsmoor La
Bristol, Lyde Green
BS16 . . . .**43** B4
Bristol, New England
BS16 . . . .**43** A4
Hoylake Dr BS30. . . . .**61** A2
Huckford La BS36. . . .**31** B4
Huckford Rd BS36 . . .**18** C1
Huckley Way BS32 . . .**17** A2
Hudds Hill Gdns 9
BS5. . . . .**58** B4
Hudd's Hill Rd BS5. . .**58** B4
Hudd's Vale Rd BS5. .**58** A4
Hughenden Rd
Bristol, Clifton BS8 . . .**47** B2
Bristol, Horfield BS7 . .**38** A1
Hughes Gdns BS7. . . .**38** C4
Hulbert CI BS4 . . . . . .**66** C2
Hulse Rd BS4 . . . .**65** C1
Humberstan Wlk
BS11 . . . .**34** A4
Humber Way BS11 . . .**10** B1
Humphry Davy Way 6
BS8 . . . .**54** B1
Humphrys Barton
BS4 . . . .**58** B3
Hungerford CI BS4. . .**74** A4
Hungerford Cres
BS4 . . . .**66** A1
Hungerford Gdns
BS4 . . . .**74** A4
Hungerford Rd BS4. .**74** A4
Hungerford Wlk
BS4 . . . .**66** A1
Hung Rd BS11 . . . .**34** A1
Hunters CI BS15 . . . . .**59** B1
Hunters Dr BS15 . . . . .**53** A1
Hunters Rd BS15 . . . . .**59** B1
Hunters Rd E BS15. . .**67** B4
Hunter's Way BS34 . .**27** C3
Huntingham Rd
BS13 . . . .**78** B4
Hunts Ground Rd
BS34 . . . .**29** A4
Hunts La BS7 . . . .**38** A2
Hurle Cres BS8 . . . . . .**47** C1
Hurle Rd BS8 . . . .**47** C1
Hurlingham Rd BS7. .**49** A2
Hurn La BS31. . . . .**83** B3
Hursley Hill BS14 . . . .**81** C1
Hurston Rd BS4 . . . . .**71** C4
Hurst Rd BS4 . . . .**72** B4
Hurst Wlk BS4. . . . . . .**72** B4

Hurstwood Rd BS16. .**41** C1
Hutton CI
Bristol BS9 . . . .**36** A3
Keynsham BS31 . . . . . .**83** B2
Huyton Rd BS5 . . . . . .**50** C3
Hyde Apartments
BS6 . . . .**48** B3
Hydes The BS31. . . . . .**76** B2
Hyland Gr BS9. . . . . . .**36** B4

I

Ida Rd 2 BS5. . . . .**57** B4
Iddesleigh Rd BS6. . .**47** C3
Idstone Rd BS16 . . . . .**51** C4
Ilchester Cres BS13 . .**63** A1
Ilchester Rd BS13. . . .**71** A4
Iles CI BS15 . . . .**67** C4
Ilex CI BS13 . . . .**70** B2
Ilminster Ave BS4. . . .**63** C3
Ilminster Avenue Prim
Sch BS4 . . . .**72** C4
Ilsyn Gr BS14 . . . .**73** C3
Imber Court CI
BS14 . . . .**73** A4
Imperial Arc 11 BS3 .**63** C4
Imperial Pk BS13. . . .**71** B2
Imperial Rd
Bristol BS14 . . . .**73** B4
8 Bristol, Clifton
BS6 . . . .**47** C1
Imperial Wlk BS14. . .**65** A1
Ingleside Rd BS15 . . .**52** A1
Ingmire Rd BS5. . . . . .**49** C3
Inkerman CI BS7. . . . .**38** A3
Inn Cotts BS11. . . . . . .**34** C3
Innox Gdns BS13. . . . .**70** C1
Inns Court Ave BS4. .**71** C3
Inns Court CI BS4 . . . .**71** C2
Inns Court Gn BS4 . . .**71** C3
Instow Rd BS4. . . . . . .**72** A4
Instow Wlk BS4. . . . . .**72** A4
International Trad Est
BS11 . . . .**21** C2
Interplex 16 BS32 . . . .**9** A3
IO Ctr BS11. . . . .**11** A1
Ipswich Dr BS4 . . . . . .**58** A2
Irby Rd BS3. . . . .**62** C3
Irena Rd BS16 . . . .**51** A3
Ireton Rd BS3 . . . .**63** A3
Ironchurch Rd BS11. .**10** A1
Ironmould La
Bristol BS4 . . . .**66** C1
Keynsham BS31. . . . . .**74** C4
Irving CI BS16 . . . .**52** C4
Irving Ho BS1. . . . .**84** C3
I.S.F. Rd BS11. . . . .**22** A3
Island Gdns BS16 . . . .**50** A4
Island Trad Pk BS11. .**22** A1
Isleys Ct BS30 . . . .**68** B3
Islington Rd BS3. . . . .**63** B4
Ison Hill Rd BS10 . . . .**24** B3
Ivor Rd BS5. . . . .**57** B4
Ivy La BS16 . . . .**51** B3
Ivy Lodge 4 BS9 . . . .**36** C3
Ivywell Rd BS9. . . . . . .**46** C3

J

Jack Knight Ho BS7. .**38** B1
Jack Price CI BS13. . . .**79** B3
Jackson CI BS35 . . . . . .**3** B3
Jacob Ct BS2 . . . .**86** C3
Jacobs Bldg The
BS8 . . . .**84** B3
Jacob's Ct BS1 . . . .**85** C2
Jacob St
Bristol BS2 . . . .**86** B3
Bristol BS2 . . . .**86** C3
Jacob's Wells Rd
BS8 . . . .**85** B2
Jamaica St BS2. . . . . .**86** B4
James CI BS16. . . . . . .**52** C4
James St BS16 . . . .**52** C3

James St
Bristol, Baptist Mills
BS2 . . . .**49** B2
Bristol BS5 . . . .**86** C4
Jane St BS5 . . . .**57** A3
Jarrets Rd BS10 . . . . . .**26** B2
Jarvis St BS5 . . . .**57** A2
Jasmine Gr BS11 . . . . .**24** A2
Jasper St BS3 . . . .**63** A3
Jean Rd BS4. . . . .**66** A2
JEFFERIES HILL **59** B1
Jefferies Hill Bottom
BS15. . . . .**59** A1
Jeffery Ct BS30. . . . . .**61** A2
Jeffreys Ct 9 BS16 . .**50** C3
Jekyll CI BS16 . . . .**40** A4
Jellicoe Ave BS16. . . .**40** A4
Jennings Ct 1 BS3 . .**62** C4
Jersey Ave BS4 . . . . . .**66** B4
Jessop Cres BS10. . . .**25** B1
Jessop Ct BS1. . . . .**87** B2
Jessop Underpass
BS3 . . . .**62** B4
Jim O'Neil Ho BS11 . .**33** C3
Jinty La BS16. . . . .**53** C2
Jocelyn Rd BS7. . . . . .**38** B3
Jockey La BS5. . . . . . .**58** C4
John Cabot City Tech
Coll BS15 . . . .**59** B3
John Cabot Ct BS1. . .**85** A1
John Carr's Terr
BS8 . . . .**85** B2
John Cozens Ho 6
BS2 . . . .**86** C3
John James Ct BS7. . .**39** A3
John Repton Gdns
BS10 . . . .**25** C2
Johnson Dr BS30 . . . .**60** B1
Johnson Rd BS16. . . . .**43** B1
Johnsons La BS5 . . . . .**50** B1
Johnsons Rd
Bristol BS5 . . . .**50** A1
1 Bristol, Moorfields
BS5 . . . .**57** B4
John St
Bristol, Baptist Mills
BS2 . . . .**49** B2
Bristol BS1 . . . .**86** A3
Bristol, Two Mile Hill
BS15 . . . .**59** B4
John Wesley Ct 10
BS16 . . . .**41** C1
John Wesley Rd
BS5 . . . .**59** A2
John Wesley's Chapel
('The New Room') *
BS1 . . . .**86** B3
Jonny Ball La BS2 . . .**86** A3
Jordan Wlk BS32 . . . .**16** B4
Joyce CI BS7 . . . .**38** C4
Joy Hill BS8 . . . .**54** B2
Jubilee Cres BS16 . . . .**42** C2
Jubilee Ct BS4. . . . . . .**65** C4
Jubilee Ho BS34 . . . . .**16** A4
Jubilee Pl
Bristol BS1 . . . .**87** A1
Bristol, Woodstock
BS15 . . . .**60** B3
Jubilee Rd
Bristol, Baptist Mills
BS2 . . . .**49** B2
Bristol, Crew's Hole
BS5 . . . .**58** B3
Bristol, Staple Hill
BS15 . . . .**52** C3
Bristol, Upper Knowle
BS4 . . . .**65** B2
Jubilee St BS2 . . . .**87** C2
Jubilee Way BS11. . . .**21** C2
Julian CI BS9 . . . .**46** C3
Julian Ct BS9 . . . .**46** C3
Julian Rd BS9 . . . .**46** C3
Julius CI BS16 . . . .**43** B2
Julius Rd BS7 . . . .**48** B3

Junction Rd BS4......65 B4
Junction Way BS15,
BS16................53 C3
Juniper Ct ② BS5 ..50 A2
Juniper Way BS34...17 B3
Jupiter Rd BS34.....14 C3
Justice Rd BS16......51 B3
Jutland Rd BS11.....21 C1

K

Karelean Ct BS10 ....26 B3
Kathdene Gdns BS7..49 A3
Keats Ct BS7 ....38 C4
Keble Ave BS13......70 B1
Keel Cl BS5..........58 B2
Keen's Gr BS35 ......3 A3
Keepers La BS7......49 A3
Keep The BS30.......61 C1
Keg Store The BS1 ..87 B2
Keinton Wlk BS10...25 B2
Kelbra Cres BS36 ...19 C2
Kellaway Ave BS7...37 C1
Kellaway Cres BS9 ..37 C2
Kellaway Ct BS6 ....37 C1
Kelston Gdns BS10 ..37 C4
Kelston Gr BS15 ....60 A2
Kelston Rd
  Bristol BS10 ....37 C4
  Keynsham BS31......75 C1
Kelston Wlk BS16...52 A4
Kemble Cl BS15 .....60 A2
Kemble Gdns BS11...34 B1
Kemble Ho BS34......8 A4
Kemperleye Way
  BS32................16 B3
Kempton Cl ② BS16 .31 A1
Kencot Wlk BS13 ....79 A3
Kendall Gdns BS16...52 B4
Kendall Rd BS16.....52 B4
Kendal Rd BS7.......38 C3
KENDLESHIRE 31 B4
Kendon Dr BS10 .....37 C3
Kendon Way BS10 ...37 C4
Kenilworth Cl BS31 ..82 B4
Kenilworth Dr BS30..69 A2
Kenilworth Rd BS6...48 A1
Kenmare Rd BS4.....64 A1
Kenmore Cres BS7...26 C1
Kenmore Dr BS7.....26 C1
Kenmore Gr BS7.....26 C1
Kennard Cl BS15.....59 B3
Kennard Rd BS15.....59 B4
Kennard Rise BS15...59 B4
Kenn Court BS4......72 A3
Kennel Lodge Rd
  BS3................62 A4
Kenneth Rd BS4 .....65 C2
Kennet Rd BS31......83 B4
Kennington Ave
  Bristol, Bishopston
  BS7................49 A3
  ③ Bristol, Two Mile Hill
  BS15................52 B1
Kennion Rd BS5.....58 C4
Kennmoor Cl BS30...60 C2
Kenn Rd BS5.........58 C3
Kensal Ave BS3......64 A3
Kensal Rd BS3.......64 A3
Kensington Apartments
  BS6................48 A3
Kensington Ct BS8..84 A4
Kensington Ho ⑤
  BS5................58 C4
KENSINGTON
  PARK 65 B3
Kensington Park Rd
  BS4................65 B2
Kensington Pk ⑫
  BS5................49 B1
Kensington Pl BS8..84 A4
Kensington Rd
  Bristol, Redland
  BS6................48 A1

Kensington Rd continued
  ③ Bristol, St George
  BS5................58 C4
  ⑦ Bristol, Staple Hill
  BS16................52 B4
Kent Cl BS34 ....28 B4
Kent Mews BS16......40 A3
Kenton Ho BS34 ......8 A1
Kenton Mews BS9....37 B1
Kent Rd BS7.........48 C4
Kents Gn BS15.......52 C2
Kent St BS3 ....63 B3
Kenwood Cl BS15....53 A1
Kerry Rd BS4........64 A1
Kersteman Rd BS6...48 A3
Kestrel Cl BS34 .....14 C4
Keswick Wlk BS10 ...26 A2
Ketch Rd BS3........64 B3
Kewstoke Rd BS9....46 C4
Kew Wlk BS4 ....73 B4
Keynsham
KEYNSHAM 82 C3
Keynsham By-Pass
  BS31................76 A3
Keynsham Hospl
  BS31................83 A4
Keynsham Prim Sch
  BS31................75 C1
Keynsham Rd BS30,
  BS31................76 C4
Keynsham Sta BS31..76 B2
Keys Ave BS7........38 B3
Kilbirnie Rd BS14....80 C3
Kilburn Ct ⑰ BS5....57 A4
Kilburn St ⑱ BS5....57 A4
Kildare Rd BS4 ......63 C1
Kilmersdon Rd
  BS13................79 A4
Kilminster Cl BS34...16 B3
Kilminster Rd BS11 ..33 C3
Kiln Cl BS15 ....51 C2
Kiln Ct BS5...........57 A4
Kilnhurst Cl BS30....68 B2
Kilvert Cl BS4 ....57 C1
Kimberley Ave BS16 .41 B1
Kimberley Cl BS16...42 B3
Kimberley Cres
  BS16................41 B1
Kimberley Rd
  Bristol, Fishponds
  BS16................41 B1
  Bristol, Kingswood
  BS15................52 B1
Kinema Ho BS4......65 B4
King Dick's La ⑦
  BS5................58 B4
King Edward Cl
  BS14................72 C2
Kingfisher Cl BS32....9 C4
Kingfisher Dr BS16 ..40 A2
King George's Rd
  BS13................70 B1
King George V Pl
  BS1................87 A2
King John's Rd
  BS15................51 C2
King Rd BS4.........65 B1
King Road Ave BS11 .21 C2
Kings Ave BS15......67 A4
King's Ave BS6, BS7 .48 A4
Kings Chase BS15 ...59 C4
Kingscote Pk BS5....59 A2
Kingscourt Cl BS14...80 C4
Kings Ct
  Bristol BS1.........87 A2
  Bristol, Little Stoke
  BS34................16 A2
  Bristol, St Pauls BS1..86 B4
  Bristol, Southville
  BS3................63 B4
  ② Bristol, Withywood
  BS13................78 B4
KINGSDOWN 86 A4
Kingsdown Par BS6..86 A4

Kings Dr
  Bristol, Hanham
  BS15................67 A4
  Bristol, Stoke Gifford
  BS34................29 B4
King's Dr BS7 ....48 A4
Kingsfield La
  Bristol, Longwell Green
  BS15................60 A1
  Bristol, Mount Hill
  BS30................68 A4
Kingsfield Rdbt
  BS15................60 A1
Kingsfield Sch BS15 .60 C4
King's Forest Prim Sch
  BS15................53 A2
King's Head La BS13 70 B3
Kingshill Ho BS4.....65 A1
Kingshill Rd BS4.....65 A1
Kingsholme Rd
  BS15................52 B1
Kingsholm Rd BS10 ..37 C4
Kingsland Cl ① BS2 .56 C2
Kingsland Rd BS2....56 C2
Kingsland Road Bridge
  ③ BS2.............56 C2
Kingsland Trad Est
  BS2................86 C3
Kingsleigh Ct BS15 ..60 B3
Kingsleigh Gdns
  BS15................60 B3
Kingsleigh Pk BS15 ..60 B3
Kingsley Ho
  Bristol BS2.........87 C2
  Bristol, Westbury on Trym
  BS9.................36 C4
Kingsley Pl ① BS3 ..63 B4
Kingsley Rd
  Bristol, Lower Easton
  BS5.................50 A1
  Bristol, Montpelier
  BS6.................48 B2
Kingsmarsh Ho ⑤
  BS5.................57 A3
Kingsmead Rd BS5 ..51 B1
Kingsmead Wlk BS5 .51 B1
Kingsmill BS9 ....35 C1
King's Parade Ave ④
  BS8.................47 C1
King's Parade Mews
  BS8.................47 C1
Kings Park Ave BS2..57 B2
King Sq BS2.........86 A4
King Square Ave
  BS2................86 A4
Kings Quarter
  Apartments ⑭
  BS2................86 A4
King's Rd
  Bristol BS8.........84 A3
  Bristol, Kensington Park
  BS4.................65 B3
Kings Sq BS30.......77 C4
King St
  Avonmouth BS11.....21 B1
  Bristol BS1.........87 A2
  Bristol, Lower Easton
  BS5................50 A1
  Bristol, St George
  BS15................59 A4
Kingston Cl BS16....42 C3
Kingston Dr BS16....42 C3
Kingston Rd BS3.....63 B4
Kingstree St BS4.....64 C4
Kingsway
  Bristol, Little Stoke
  BS34................16 A2
  Bristol, St George
  BS5.................59 A3
Kingsway Ave BS15 ..59 A4
Kingsway Cres BS15 .59 B4
Kingsway Pk BS30 ...61 A2

Kingsway Sh Prec
  BS5................59 A3
Kingswear Rd BS3 ...63 C2
Kings Weston Ave
  BS11................34 A4
Kingsweston Down
  Nature Res ★ BS9,
  BS11................21 A1
Kings Weston La
  Avonmouth BS11 ....22 C3
  Bristol BS11.........34 C4
Kings Weston Rd BS11,
  BS10................24 A1
Kingsweston Sch
  BS11................34 C4
Kings Wlk BS13......70 A3
KINGSWOOD 60 A4
Kingswood Douglas Ind
  Est BS15............59 C3
Kingswood Foundation
  Est BS15............59 B3
Kingswood Heritatge
  Mus ★ BS30........61 A2
Kingswood Hts
  BS15................52 B1
Kingswood Ind Est
  BS30................68 B4
Kingswood Trad Est
  BS15................52 B1
King William Ave
  BS1................87 A2
King William St BS3 .63 A4
Kinsale Rd BS14 .....73 B3
Kinsale Wlk BS4.....64 A1
Kinvara Rd BS4......72 A4
Kipling Rd BS7 ......27 C1
Kirkby Rd BS11......23 B1
Kirkstone Gdns
  BS10................26 A2
Kirkstone Ho BS34...15 B4
Kirtlington Rd BS5...49 C3
Kite Hay Cl BS16.....40 A1
Kites Cl BS32..........9 A2
Knapps La BS5.......50 C2
Kneller Cl BS11......34 C4
Knighton Rd BS10 ...26 C1
Knightsbridge Pk
  BS13................80 A4
Knights Cl BS9 ......37 B2
Knightstone Ct BS5..50 B2
Knightstone Gdns
  BS4.................65 A2
Knightstone Ho ①
  BS2................86 A4
Knightstone Lodge
  BS6................48 B1
Knightstone Mount
  BS5................58 C2
Knightstone Pl
  BS15................67 A2
Knightstone Rise ⑤
  BS5................58 B4
Knightstone Sq
  BS14................73 B1
Knightstone Wlk
  BS2................84 C4
Knightwood Rd
  BS34................17 A1
Knole Cl BS32........8 A4
Knole Ct BS10........25 B3
Knole La BS10........25 C3
Knole Pk BS32........8 A3
Knoll Ct BS9.........46 B3
Knoll Hill BS9.......46 B3
Knovill Cl BS11......23 C2
KNOWLE 64 B3
KNOWLE PARK 64 C1
Knowle Park Jun Sch
  BS4................64 C1
Knowle Rd BS2......64 B3
Knowsley Rd BS16...50 C3
Kyght Cl BS15.......60 C4
Kylross Ave BS14....73 A1
Kynges Mill Cl BS16..40 C3

Kyngstone Ct ⑩
  BS16................50 C3

L

Labbott The BS31 ....76 A1
Laburnum Gr BS16...51 C4
Laburnum Rd BS15 ..59 B1
Laburnum Wlk BS31 .82 A3
Lacey Rd BS14.......74 B2
Lacock Dr BS30......60 B1
Ladd Cl BS15.........60 B3
Ladies Mile BS8 .....47 A1
Ladman Gr BS14.....74 A2
Ladman Rd BS14 ....74 A1
Ladysmith Rd BS6...47 C4
Lakemead Gdns ③
  BS13................78 B4
Lakemead Gr BS13...70 B2
Lake Rd BS10........37 B4
Lakeside BS16.......50 C3
Lake View BS16......51 A3
Lake View Rd BS5....57 C4
Lakewood Cres
  BS10................37 A4
Lakewood Rd BS10 ..37 A4
La Maison BS5.......51 B2
Lambert Pl BS4......71 C2
Lamb Hill BS5 ....58 B3
Lambley Rd BS5 .....58 A4
Lambourn Cl BS3....63 C3
Lambourn Rd BS31 ..83 B4
Lambrook Rd BS16...51 B4
Lamb St BS2.........86 C3
Lamington Cl BS13 ..70 B2
Lamord Gate BS34...16 C1
Lampeter Rd BS9....36 C3
Lampton Ave BS13...80 A3
Lampton Gr BS13....80 A3
Lanaway Rd BS16....41 A2
Lancashire Rd BS7...48 C3
Lancaster Cl BS34 ...28 B4
Lancaster Rd BS2....49 B2
Lancaster St ⑩ BS5..57 B3
Lancelot Rd BS16....40 A4
Landmark Ct BS1....85 C1
Landrail Wlk BS16...40 B2
Landseer Ave BS7 ...39 A3
Land The BS36.......20 A3
Lanercost Rd BS10...26 A2
Lanesborough Rise
  BS14................73 C3
Lanes Dairy BS34 ...27 B3
Lanes End BS4 ......65 B1
Lane The BS35.........6 A2
Langdale Ct BS34....15 B4
Langdale Rd BS16...51 A4
Langdown Ct BS14...71 A1
Langfield Cl BS10....24 C3
Langford Rd BS13 ...70 B2
Langford Way BS15 ..60 A3
Langham Rd BS4.....65 A2
Langhill Ave BS4.....71 C3
Langley Cres BS3....62 A1
Langley Mow BS16...43 A3
Langsdown Ho ⑦
  BS2................49 A1
Langthorn Cl BS36...20 A3
Langton Court Rd
  BS4................57 C1
Langton Ct ⑪ BS16..50 C3
Langton Ho ⑨ BS2 ..86 C3
Langton Pk BS3......63 B4
Langton Rd BS4 .....57 C1
Langton Way BS4....58 B2
Lansdown Cl BS15...52 B2
Lansdown BS16......30 A1
Lansdowne Ct ⑧
  BS5................56 C4
Lansdown Ho BS15 ..52 B2
Lansdown Pl BS8 ....84 A3

Lansdown Rd
Bristol BS8 . . . .**84** A3
Bristol, Kingswood
BS15 . . . .**52** B2
Bristol, Redland BS6. . .**48** A1
6 Bristol, Upper Easton
BS5 . . . .**57** A4
Lansdown Terr BS6 . .**37** C1
Lansdown View
BS15 . . . .**60** B4
Laphams Ct **1** BS30 .**68** B4
Lapwing Cl BS32. . . . . . .**9** B2
Lapwing Gdns BS16. .**40** B2
Larch Rd BS15 . . . .**52** C3
Larch Way BS34 . . . . . .**14** C3
Larkfield BS36. . . . .**20** B3
Larks Field BS16. . . . . .**40** A1
Larksleaze Rd BS30. .**68** B2
Lasbury Gr BS13 . . . . . .**71** B1
Latchmoor Ho BS13. .**70** C4
Latimer Cl BS4 . . . .**66** A4
Latton Rd BS7 . . . .**38** B4
Launceston Ave
BS15 . . . .**59** A1
Launceston Rd
BS15 . . . .**51** C1
Laurel St BS15. . . . .**59** C4
Laurels The
Bristol, Catbrain
BS10 . . . .**13** B2
Bristol, Mangotsfield
BS16 . . . .**42** C2
Laurie Cres BS9 . . . . . .**37** C2
Laurie Lee Ct **3**
BS30 . . . .**60** C1
Lavender Ct BS5. . . . . .**51** A1
Lavender Way BS32. .**17** A3
Lavers Cl BS15. . . . .**60** A2
Lavington Rd BS5. . . . .**59** A2
Lawford Ave BS34 . . . .**16** A2
Lawfords Gate BS2 . .**86** C3
Lawfords Gate Ho **17**
BS2 . . . .**86** C3
Lawford St BS2 . . . .**86** C3
Lawn Ave BS16 . . . .**41** A1
Lawn Rd BS16 . . . .**41** A1
Lawns The BS11 . . . . . .**34** A3
Lawnwood Ind Units **14**
BS5 . . . .**57** A4
Lawnwood Rd **15**
BS5 . . . .**57** A4
Lawrence Ave BS5. . . .**49** C1
Lawrence Cl BS15 . . . .**53** B2
Lawrence Gr BS9 . . . . .**37** A1
Lawrence Hill BS5 . . . .**57** A3
Lawrence Hill Ind Pk
BS5 . . . .**57** A4
Lawrence Hill Rdbt
BS5 . . . .**56** C3
Lawrence Hill Sta
BS5 . . . .**57** A4
**LAWRENCE
WESTON** **23** B1
Lawrence Weston Rd
Avonmouth BS11 . . . .**23** A4
Bristol BS11 . . . .**23** B2
Laxey Rd BS7 . . . .**38** B3
Lays Dr BS31 . . . .**75** B1
Lays Farm Bsns Ctr
BS31. . . . .**82** A4
Lays Farm Trad Est
BS31. . . . .**82** A4
Lea Croft BS13. . . . .**78** C4
Leading Edge The
BS8 . . . .**85** B2
Leaholme Gdns
BS14. . . . .**80** C3
Leap Vale BS16 . . . . . .**42** C4
Leap Valley Cres
BS16. . . . .**42** C4
Lear Cl BS30. . . . .**61** A1

Leda Ave BS14. . . . . . .**72** C3
Ledbury Rd BS16 . . . .**52** A4
Lee Cl BS34 . . . .**15** A4
Leeming Way BS11 . .**33** B4
Lees Ct BS15 . . . .**52** C1
Lees Hill BS15 . . . .**52** C2
Lees La BS30 . . . .**61** C1
Leicester Sq BS16 . . .**52** B3
Leicester St **6** BS3 . .**63** C4
Leicester Wlk BS4 . . .**58** B1
Leigh Ct BS9 . . . .**46** B3
Leigh Rd BS8 . . . .**84** B4
Leigh St BS3 . . . .**62** C4
Leighton Rd
Bristol, Southville
BS3 . . . .**63** A4
Bristol, Upper Knowle
BS4 . . . .**65** A2
Leigh Woods Forest
Walks * BS8. . . . .**46** A1
Leinster Ave BS4 . . . .**71** C4
Leisure Rd BS15 . . . . .**60** A1
Lemon La BS2. . . . .**86** C4
Lena Ave **3** BS5 . . . . . .**50** A1
Lena St BS5 . . . .**50** A1
Lennox Way BS11 . . . .**21** C1
Lenover Gdns BS13 . .**79** A4
Leonard La BS1. . . . . . .**86** A3
Leonard Rd BS5 . . . . . .**57** C3
Leonards Ave BS5 . . .**50** A1
Leopold Rd BS6 . . . . . .**48** C2
Les Brown Ct BS2. . . .**87** C2
Lescren Way BS11 . . . .**22** B1
Lewington Rd BS16. .**52** A4
Lewins Mead BS1. . . .**86** A3
Lewis St **9** BS5 . . . . . .**57** C3
Lewis Cl
Bristol, Emerson's
Green BS16. . . . .**43** B1
Bristol, North Common
BS30. . . . .**61** C1
Lewis Rd BS13. . . . .**70** C4
Lewis St BS2 . . . .**57** A1
Lewton La BS36 . . . . . .**18** C3
Leyland Wlk BS13. . . .**78** B4
Leyton Villas BS6 . . . .**47** C2
Liberty Gdns BS1 . . . .**85** C1
Lichfield Rd BS4. . . . . .**58** A2
Lilac Cl BS10 . . . .**26** A1
Lilac Ct BS31 . . . .**82** A4
Lillian St **5** BS5 . . . . . .**57** B4
Lilstock Ave BS7. . . . . .**49** A4
Lilton Wlk BS13. . . . . . .**62** C1
Lilymead Ave BS4. . . .**64** C3
Lime Cl BS10 . . . .**25** C3
Lime Ct BS31 . . . .**82** A4
Lime Kiln Cl BS34. . . . .**28** B3
Lime Kiln Gdns BS32. .**9** B2
Lime Kiln Rd BS1. . . . .**85** B2
Limekilns Cl BS31 . . . .**76** B1
Lime Rd
Bristol, Hanham
BS15 . . . .**58** C1
Bristol, Southville
BS3 . . . .**63** A4
Limerick Rd BS6. . . . . .**48** A2
Limes The BS16 . . . . . .**29** C1
Lime Tree Gr BS20 . . .**45** C3
Lime Trees Rd BS9 . . .**37** C2
Lincoln Cl BS31. . . . . . .**82** A4
Lincoln Ct BS16. . . . . . .**39** C2
Lincoln St BS5 . . . .**57** A3
Lincombe Ave BS16. .**41** C2
Lincombe Rd BS16. . .**41** B2
Linden Cl
Bristol BS14 . . . .**74** A3
Bristol, Mayfield Park
BS16 . . . .**51** B2
Winterbourne BS36 . .**18** C2
Linden Dr BS32. . . . . . .**16** C4
Linden Grange BS6 . .**48** A3
Linden Ho BS16 . . . . . .**39** B1

Linden Quarter **13**
BS3 . . . .**63** B3
Linden Rd BS6. . . . .**47** C4
Lindon Ct **4** BS15 . . .**51** C1
Lindon Ho BS4 . . . .**66** A3
Lindrea St **3** BS3. . . . .**63** A3
Lindsay Rd BS7 . . . . . .**49** B4
Lines Way BS14 . . . . . .**81** B3
Lingfield Pk BS16 . . . .**31** A2
Link Rd BS34 . . . .**27** C3
Linnell Cl BS7 . . . .**39** A2
Linnet Cl BS34. . . . .**14** C4
Lintern Cres BS30 . . . .**61** A2
Lintham Dr BS15. . . . . .**60** B2
Linton's Wlk BS14 . . . .**72** C3
Lisburn Rd BS4. . . . . . .**64** A1
Litfield Pl BS8 . . . .**54** B3
Litfield Rd BS8 . . . .**54** B4
Little Ann St BS2,
BS5 . . . .**86** C4
Little Birch Croft
BS14. . . . .**80** C3
Little Bishop St BS2. .**86** B4
Little Caroline Pl **4**
BS8 . . . .**54** B1
Littlecross Ho BS3 . . .**63** A4
Little Dowles BS30. . .**68** C4
Little George St
BS2. . . . .**86** C4
Little Green La BS35 . .**2** B3
Little Hayes BS16 . . . .**41** A2
Little Headley Cl
BS13. . . . .**71** A3
Little King St BS1. . . . .**87** A2
Little Mdw BS34 . . . . . .**17** B2
Little Mead BS11 . . . . .**23** C1
Little Mead Prim Sch
BS10 . . . .**26** A2
Little Paradise BS3 . .**63** C3
Little Parr Cl BS16 . . .**39** B1
Little Paul St BS2. . . . .**84** C4
LITTLE STOKE **16** B3
Little Stoke La BS34. .**16** B2
Little Stoke Prim Sch
BS34. . . . .**16** B2
Little Stoke Rd BS9 . .**46** C4
Little Thatch Cl
BS14. . . . .**73** B2
Littleton Rd BS34 . . . . .**8** A1
Littleton St **4** BS5. . . .**50** A1
Little Withey Mead
BS9 . . . .**36** B1
Littlewood Cl BS14 . .**81** A3
Livingstone Mews **11**
BS3 . . . .**63** B3
Llanarth Villas **3**
BS6. . . . .**48** B1
Llewellyn Ct BS9 . . . . .**36** C4
Lockemor Rd BS13. . .**80** B4
Lock Gds BS13 . . . .**70** A3
Lockingwell Rd
BS31. . . . .**75** C1
LOCKLEAZE **39** B3
Lockleaze Prim Sch
BS7. . . . .**39** A2
Lockleaze Rd BS7 . . .**38** C2
Lodge Causeway Trad
Ctr BS16 . . . .**51** A4
Lodge Cswy BS16. . . .**51** B3
Lodge Ct BS9. . . . .**46** C4
Lodge Dr BS30 . . . .**69** B2
Lodge Hill BS15 . . . . . .**52** A2
Lodge Pl BS1. . . . .**84** C3
Lodge Rd BS15 . . . .**52** A1
Lodgeside Ave BS15 .**52** A1
Lodgeside Gdns
BS15. . . . .**52** A1
Lodge St BS1. . . . .**84** C3
Lodge Wlk BS16 . . . . . .**41** C2
Lodore Rd BS16 . . . . . .**51** A3
LODWAY **33** A1
Lodway BS20 . . . .**45** B4
Lodway Cl BS20 . . . . . .**33** B1

Lodway Gdns BS20 . .**45** B4
Lodway Rd BS4. . . . . . .**65** B2
Logan Rd BS7 . . . .**48** B3
Logus Ct **14** BS30 . . . .**68** B4
Lombard St BS3 . . . . . .**63** C4
Lomond Rd BS7 . . . . . .**27** A1
Londonderry Farm
BS30 . . . .**76** C4
London Rd
Bristol, St Pauls
BS2 . . . .**49** A1
Bristol, Warmley
BS30 . . . .**61** C3
London St BS15. . . . . . .**59** C4
Long Acre Rd BS14 . .**80** C3
Long Acres Cl BS9 . . .**35** C3
Long Beach Rd
BS30 . . . .**69** A3
Longbrook Trad Est
BS3 . . . .**62** A3
Long Cl
Bristol, Fishponds
BS16 . . . .**41** B2
Bristol, Little Stoke
BS32 . . . .**16** C2
Long Cross
Bristol, Lawrence
Weston BS11 . . . .**23** C2
Bristol, Shirehampton
BS11 . . . .**34** B3
Longden Rd BS16. . . .**42** B2
Long Eaton Dr BS14. .**73** B3
Longfield Rd BS7 . . . . .**48** C3
Longford Ave BS10. . .**37** C4
Long Fox Manor
BS4 . . . .**66** C1
Long Handstones
BS30 . . . .**68** C4
Longlands Ho **13**
BS5 . . . .**57** B3
Longleat Cl BS9 . . . . . .**37** B1
Long Mdw BS16 . . . . . .**39** C2
Longmead Ave BS7 . .**37** C1
Longmead Croft
BS13. . . . .**78** B4
Longmeadow Rd
BS31. . . . .**82** A4
Longmead Rd BS16 . .**31** C1
Longmoor Ct BS3. . . .**62** C2
Longmoor Rd BS3 . . .**62** C2
Longney Pl BS34. . . . . . .**8** A1
Long Rd BS16 . . . .**52** A4
Longreach Gr BS14 . .**73** C2
Long Row BS1. . . . .**87** B2
Longway Ave BS13,
BS14. . . . .**80** B4
LONGWELL GREEN.**68** A3
Longwell Green Prim
Sch BS30 . . . .**68** B3
Longwell Green Trad
Pk BS30 . . . .**68** A4
Longwell Ho BS30 . . .**68** B3
Longwood BS4 . . . .**66** C2
Lons Cl BS30 . . . .**69** B1
Lonsdale Bsns Ctr
BS15. . . . .**52** A2
Lorain Wlk BS10. . . . . .**25** A4
Lorton Cl BS10 . . . .**25** C1
Lorton Rd BS10. . . . . . .**25** C1
Loughman Cl **2**
BS15. . . . .**60** A4
Louisa St BS2 . . . .**87** C2
Louise Ave BS16 . . . . .**42** C1
Lovell Ave BS30. . . . . .**69** C4
Lovell's Hill BS15 . . . .**59** A1
Lovells The BS20. . . . .**45** A4
Loveridge Ct BS36 . . .**19** C3
Loveringe Cl BS10 . . .**25** A4
Lowbourne BS14 . . . .**72** B2
Lower Ashley Rd
Bristol, Baptist Mills
BS2, BS5 . . . .**49** B1
18 Bristol, St Pauls
BS2 . . . .**49** A1

Lower Castle St BS1 .**86** B3
Lower Chapel La
BS36. . . . .**20** A3
Lower Chapel Rd
BS15 . . . .**59** B1
Lower Cheltenham Pl
BS6. . . . .**49** A1
Lower Church La
BS2. . . . .**86** A3
Lower Clifton Hill
BS8 . . . .**85** B2
Lower Cock Rd
BS15 . . . .**60** B3
Lower College St
BS1. . . . .**85** C2
Lower Conham Vale
BS15 . . . .**58** C1
LOWER EASTON **50** B2
Lower Fallow Cl
BS14. . . . .**80** B3
Lower Gay St BS2. . . .**86** A4
Lower Grove Rd
BS16. . . . .**51** A4
Lower Guinea St
BS1. . . . .**87** A1
Lower Hanham Rd
BS15 . . . .**59** B2
Lower High St BS11. .**33** C3
Lower Ho BS34 . . . .**27** B3
Lower House Cres
BS34. . . . .**27** C4
Lower Knole La
BS10. . . . .**25** B3
LOWER KNOWLE **64** A1
Lower Lamb St BS1 . .**85** C2
Lower Maudlin St
BS1. . . . .**86** A3
Lower Park Row
BS1. . . . .**86** A3
Lower Redland Mews
2 BS6 . . . .**47** C2
Lower Redland Rd
BS6. . . . .**47** C2
Lower Sidney St
BS3 . . . .**62** C2
**LOWER
SOUNDWELL** **53** A2
Lower Station App Rd
BS1. . . . .**87** C1
Lower Station Rd
6 Bristol, Ridgeway
BS16 . . . .**51** B4
Bristol, Staple Hill
BS16 . . . .**52** A4
Lower Stone Cl
BS36. . . . .**20** A3
Lower Thirlmere Rd
BS34. . . . .**15** B4
Lowlis Cl BS10. . . . .**25** A3
Lowther Rd BS10 . . . .**26** A2
Loxton Sq BS14. . . . . . .**72** C2
Lucas Cl BS4 . . . .**65** C1
Luccombe Hill BS6 . .**47** C2
Luckington Rd BS7 . .**38** A4
Luckley Ave BS13 . . . .**71** B1
Luckwell Prim Sch
BS3. . . . .**62** C3
Luckwell Rd BS3. . . . . .**63** A3
Lucky La BS3 . . . .**63** C4
Ludlow Cl
Bristol, St Pauls
BS2 . . . .**49** A1
Bristol, Willsbridge
BS30 . . . .**69** A2
Keynsham BS31 . . . . .**75** C1
Ludlow Ct BS30. . . . . . .**69** A1
Ludlow Rd BS7 . . . .**38** C3
Ludwell Cl BS36 . . . . . .**18** B1
Lullington Rd BS4 . . . .**65** A2
Lulsgate Rd BS13 . . . .**70** C4
Lulworth Cres BS16. .**42** C4
Lulworth Rd BS31. . . .**82** C4
Lurgan Wlk BS4 . . . . . .**63** C1
Lutyens Cl BS16 . . . . . .**40** A4

Lux Furlong BS9 . . . . . .35 A3
Luxton St BS5 . . . . . . .57 A4
Lyddington Rd BS7 . .38 B4
Lyde Green Rdbt
BS16 . . . . .43 A4
Lydford Wlk BS3. . . . .63 B2
Lydiard Croft BS15. . .67 B4
Lydney Rd
Bristol, Southmead
BS10 . . . . .26 B1
Bristol, Staple Hill
BS16 . . . . .52 C4
Lydstep Terr BS3. . . . .63 B4
Lynch Ct BS30 . . . . . . .68 B4
Lyncombe Wlk BS16 .51 C2
Lyndale Ave BS9 . . . . .35 C1
Lyndale Rd BS5. . . . . .57 C4
Lynde Cl BS13 . . . . . . .79 A4
Lyndhurst Rd
Bristol BS9 . . . . .36 B3
Keynsham BS31 . . . . .83 A3
Lynmouth Rd 🔳
BS2. . . . . .49 B2
Lynn Rd BS16 . . . . . . .39 C1
Lynton 🔳 BS15 . . . . . .60 C4
Lynton Pl 🔳 BS5. . . . .57 B4
Lynton Rd BS3. . . . . . .63 C2
Lynton Way BS16 . . . .29 C1
Lynwood Ct BS13. . . . .71 A2
Lynwood Rd BS3. . . . .63 A2
Lyons Court Rd
BS14 . . . . .73 C3
Lyppiatt Rd BS5 . . . . .57 C4
Lyppincourt Rd
BS10 . . . . .25 B3
Lysander Rd BS10,
BS34. . . . . .14 A2
Lysander Wlk BS34 . .16 C1
Lytchet Dr BS16 . . . . .42 B4
Lytes Cary Rd BS31 . .83 B3
Lytham Ho BS4 . . . . . .65 C1
Lytton Gr
Bristol BS7 . . . . .38 C4
Keynsham BS31 . . . . .76 C1
Lyveden Gdns BS13 . .71 A1

M

Mabberley Cl BS16. . .43 B1
McAdam Way BS1 . . . .
MacAuley Rd BS7 . . . .38 C4
MacDonald Wlk 🔳
BS15 . . . . .59 C4
Macey's Rd BS13 . . . .79 C3
Machin Cl BS10. . . . . .25 A3
Machin Gdns BS10. . .25 B3
Machin Rd BS10 . . . . .25 B3
Mackie Ave BS34 . . . .27 C4
Mackie Gr BS34 . . . . .27 C2
Mackie Rd BS34 . . . . .27 C2
McLaren Rd BS11. . . .21 C1
Macrae Ct BS15 . . . . .60 A4
Madeline Rd BS16 . . .51 A2
Maesbury BS15. . . . . .60 A2
Maesbury Rd BS31. . .83 B2
Maesknoll Rd BS4 . . .64 C2
Magdalena Ct BS1. . .87 B1
Magdalene Pl BS2 . . .49 A1
Maggs Cl BS10 . . . . . .26 A3
Maggs La
Bristol BS5 . . . . .50 C2
Whitchurch BS14 . . . .81 B4
Magpie Bottom La
Bristol, Kingswood
BS15 . . . . .59 B2
Bristol, St George
BS5 . . . . .59 A2
MAIDEN HEAD 78 B1
Maidenhead Rd
BS13 . . . . .79 C3
Maiden Way BS11 . . .33 B4
Maidstone St BS3. . . .64 B3
Main Dr BS10. . . . . . . .24 C1
Main Rd BS16 . . . . . . .43 C1

Main View BS36. . . . . .20 B3
Maisemore Ave BS34 . .8 C1
Makin Cl BS30. . . . . . .61 B1
Malago BS3 . . . . .63 C3
Malago Vale Trad Est
BS3 . . . . .63 C3
Malago Wlk BS13 . . . .78 A4
Malden Mead BS14 . .72 C1
Maldowers La 🔳
BS5 . . . . .58 C4
Mallard Cl
Bristol BS32 . . . . .9 B2
Bristol, Crofts End
BS5 . . . . .51 A1
Mall Galleries The
BS1. . . . . .86 B3
Mall The BS8 . . . . . . .54 B3
Mall The BS34 . . . . . .14 B2
Malmains Dr BS16 . . .29 C1
Malmesbury Cl
Bristol, Bishopston
BS6 . . . . .48 A4
Bristol, Longwell Green
BS30 . . . . .60 B1
Malvern Ct BS5. . . . . .58 B3
Malvern Dr BS30. . . . .61 B1
Malvern Rd
Bristol, Crew's Hole
BS5 . . . . .58 B3
Bristol, Kensington Park
BS4 . . . . .65 C3
Mancroft Ave BS11 . .34 B3
MANGOTSFIELD 42 B2
Mangotsfield CE Prim
Sch BS16. . . . . .43 A2
Mangotsfield Rd
BS16 . . . . .42 C1
Mangotsfield Sch
BS16 . . . . .53 C4
Manilla Rd BS8 . . . . . .84 A3
Manor Cl
Easton-in-G BS20 . . . .44 C4
Frampton Cotterell
BS36 . . . . .20 A2
Manor Coalpit Heath
CE Prim Sch The
BS36. . . . . .20 B2
Manor Court Dr BS7 .38 A3
Manor Ct
Bristol, Fishponds
BS16 . . . . .50 C4
🔳 Bristol, Upper Easton
BS5 . . . . .49 C1
Manor Farm BS32 . . .16 B4
Manor Farm Cres
BS32 . . . . .16 B4
Manor Gardens Ho
BS16 . . . . .40 B1
Manor Gr
Bristol BS34 . . . . .8 C2
Bristol, Mangotsfield
BS16 . . . . .53 B4
Manor Ho
🔳 Bristol, Lower
Easton BS5 . . . . .49 C1
Bristol, Tyndall's Park
BS2 . . . . .84 C3
Manor La BS36 . . . . . .19 A3
Manor Pk BS6 . . . . . . .47 C3
Manor Pl
Bristol, Frenchay
BS16 . . . . .30 A1
Bristol, Stoke Gifford
BS34 . . . . .29 B4
Manor Rd
Bristol, Bishopston
BS7 . . . . .48 C4
Bristol, Bishopsworth
BS13 . . . . .70 C2
Bristol, Fishponds
BS16 . . . . .40 C1
Bristol, Mangotsfield
BS16 . . . . .53 B4
Mansfield St BS3 . . . .63 B2

Manston Cl BS14 . . . .73 B2
Manworthy Rd BS4 . .65 C3
Manx Rd BS7 . . . . .36 A3
Maple Ave BS16 . . . . .52 A3
Maple Cl
Bristol BS14 . . . . .73 C1
Bristol, Little Stoke
BS34 . . . . .16 A3
Bristol, Oldland BS30 . .69 A4
Maple Ct
Bristol BS9 . . . . .36 B4
🔳 Bristol BS15 . . . . . .52 B1
Maple Ho BS2 . . . . . . .86 A4
Maple Leaf Ct BS8 . .84 A3
Mapleleaze BS4 . . . . .65 C3
Maplemeade BS7. . . .48 A4
Maple Rd
Bristol, Horfield
BS7 . . . . .38 A1
Bristol, St Anne's
BS4 . . . . .57 C1
Maplestone Rd
BS14 . . . . .80 C3
Maple Wlk BS31. . . . .82 B4
Mapstone Cl BS16 . . .29 C3
Marbeck Rd BS10. . . .25 C1
Mardale Cl BS10. . . . .26 A2
Marden Rd BS31. . . . .83 B4
Mardon Rd BS4. . . . . .57 C2
Mardyke Ferry Rd
BS1. . . . . .85 B1
Margaret Rd 🔳
BS13 . . . . .78 B4
Margate St BS3. . . . . .64 B3
Marguerite Rd BS13 .70 B3
Marigold Wlk BS3 . . .62 C2
Marina Gdns BS16 . . .50 C3
Marine Par BS20. . . . .33 B1
Mariners Dr BS9. . . . .46 B4
Mariners' Path BS9 . .46 C3
Mariner's Way BS20 .33 B1
Marion Rd BS15 . . . . .67 A3
Marion Wlk BS5 . . . . .58 C3
Marissal Cl BS10. . . . .24 C3
Marissal Rd BS10 . . . .24 C3
Mariston Way BS30. . .61 B2
Maritime Heritage
Ctr★ BS1. . . . . .85 B1
Marjoram Pl BS32 . . .17 A3
Market Gate BS2 . . . .86 C3
Marketside BS2 . . . . .65 A4
Market Sq BS16 . . . . .52 A3
Mark La BS1. . . . . .85 C2
Marklands BS9 . . . . . .46 C3
Marksbury Rd BS3. . .63 C2
Marlborough Ave 🔳
BS16 . . . . .50 C3
Marlborough Dr
BS16 . . . . .29 C1
Marlborough Flats 🔳
BS2 . . . . .86 A4
Marlborough Hill
BS2 . . . . .86 A4
Marlborough Hill Pl
BS2 . . . . .86 A4
Marlborough Ho 🔳
BS2 . . . . .86 A4
Marlborough St
Bristol BS2 . . . . .86 A4
Bristol, Eastville BS5 . .50 C3
Marlepit Gr BS13 . . . .70 B2
Marlfield Wlk BS13 . .70 A3
Marling Rd BS5. . . . . .58 B4
Marlwood Dr BS10. . .25 B3
Marmaduke St BS3 . .64 B3
Marmion Cres BS10. .25 A3
Marne Cl BS14. . . . . . .73 C1
Marshall Ho 🔳
BS16 . . . . .51 A4
Marshall Wlk BS4. . . .71 C3
Marsham Way BS30. .68 B4
Marsh Cl BS36. . . . . . .18 C1
MARSH COMMON . . .5 C4

Marsh Common Rd
BS35. . . . . .5 C3
Marshfield Pk BS16. .41 B4
Marshfield Rd
Bristol, Frenchay
BS16 . . . . .41 B4
Bristol, Hillfields
BS16 . . . . .52 A4
Marsh La
Bristol, Ashton Vale
BS3 . . . . .63 A2
Bristol, Barton Hill
BS5 . . . . .57 B2
Easton-in-G BS20 . . . .44 C4
Portbury BS20 . . . . . .32 B2
Marsh Lane Ind Est
BS20 . . . . .32 B3
Marsh Rd BS3 . . . . . . .62 B3
Marsh St
Avonmouth BS11 . . . .33 B4
Bristol BS1 . . . . .87 A2
Marston Rd BS4 . . . . .65 A3
Martcombe Rd BS20 .45 B2
Martha's Orch BS13. .70 A3
Martin Cl BS34 . . . . . .14 C4
Martin Ct 🔳 BS16. . . .50 C3
Martingale Rd BS4. . .65 C4
Martins Cl BS15 . . . . .59 B1
Martin's Rd BS15 . . . .59 B1
Martin St 🔳 BS3. . . . .63 A3
Martock Cres BS3 . . .63 B1
Martock Rd
Bristol BS3 . . . . .63 B2
Keynsham BS31 . . . . .83 B3
Marwood Rd BS4 . . . .72 A4
Marybush La BS2 . . . .86 B3
Mary Carpenter Pl 🔳
BS2. . . . . .49 A1
Mary Ct BS5 . . . . .57 C4
Marygold Leaze
BS30 . . . . .68 C4
Mary Seacole Ct 🔳
BS2. . . . . .49 B2
Mary St BS5 . . . . .57 C4
Mascot Rd BS3 . . . . . .63 C3
Masefield Way BS7 . .38 C2
Maskelyne Ave
BS10 . . . . .37 C3
Masons View BS36. . .19 A3
Matchells Cl BS4 . . . .58 A2
Materman Rd BS14 . .74 B2
Matford Cl
Bristol BS10 . . . . .26 B4
Winterbourne BS36 . . .18 C1
Matthews Cl BS14 . . .74 B2
Matthew's Rd 🔳
BS5 . . . . .57 B3
Maules La BS16. . . . . .29 A2
Maunsell Rd BS11 . . .23 C2
Maurice Rd BS6 . . . . .48 C2
Mautravers Cl BS32. .16 B3
Mawdeley Ho 🔳
BS3. . . . . .63 B4
Maxse Rd BS4 . . . . . . .65 A2
Maybec Gdns BS5 . . .58 C2
Maybourne Ave 66 C2
Maycliffe Pk BS6 . . . .49 A2
Mayfield Ave BS16 . .51 B2
Mayfield Ct BS16 . . . .51 B3
MAYFIELD PARK 51 B2
Mayfield Pk BS16 . . . .51 B2
Mayfield Pk N BS16 . .51 B2
Mayfield Pk S BS16 . .51 B2
Mayfields BS31 . . . . . .76 A1
Maynard Cl BS13 . . . .71 B1
Maynard Rd BS13. . . .71 B1
Mayors Bldgs BS16 . .41 A1
May Park Prim Sch
BS5 . . . . .50 A4
Maypole Ct 🔳 BS15. .59 A2
Mays Cl BS36. . . . . . . .20 B3
May St BS15. . . . . .52 A1
Maytree Ave BS13 . . .71 A3
Maytree Cl BS13 . . . . .71 A3

Maytrees BS5 . . . . . . .50 A2
May Tree Wlk BS31. . .82 A3
Mayville Ave BS34 . . .27 B3
Maywood Ave 🔳
BS16 . . . . .51 C4
Maywood Cres BS16 .51 C4
Maywood Rd BS16. . .52 A4
Maze St BS5. . . . . .57 A2
Mead Cl BS11 . . . . . . .34 A2
Mead Ct BS36 . . . . . . .18 C2
Meadgate BS16. . . . . .43 A3
Meadowbrook Prim
Sch BS32. . . . . .16 C4
Meadow Cl BS16. . . . .42 B3
Meadow Court Dr
BS30. . . . . .69 B3
Meadowcroft BS16 . .42 C4
Meadow Gr BS11 . . . .33 C3
Meadowland Rd
BS10 . . . . .24 C4
Meadow Mead BS36 .19 C4
Meadowside Dr
BS14 . . . . .80 C3
Meadows Prim Sch The
BS30 . . . . .77 C4
Meadow St BS11. . . . .21 B1
Meadows The BS15 . .67 C4
Meadowsweet Ave
BS34 . . . . .27 C3
Meadow Vale BS5. . . .51 B1
Meadow View BS36 . .20 B3
Meadow Way BS32 . .16 C3
Mead Rd BS34. . . . . . .17 A1
Mead Rise BS3 . . . . . .64 B4
Mead St BS4 . . . . .87 C1
Meads The BS16 . . . . .42 B3
Mead The BS34 . . . . . .27 C4
Meadway BS9 . . . . . . .35 B2
Meardon Rd BS14. . . .74 A2
Mede Cl BS1 . . . . .87 B1
Media Ho BS8 . . . . . . .84 B3
Medical Ave BS2,
BS8. . . . . .84 C3
Medway Cl BS31. . . . .83 B3
Medway Dr
Frampton Cotterell
BS36. . . . . .19 C3
Keynsham BS31 . . . . .83 B3
Meere Bank BS11. . . .23 C1
Meg Thatcher's Gdns
BS5 . . . . .59 A3
Meg Thatchers Gn
BS5 . . . . .59 A3
Melbourne Rd BS7. . .48 B4
Melbury Rd BS4 . . . . .64 C2
Melita Rd BS6 . . . . . . .48 C3
Mellent Ave BS13. . . .79 B3
Mells Cl BS31. . . . . . . .83 B2
Melrose Ave BS8 . . . .84 B4
Melrose Pl BS8 . . . . . .84 B4
Melton Cres BS7. . . . .38 C3
Melville Rd BS6. . . . . .47 C1
Melville Terr BS3 . . . .63 B3
Melvin Sq BS4. . . . . . .64 A1
Memorial Cl BS15 . . .67 A4
Memorial Rd BS15. . .67 A4
Memorial Stadium
(Bristol Rovers FC)★
BS7 . . . . .38 B2
Mendip Cl BS31 . . . . .75 C1
Mendip Cres BS16 . . .42 C4
Mendip Ct BS16 . . . . .28 C1
Mendip Rd BS3 . . . . . .63 C3
Mendip View Ave
BS16 . . . . .51 B3
Menhyr Gr BS10 . . . . .25 C3
Mercer Ct BS14. . . . . .73 A4
Merchants Almshouses
BS1 . . . . .87 A2
Merchants Ct BS8 . . .85 A1

Merchants Quay
BS1 . . . . .87 A1
Merchants Rd
Bristol BS8 . . . . .84 A3
Bristol, Hotwells BS8 . .85 A1
Merchants Row BS1 . .85 C1
Merchant St BS1 . . . . .86 B3
Merchants Trad Pk
BS2 . . . . .57 B2
Mercia Dr BS2 . . . . . . .49 B2
Meredith Ct BS1 . . . . .85 A1
Merfield Rd BS4 . . . . . .65 A2
Meridian Pl BS8 . . . . . .84 B3
Meridian Rd BS6 . . . . .48 A1
Meridian Vale BS8 . . .84 B3
Meriet Ave BS13 . . . . .79 A4
Merioneth BS8 . . . . . . .55 A1
Meriton St BS2 . . . . . . .57 A1
Merlin Cl BS9 . . . . .36 B4
Merlin Ct BS10 . . . . . . .37 A3
Merlin Rd BS10,
BS34 . . . . .14 A2
Merrett Ct BS7 . . . . . . .39 A2
Merrick Ct BS1 . . . . . . .87 A1
Merrimans Rd BS11. .33 C4
Merryweather Cl
BS32 . . . . .16 B4
Merryweathers BS4. .66 A2
Merrywood Cl [5]
BS3 . . . . .63 B4
Merrywood Ct BS4. . .65 B4
Merrywood Rd BS3 . .63 B4
Merstham Rd [13]
BS2 . . . . .49 B2
Merton Rd BS7 . . . . . . .38 A1
Mervyn Rd BS7 . . . . . .48 C4
Meryl Ct BS6 . . . . .47 C1
Metford Gr BS6. . . . . . .47 C3
Metford Pl BS6 . . . . . . .48 A3
Metford Rd BS6 . . . . . .48 A3
Metropolitan The
BS1 . . . . .87 B1
Middle Ave BS1. . . . . . .87 A2
Middleford Ho BS13 .79 B4
Middle Rd BS15 . . . . . .53 A3
Middleton Rd BS11 . .34 B4
Midland Mews BS2 . .86 C3
Midland Rd
Bristol BS2 . . . . .86 C3
Bristol, Staple Hill
BS16 . . . . .52 B4
Midland Road Bsns Pk
BS16 . . . . .52 B4
Midland St BS2 . . . . . . .87 C2
Midland Terr BS16 . . .51 A3
Mildred St BS5 . . . . . . .57 B3
Miles Ct
Bristol, Cadbury Heath
BS30 . . . . .68 B4
Bristol, Clifton BS8 . . . .47 B1
Miles Rd BS8 . . . . .47 B1
Mile Wlk BS14 . . . . . . .72 C2
Milford St BS3 . . . . .63 B4
Millard Cl BS10 . . . . . . .26 B2
Millar Ho BS8 . . . . .84 A3
Mill Ave BS1. . . . . .87 A2
Millbank Cl BS4 . . . . . .66 A3
Millbook Ct [3] BS6 . .48 C1
Millbrook Ave BS4. . .66 B3
Millbrook Cl BS30 . . .61 B2
Mill Cl BS36 . . . . .20 A3
Millennium Cl BS36. .20 B3
Millennium Prom
BS1 . . . . .85 C1
Millers Cl BS20 . . . . . . .45 B4
Millers Dr BS30 . . . . . .61 C1
Millfield Dr BS30 . . . . .61 B2
Millground Rd BS13 .70 B1
Millgrove St N BS2. . .86 A4

Mill Ho
[11] Bristol, Baptist Mills
BS5 . . . . .49 B1
Bristol BS1 . . . . .87 A1
Milliman Cl BS13 . . .71 B1
Mill La
Bristol, Southville
BS3 . . . . .63 C4
Bristol, Warmley
BS30 . . . . .61 B1
Portbury BS20 . . . . . . .44 A3
Millmead Ho BS13 . .79 B4
Millpill Cl BS9 . . . . . . .35 C1
Millpond Prim Sch
BS5 . . . . .49 B1
Millpond St [10] BS5 . .49 B1
Millpool Ct BS10. . . .37 A4
Mill Rd BS36. . . . . .30 B4
Mill Steps BS36 . . . . .30 C4
Millward Gr BS16 . . . .52 A4
Milner Gn BS30 . . . . . .60 C1
Milner Rd BS7 . . . . . . .38 B1
Milsom St BS5 . . . . .56 C4
Milton Pk [1] BS5 . . . .57 B3
Milton Rd BS7 . . . . .38 A2
Miltons CI BS13 . . . . . .79 C4
Milverton Gdns BS6 .49 A2
Milward Rd BS31 . . . .76 A2
Mina Rd BS2 . . . . .49 B2
Minehead Rd BS4. . . .64 B1
Minor's La BS10 . . . . .11 B4
Minsmere Rd BS31 . .83 B4
Minton Cl BS14 . . . . . .73 A1
Minto Rd BS2 . . . . .49 B2
Minto Road Ind Ctr [9]
BS2 . . . . .49 B2
Mitchell La BS1. . . . . .87 B2
Mitchell Wlk BS30 . .61 C3
Mivart St BS5. . . . . .49 C2
Modecombe Gr
BS10 . . . . .25 A3
Mogg St BS2 . . . . .49 B2
Molesworth Cl BS13 .78 C4
Molesworth Dr
BS13 . . . . .78 C4
Monarch Ct BS16 . . . .31 B1
Monarch Ho [1] BS3. .63 A3
Monica Willis Ho [18]
BS3 . . . . .63 B3
Monk Rd BS7 . . . . .48 B4
Monks Ave BS15 . . . .59 A4
Monk's Park Ave
BS7 . . . . .38 A4
Monks Park Sch
BS7 . . . . .38 A4
Monks Park Way
BS7 . . . . .38 A4
Monkton Rd BS15. . . .59 A1
Monmouth Ct BS20 .33 B4
Monmouth Hill BS32 .7 C4
Monmouth Rd
Bristol BS7 . . . . .48 B4
Keynsham BS31 . . . . . .75 C1
Pill BS20 . . . . .33 B1
Monmouth St BS3 . . .64 B3
Monsdale Cl BS10 . . . .25 B3
Monsdale Dr BS10 . . .25 B2
Montague Cl BS34 . . .16 C1
Montague Ct [4]
BS2 . . . . .86 A4
Montague Flats [6]
BS2 . . . . .86 A4
Montague Hill BS2. . .86 A4
Montague Hill S [5]
BS2 . . . . .86 A4
Montague Pl BS6. . . . .86 A4
Montague St BS1 . . . .86 A4
Montgomery St BS3 .64 B3
MONTPELIER 48 C2
Montpelier Central [1]
BS6 . . . . .48 C1
Montpelier Ct BS6. . .48 C2
Montpelier Sta BS6. .48 C2
Montreal Ave BS7 . . .38 C4

Montreaux Ct [9]
BS16 . . . . .52 B3
Montreaux Ho [2]
BS5 . . . . .58 C3
Montrose Ave BS6 . . .48 A1
Montrose Dr BS30 . . .61 A2
Montrose Pk BS4 . . . .65 C2
Montroy Cl BS9 . . . . . .48 C1
Mont The [2] BS6. . . . .48 C1
Moon St BS2 . . . . .49 B2
Moor Croft Dr BS30. .68 B3
MOOREND 30 C2
Moorend Farm Ave
BS11 . . . . .10 C1
Moorend Gdns BS11 .34 B3
Moorend Rd BS16 . . .30 B3
MOORFIELDS. 57 B4
Moorfields Ho BS5. . .57 B3
Moor Gr BS11 . . . . .34 A1
Moorgrove Ho BS9 . .35 B3
Moorhill St [17] BS5. .49 C1
Moor House Cvn Pk
BS10 . . . . .23 B4
Moorhouse La BS10 .23 C4
Moorings The BS20 . .45 B4
Moorlands Rd
Bristol, Mayfield Park
BS16 . . . . .51 B2
Bristol, Ridgeway
BS16 . . . . .51 A3
Moravian Ct [4]
BS15 . . . . .59 C4
Moravian Rd BS15 . . .59 C4
Moravian Rd Bsns Pk
BS15 . . . . .59 C4
Morden Wlk BS14. . . .73 C3
Moreton Cl BS14. . . . .80 C4
Morgan St BS2 . . . . . .49 A1
Morley Ave BS16. . . . .53 B4
Morley Cl
Bristol, Little Stoke
BS34 . . . . .16 A3
Bristol, Staple Hill
BS16 . . . . .52 B4
Morley Rd
Bristol, Staple Hill
BS3 . . . . .63 B4
Bristol, Staple Hill
BS16 . . . . .52 B3
Morley Sq BS7. . . . . . .48 C4
Morley St
Bristol, Baptist Mills
BS2 . . . . .49 A1
Bristol, Russell Town
BS5 . . . . .57 A3
Morley Terr [1] BS15. .52 B1
Mornington Rd [14]
BS8 . . . . .47 B2
Morpeth Rd BS4. . . . .71 C4
Morris Rd BS7 . . . . . . .38 C1
Morse Rd BS5 . . . . .57 B3
Mortimer Rd
Bristol BS8 . . . . .84 A3
Bristol, Filton BS34. . . .27 C2
Morton St BS5. . . . . . . .57 A3
Motorway Distribution
Ctr BS11. . . . . .22 C2
Mountain Mews [5]
BS5 . . . . .58 C3
Mount Cl BS36. . . . . . .19 A4
Mount Cres BS36 . . . .18 C1
Mount Gdns BS15. . . .59 C2
MOUNT HILL. 60 A2
Mount Hill Rd BS15 .59 C2
Mount Pleasant
Hallen BS10 . . . . .24 A4
Pill BS20 . . . . .45 C4
Mount Pleasant Terr
BS3 . . . . .63 B4
Mow Barton BS13 . . .70 B2
Mowbray Rd BS14 . . .73 B3
Mowcroft Rd BS13. . .79 C4
Moxham Dr BS13 . . . .79 B4
Muirfield BS30 . . . . . .60 C2

Mulberry Cl [1] BS15 .60 A4
Mulberry Dr BS15. . . .65 C4
Mulberry Gdns [10]
BS16 . . . . .52 B3
Mulberry Wlk BS9 . . .35 B4
Muller Ave BS7 . . . . . .49 A4
Muller Rd BS5, BS7 . .49 C3
Mulready Cl BS7. . . . .39 B2
Murdoch Sq BS7. . . . .38 B4
Murford Ave BS13 . . .79 A4
Murford Wlk BS13 . . .79 A4
Murray St [9] BS3. . . .63 B4
**Museum of Bristol (due
to open 2009)**
BS1 . . . . .87 A1
Musgrove Cl BS11 . . .24 A2
Myrtle Ct BS3 . . . . .63 A4
Myrtle Dr BS11 . . . . . .34 A1
Myrtle Hill BS20 . . . . .33 B1
Myrtle Rd BS2. . . . . . . .84 C4
Myrtle St BS3. . . . . .63 A4

N

Nags Head Hill BS5 . .58 C3
Nailsea Cl BS13. . . . . .70 C3
Napier Ct BS1 . . . . . . .85 B1
Napier Ho BS6. . . . . . .47 C2
Napier Miles Rd
BS11 . . . . .34 C4
Napier Rd
Avonmouth BS11 . . . . .21 C1
Bristol, Baptist Mills
BS5 . . . . .49 C2
Bristol, Redland BS6. . .47 C2
Napier Sq BS11. . . . . .21 B1
Napier St BS5 . . . . .57 A2
Narroways Rd BS2 . . .49 B3
Narrow La BS16 . . . . .52 C4
Narrow Plain BS2. . . .87 B2
Narrow Quay BS1. . . .87 A1
Naseby Wlk BS5 . . . . .51 A1
Nash Cl BS31 . . . . .76 C1
Nash Dr BS7 . . . . .39 B3
Neads Dr BS30 . . . . . .61 B1
Neale Way BS11. . . . . .22 A1
Neate Ct BS34 . . . . . . .16 A4
Neath Rd BS5 . . . . .57 C4
Nelson Ho
[6] Bristol BS1 . . . . . . .86 A4
[8] Bristol, Staple Hill
BS16 . . . . .41 C1
Nelson Par [10] BS3 . .63 C4
Nelson Rd
Bristol BS16 . . . . .41 C1
[4] Bristol, Staple Hill
BS16 . . . . .52 B4
Nelson St
Bristol, Ashton Vale
BS3 . . . . .62 C2
Bristol BS1 . . . . .86 A3
Neston Wlk BS4 . . . . .72 B4
NETHAM 57 C3
Netham Ct [22] BS5 . .57 C3
Netham Gdns [21]
BS5 . . . . .57 C3
Netham Park Ind Est
BS5 . . . . .57 C2
Netham Rd BS5 . . . . . .57 C2
Netham View Ind Pk [20]
BS5 . . . . .57 C3
Nettlestone Cl BS10 .24 C4
Nevalan Dr BS5. . . . . .58 C2
Neville Rd BS15. . . . . .52 C2
Nevil Rd BS7 . . . . .48 C4
New Bldgs BS16 . . . . .51 A4
Newbrick Rd BS34. . .17 B1
Newbridge Cl BS4 . . .57 C1
Newbridge Ho BS9 . .46 A4
Newbridge Rd BS4. . .58 A2
Newbridge Trad Est
BS4 . . . . .57 C1

New Brunswick Ave
BS5 . . . . .59 A3
Newbury Rd BS7. . . . .38 C3
New Charlotte St
BS3 . . . . .63 C4
New Charlton Way
BS10 . . . . .13 B2
**NEW
CHELTENHAM** 53 A1
New Cheltenham Rd
BS15 . . . . .52 C1
Newcombe Dr BS9. . .46 A4
Newcombe Rd BS9 . .36 B3
NEW ENGLAND. 43 A3
Newent Ave BS15. . . .59 A3
New Fosseway Rd
BS14 . . . . .73 A2
New Fosseway Sch
BS14 . . . . .73 A2
Newfoundland Rd
[6] Bristol, Baptist Mills
BS2 . . . . .49 B1
Bristol BS2 . . . . .86 C4
Newfoundland St
BS2 . . . . .86 C4
Newfoundland Way
BS2 . . . . .86 C4
Newgate BS1. . . . . . . .86 B3
New John St [7] BS3 .63 B3
New Kings Ct BS7 . . .48 A4
New Kingsley Rd
BS2 . . . . .87 C2
Newland Dr BS13. . . .78 C4
Newland Hts [12] BS2 .49 A2
Newland Rd BS13 . . .78 C3
Newlands Ave BS36 .20 A3
Newlands Rd BS31. . .82 B4
Newlands The BS16 .41 A3
Newland Wlk BS13. . .78 C3
NEWLEAZE 27 C2
Newleaze BS34 . . . . . .27 B2
New Leaze BS32 . . . . . .9 A3
Newleaze Ho BS34. . .27 B2
Newlyn Ave BS9 . . . . .35 C1
Newlyn Wlk BS4 . . . . .65 A1
Newmarket Ave [11]
BS1 . . . . .86 A3
New Mdws BS14 . . . .72 C2
Newnham Cl BS14 . . .73 C3
Newnham Pl BS34 . . .28 A1
New Oak Prim Sch
BS14 . . . . .72 C4
Newport Rd BS20. . . .33 B1
Newport St BS3 . . . . .64 C4
Newquay Rd
Bristol BS4 . . . . .64 B1
Bristol BS4 . . . . .72 B4
New Queen St
Bristol, St George
BS15 . . . . .59 A4
Bristol, Windmill Hill
BS3 . . . . .64 A4
New Rd
Bristol, Filton BS34. . . .27 A3
Bristol, Harry Stoke
BS34 . . . . .28 B3
Pill BS20 . . . . .45 B4
New Room The (John
Wesley's Chapel) *
BS1 . . . . .86 B3
Newry Wlk BS4 . . . . . .64 A1
New Sandringham Ho
[6] BS7 . . . . .48 B2
Newsome Ave BS20. .45 B4
New St BS2. . . . . .86 C4
New Stadium Rd
BS5 . . . . .49 C3
New Station Rd
BS16 . . . . .51 B4
New Station Way
BS16 . . . . .51 B4
New Street Flats [4]
BS2 . . . . .86 C4
New Thomas St BS2. .87 C2

NEWTON 56 C3
Newton Cl BS15 . . . . .53 B1
Newton Dr BS30 . . . . .60 C1
Newton Rd BS30. . . . .60 C1
Newton St BS5 . . . . . .56 C4
New Walls BS2 . . . . . .64 B4
New Wlk BS15. . . . . . .59 A1
Niblett Cl BS15 . . . . . .60 B2
Niblett's Hill BS5 . . . .58 C2
Nibley Rd BS11 . . . . . .34 A1
Nicholas La BS5 . . . . .58 C2
Nicholas Rd BS5. . . . .49 C1
Nicholas St BS3 . . . . .64 A4
Nicholettes BS30 . . . .61 C1
Nicholls Cl BS36. . . . .18 C3
Nicholls La BS36. . . . .18 C2
Nigel Pk BS11 . . . . . . .34 A3
Nightingale Cl
Bristol BS4 . . . . .58 A2
Frampton Cotterell
BS36 . . . . .19 B2
Nightingale Ct BS4 . .65 C3
Nightingale La BS36 . .19 B4
Nine Tree Hill 16
BS1. . . . . .48 C1
Ninth Ave BS7 . . . . . . .27 C1
Noble Ave BS30. . . . . .69 B4
Norfolk Ave
Bristol BS2 . . . . .86 B4
Bristol, Montpelier
BS6 . . . . .48 C2
Norfolk Gr BS31 . . . . .82 A4
Norfolk Hts 10 BS2. . .86 B4
Norfolk Pl BS3 . . . . . . .63 B3
Norland Rd BS8 . . . . .54 B4
Norley Rd BS7 . . . . . . .38 B3
Normanby Rd 20
BS5 . . . . .49 C1
Norman Gr BS15. . . . .52 B2
Norman Rd
Bristol, Baptist Mills
BS2 . . . . .49 B2
Bristol, Warmley
BS30 . . . . .61 A4
Norman's Cotts
BS36 . . . . .18 B3
Normans Way BS20. .32 A3
Normanton Rd 18
BS8 . . . . .47 B2
Norrisville Rd 9
BS6 . . . . .48 C1
North Cnr 8 BS3 . . . .63 A3
North Contempris
BS8 . . . . .84 A3
Northcote Ho BS8 . .84 A3
Northcote Rd
Bristol, Clifton BS8 . . .47 A1
Bristol, Crew's Hole
BS5 . . . . .58 A3
Bristol, Mangotsfield
BS16 . . . . .42 B2
Northcote St 18 BS5 .49 C1
North Croft BS30 . . . .69 C4
North Ct BS23 . . . . . . .9 B3
North Devon Rd
BS16 . . . . .40 C1
Northend Ave BS15 . .52 B2
Northend Gdns
BS15 . . . . .52 B2
Northend Ave BS15 . .59 C1
Northfield Ho 10
BS3 . . . . .63 B4
Northfield Rd BS5 . . .59 A3
North Gr BS20 . . . . . .45 B4
North Green St 12
BS8 . . . . .54 B2
Northleach Wlk
BS11 . . . . .34 B1
Northover Ct BS35. . . .3 C1
Northover Rd BS9 . . .25 B1
North Pk BS15. . . . . . .52 C1

North Rd
7 Bristol BS3 . . . . . . .62 C4
Bristol, Montpelier
BS6 . . . . .48 C2
Bristol, Stoke Gifford
BS34 . . . . .29 A4
Winterbourne BS36 . .19 A3
North St
Bristol BS1 . . . . .86 B4
Bristol, Downend
BS16 . . . . .42 A1
Bristol, Oldland Common
BS30 . . . . .69 B4
Bristol, Southville
BS3 . . . . .63 A3
Northumberland Rd
BS6 . . . . .48 B2
Northumbria Dr
BS9 . . . . .47 C4
North View
Bristol BS6 . . . . .47 B4
Bristol, Mangotsfield
BS16 . . . . .42 A1
Bristol, Upper Soundwell
BS16 . . . . .52 B4
NORTHVILLE 27 B1
Northville Rd BS7. . . .27 B1
North Way BS34 . . . . .27 C4
Northwick Rd BS7 . . .38 B4
Northwoods Wlk
BS10 . . . . .26 B3
Norton Cl BS15 . . . . . .60 B3
Norton Ho
7 Bristol BS1 . . . . . .87 B1
Bristol, Patchway
BS34 . . . . .8 A1
Norton La BS14. . . . . .81 B2
Norton Rd BS4 . . . . . .64 C3
Norwich Dr BS4 . . . . .58 A2
Nottingham Rd BS7. .48 C2
Nottingham St BS3 . .64 B3
Nova Scotia Pl BS1 . .85 A1
Nova Way BS11 . . . . . .21 C1
Novers Cres BS4. . . . .71 B4
Novers Hill BS4. . . . . .71 B4
Novers Hill Trad Est
BS3 . . . . .63 B1
Novers La BS4 . . . . . . .71 C3
NOVERS PARK. 71 C4
Novers Park Cl BS4 . .63 B1
Novers Park Dr BS4. .71 B4
Novers Park Rd BS4 .71 C4
Novers Rd BS4 . . . . . .71 B4
Nugent Hill BS6 . . . . .48 B1
Nunney Cl BS31. . . . . .83 B2
Nursery Gdns BS10 . .25 B3
Nursery The BS3. . . . .63 A3
Nutfield Gr BS34. . . . .27 C2
Nutfield Ho BS34 . . . .27 C1
Nutgrove Ave BS3 . . .64 A3
Nuthatch Dr BS16. . . .40 B2
Nuthatch Gdns
BS16 . . . . .40 C2
Nympsfield BS15 . . . .52 C2

O

Oak Cl BS34 . . . . .16 B3
Oak Ct BS14 . . . . .72 C1
Oakdale Ave BS16 . . .41 C4
Oakdale Cl BS16. . . . .42 A4
Oakdale Ct BS16. . . . .41 C3
Oakdale Rd
Bristol BS14 . . . . .72 C4
Bristol, Downend
BS16 . . . . .42 A4
Oakdale Wlk BS16 . . .42 A3
Oakdene Ave BS5. . . .50 B3
Oakenhill Rd BS4 . . . .66 A2
Oakenhill Wlk BS4 . . .66 A2
Oakfield Bsns Pk
BS15 . . . . .59 C3
Oakfield Gr BS8 . . . . .84 B4
Oakfield Mans BS8 . .84 B4

Oakfield Pl BS8. . . . . .84 B4
Oakfield Rd
Bristol BS8 . . . . .84 B4
Bristol, Kingswood
BS15 . . . . .59 C3
Keynsham BS31 . . . . .83 A2
Oak Gr BS20. . . . . .33 B1
Oakhanger Dr BS11 . .23 C1
Oakhill Ave BS30 . . . .69 B2
Oakhill La BS10. . . . . .24 A4
Oak Ho BS13 . . . . .79 C4
Oakhurst Rd BS9 . . . .36 B1
Oak La BS5 . . . . .51 A2
Oakland Rd
Bristol, Crew's Hole
BS5 . . . . .58 A4
6 Bristol, Redland
BS6 . . . . .47 C1
Oaklands Cl BS16. . . .43 A1
Oaklands Dr
Almondsbury BS32 . . . .8 B3
Bristol, Frenchay
BS16 . . . . .40 C3
Bristol, Oldland Common
BS30 . . . . .69 B2
Oaklands Rd BS16 . . .42 C1
Oakleaze BS36 . . . . . .20 B3
Oakleigh Ave BS5. . . .50 B1
Oakleigh Gdns BS30 .69 B2
Oakley Rd BS7. . . . . . .38 B3
Oakmeade Pk BS4 . . .65 A2
Oak Rd BS7 . . . . .38 A1
Oakridge Cl BS15. . . .60 C3
Oaks The BS7. . . . . . . .48 C4
Oak Tree Cl BS15. . . . .67 B3
Oaktree Cres BS32. . . .9 A2
Oaktree Ct BS11 . . . . .34 A3
Oaktree Gdns BS13 . .70 A1
Oak Tree Wlk BS31. . .82 B3
Oakwood Ave BS9 . . .37 B2
Oakwood Gdns
BS36 . . . . .20 C3
Oakwood Pk BS16 . . .51 B3
Oakwood Rd BS9 . . . .37 A2
Oatlands Ave BS14. . .72 C2
Oatley Ho BS9 . . . . . . .36 C1
Oatley Trad Est 6
BS15 . . . . .52 B1
Oberon Ave BS5 . . . . .50 C2
Okebourne Cl BS10 . .25 C4
Okebourne Rd BS10 .25 C4
Okeford Ho BS9 . . . . .36 B3
Old Acre Rd BS14. . . .80 C3
Old Ashley Hill BS6 .49 A1
Old Barrow Hill
BS11 . . . . .33 C3
Old Bread St BS2 . . . .87 C2
Old Brewery The
BS20 . . . . .45 B4
Oldbridge Rd BS14 . .81 B3
Oldbury Chase BS30 .68 C2
Oldbury Court Dr
BS16 . . . . .41 A2
Oldbury Court Prim
Sch BS16. . . . . .41 B3
Oldbury Court Rd
BS16 . . . . .40 C1
Old Church Cl BS30 . .61 C3
Old Drill Hall The
BS2 . . . . .86 C3
Old Farm La BS5. . . . .59 A2
Oldfield Pl BS8 . . . . . .54 B1
Oldfield Rd BS8. . . . . .85 A1
Old Gloucester Rd
Bristol, Stoke Gifford
BS16 . . . . .29 C4
Hambrook BS16 . . . . .29 C2
Old King Street Ct
BS1 . . . . .86 B3
Old La BS16 . . . . .43 B2
OLDLAND 68 C3
OLDLAND
COMMON. 69 C3

Oldland Common Sta★
BS30. . . . . .69 B3
Oldlands Ave BS36. . .20 A2
Old Malthouse The
BS2 . . . . .86 C4
Old Market Rdbt
BS2 . . . . .86 C3
Old Market St BS2 . . .86 C3
Oldmead Wlk BS13 . .70 A3
Old Park Hill BS2 . . . .84 C3
Old Park Rd BS11. . . .33 C3
Old Pk BS2 . . . . .84 C3
Old Police Sta The
BS4 . . . . .64 C3
Old Pooles Yd BS4 . . .66 A2
Old Priory Rd BS20 . .45 A4
Old Quarry Rd BS11. .34 A3
Old Quarry Rise
BS11 . . . . .34 B3
Old School Ho BS4. .65 C2
Old School House The
BS2 . . . . .86 C3
Old Smiths Yd BS15 . .59 C1
Old Sneed Ave BS9 . .46 B4
Old Sneed Cotts
BS9 . . . . .46 C4
Old Sneed Pk BS9 . . .46 B4
Old Sneed Rd BS9 . . .46 B4
Old Tannery The 20
BS2 . . . . .86 C3
Old Vicarage Ct
BS14 . . . . .81 B4
Old Vicarage Gn
BS31. . . . . .76 A2
Old Vicarage Pl BS8. .47 B1
Old Vicarage The
Bristol BS13 . . . . .70 B2
Bristol, Montpelier
BS6 . . . . .48 C1
Old Wesleyan Chapel
The BS16. . . . . .61 A1
Old Work Ho The
BS5 . . . . .58 A4
Olveston Rd BS7. . . . .38 A1
Olympus Cl BS34 . . . .16 B2
Olympus Rd BS34. . . .14 B3
Oram Ct BS30 . . . . . . .68 B4
Orange St BS2. . . . . . .86 C4
Orchard Ave BS1 . . . .85 C2
Orchard Bvd BS30 . . .69 A4
Orchard Cl
Bristol, Kingswood
BS15 . . . . .60 A4
Bristol, Westbury on T
BS9 . . . . .36 B1
Keynsham BS31 . . . . .75 C2
Winterbourne BS36 . .18 C1
Orchard Cotts 11
BS16 . . . . .41 C1
Orchard Cres BS11. . .33 C3
Orchard Ct
Bristol BS9 . . . . .46 A3
Bristol, Filton BS34. . .27 B2
19 Bristol, Pile Marsh
BS5 . . . . .57 C3
Orchard Dr BS13. . . . .70 C2
Orchard Gate BS32 . . .9 A2
Orchard Gdns BS15 . .60 B4
Orchard Ho **2** BS5 . .58 B4
Orchard La BS1. . . . . .85 C2
Orchard Lea BS20. . . .45 C4
Orchard Pk BS14 . . . .81 C4
Orchard Rd
Bristol, Ashley Down
BS7 . . . . .48 C4
Bristol, Crew's Hole
BS5 . . . . .58 B4
Bristol, Kingswood
BS15 . . . . .60 A4
Frampton Cotterell
BS36 . . . . .20 B3
Orchard Sq BS5 . . . . .57 C3
Orchard St BS1 . . . . . .85 C2

Orchards The
Bristol, Kingswood
BS15 . . . . .60 B3
Bristol, Shirehampton
BS11 . . . . .34 A2
Orchard The
Bristol BS34 . . . . .17 A1
Frampton Cotterell
BS36 . . . . .20 A4
Pill BS20 . . . . .45 B4
Orchard Vale BS15 . . .60 B3
Orion Dr BS34 . . . . . . .16 B2
Orland Way BS30 . . . .68 C3
Orlebar Gdns BS11 . .23 C2
Ormerod Rd BS9. . . . .36 A1
Ormonds Cl BS32 . . . .9 C1
Ormsley Cl BS34 . . . . .16 A4
Orpen Gdns BS7 . . . . .39 A1
Orpen Pk BS32 . . . . . .8 C3
Orpheus Ave BS34 . . .16 B2
Orwell Dr BS31 . . . . . .83 B4
Orwell St BS3 . . . . . . .64 A3
Osborne Ave BS7 . . . .49 A3
Osborne Cl BS34. . . . .28 B4
Osborne Rd
Bristol, Clifton BS8 . . .47 B1
Bristol, Southville
BS3 . . . . .63 B4
Severn Beach BS35 . . .2 B3
Osborne Terr 10
BS3 . . . . .63 A2
Osborne Villas BS2. . .84 C4
Osborne Wallis Ho
BS8 . . . . .85 A1
Osprey Ct BS14. . . . . .71 C1
Osprey Rd 15 BS5. . . .57 B3
Otterford Cl BS14. . . .73 A1
Ottery Cl BS11 . . . . . .23 B1
Ottrells Mead BS32 . . .9 A3
Our Lady of Lourdes RC
Prim Sch BS15 . . . . .60 A3
Our Lady of the Rosary
RC Prim Sch BS11. .34 C4
OVER. 7 B2
Overhill BS20. . . . . . . .45 C4
Over La BS35. . . . . .7 B2
Overndale Rd BS16 . .41 B2
Overnhill Ct BS16. . . .41 C1
Overnhill Rd BS16 . . .41 C1
Overnhurst Ct 2
BS16 . . . . .41 C1
Overton **5** BS4. . . . . .65 C1
Overton Rd BS6 . . . . .48 C2
Owen Gr BS9 . . . . .37 A1
Owen Henry Ho BS2 .49 B1
Owen St 18 BS5. . . . . .57 A4
Owls Head Rd BS15 . .60 C3
Oxbarton BS34 . . . . . .17 A1
Oxenhan Ct BS5 . . . . .57 C4
Oxen Leaze BS32 . . . . .9 C2
Oxford Pl
21 Bristol, Clifton
BS8 . . . . .54 B2
14 Bristol, Upper Easton
BS5 . . . . .49 C1
Oxford St
Bristol BS2 . . . . .87 C2
7 Bristol, Redfield
BS5 . . . . .57 B3
Bristol, The Dings
BS2 . . . . .56 C2
Bristol, Tyndall's Park BS2,
BS6 . . . . .84 C4
Bristol, Windmill Hill
BS3 . . . . .64 B4
Oxhouse Gdns BS10 .24 C3
Oxleaze BS13. . . . . . . .79 C4
Oxleaze La BS41. . . . .78 A3
Ozlworth BS15 . . . . . .60 C4

P

Pacquet Ho BS20 ....33 C1
Paddock Cl
 Bristol BS32 ....9 C2
 Bristol, Emerson's Green
 BS16 ....43 B2
Paddock Gdn BS14 ..28 B4
Paddocks The BS16...31 B1
Padmore Ct **7** BS5 ..57 C3
Padstow Rd BS4 .....72 B4
Page Ct BS16 ....53 A4
Page Rd BS16 ....52 B4
Pages Mead BS11 ...33 B4
Painswick Ave BS34 .15 C4
Paintworks BS4 .....65 A4
Palmdale Cl BS30....68 C2
Palmer Ave BS35 ......5 A3
Palmers Cl BS30 .....60 C2
Palmers Leaze BS34 .17 B2
Palmerston Rd BS6 ..48 A4
Palmerston St BS3 ...63 B3
Palmyra Rd BS3 .....63 A2
Pamela Ho **9** BS16 ..41 C1
Panoramic The BS1 ..84 C3
Pantile The **16** BS3 ..63 B3
Parade Ct BS5 ....51 A2
Parade The
 Bristol, Bishopsworth
 BS13 ....70 C2
 Bristol BS34 ....8 A1
 Bristol, Shirehampton
 BS11 ....34 A2
Paragon The BS8 ....54 B2
Parbrook Ct BS14....73 A1
Parfitt's Hill **8** BS5 ..58 B2
Parish The BS3 ....85 B1
Park Ave
 Bristol BS32 ....8 B2
 Bristol, Eastville BS5 ..50 B3
 Bristol, Rose Green
 BS5 ....58 A4
 Bristol, Windmill Hill
 BS3 ....64 A3
 Frampton Cotterell
 BS36 ....19 C2
 Winterbourne BS36 ...18 C3
Park Cl
 Bristol, Cadbury Heath
 BS30 ....61 A1
 Bristol, Kingswood
 BS15 ....60 A3
 Keynsham BS31 ......75 C1
Park Cres
 Bristol, Cadbury Heath
 BS30 ....61 A1
 Bristol, Frenchay
 BS16 ....30 A1
 Bristol, Rose Green
 BS5 ....58 A4
Park Edge BS5 ....58 B4
Parkers Barton BS5 ..57 A2
Parkers Cl BS10 .....26 C4
Parker St **5** BS3.....63 A3
Park Farm Ct **13**
 BS30 ....68 B4
Park Farm Village Gn
 BS36 ....19 C2
Parkfield Ave **3**
 BS5 ....57 C3
Park Gr BS9 ....37 B1
Park Hill BS11 ....34 B2
Parkhouse La BS31 ..82 A2
Parkhurst Ave **4**
 BS16 ....51 C4
Park La
 Bristol BS2 ....84 C3
 Frampton Cotterell
 BS36 ....19 C2

Parklands
 Bristol BS8 ....84 C4
 Bristol, Kingswood
 BS15 ....60 A4
Parklands Rd BS3 ...62 A4
Park Leaze BS34......7 C1
Park Pl
 Bristol, Kingsdown
 BS8 ....84 B3
 Bristol, Upper Eastville
 BS5 ....50 C3
 Bristol, Victoria Park
 BS2 ....84 C3
Park Prim Sch The
 BS15 ....60 A4
Park Rd
 Bristol BS3 ....85 B1
 Bristol, Cadbury Heath
 BS30 ....61 A1
 Bristol, Kingswood
 BS15 ....59 C4
 Bristol, Northville
 BS7 ....27 B1
 Bristol, Shirehampton
 BS11 ....34 B2
 Bristol, Staple Hill
 BS16 ....42 A1
 Bristol, Stapleton
 BS16 ....39 C1
 Keynsham BS31 ......82 C4
Park Row
 Bristol BS1 ....84 C3
 Frampton Cotterell
 BS36 ....19 B4
Parkside Ave BS36...18 C2
Parkside Gdns BS5 ..49 C4
Park St
 Bristol BS1 ....84 C3
 Bristol BS4 ....64 C4
 Bristol, Crew's Hole
 BS5 ....58 B4
 Bristol, Totterdown
 BS4 ....64 C3
Parkstone Ave BS7 ..38 B2
Park Street Ave BS1 .84 C3
Park The
 Bristol BS32 ....9 A3
 Bristol, Frenchay
 BS16 ....29 C1
 Bristol, Kingswood
 BS15 ....60 A4
 Bristol, Willsbridge
 BS30 ....69 A1
 Keynsham BS31 ......76 A2
Park View
 Bristol, Kingswood
 BS15 ....60 A3
 Bristol, Southville
 BS3 ....63 B4
Park View Ct BS16 ..42 A1
Park View Terr BS5 ..58 A4
Parkwall Cres BS30..68 B4
Parkwall Prim Sch
 BS30 ....68 C4
Parkwall Rd BS30....68 C4
Parkway BS34........29 B4
Park Way BS30 ......61 A1
Parkway N BS34.....29 B4
Parkway Trad Est **10**
 BS2 ....49 A2
Park Wlk BS20........45 C4
Park Wood Cl BS14 ..80 A4
Parliament St BS4 ...64 C4
Parnall Rd BS16 .....51 B3
Parnall Road Ind Est
 BS16 ....51 B3
Parnell Rd BS16 .....40 A3
Parry's Cl BS9 ....36 A1
Parrys Gr BS9 ....36 A1
Parry's La BS9 ....36 B1
Parslow Barton **4**
 BS5 ....58 C3
Parsons Ave BS34....17 A1

Parsons Paddock
 BS14 ....72 C3
Parson St BS3 ....63 A2
Parson Street Prim Sch
 BS3 ....63 B2
Parson Street Sta
 BS3 ....63 A2
Parsons Wlk BS30 ...61 C3
Partition St BS1 .....85 C2
Partridge Dr BS16 ...41 B2
Passage Leaze BS11 .33 C2
Passage Rd
 Bristol, Brentry
 BS10 ....25 A3
 Bristol, Westbury on Trym
 BS9 ....36 C4
Passage Road Brentry
 Hill BS9, BS10 .....25 B2
Passage St BS2......87 B2
Patch Ct BS16 ....42 C4
PATCHWAY 8 C2
Patchway Brook
 BS32 ....9 A2
Patchway CE Prim Sch
 BS34 ....8 C1
Patchway Com Coll
 BS32 ....8 C1
Patchway Sta BS34 ..16 A2
Patchway Trad Est
 BS34 ....14 C3
Patterson Ho **8**
 BS1 ....87 B1
Paul Alan Ho **21**
 BS5 ....57 B3
Paul St BS2 ....84 A4
Paulton Dr BS7......48 A4
Paultow Ave BS3 ....64 A3
Paultow Rd BS3 .....64 A3
Pavey Cl BS13 ....79 B4
Pavey Rd BS13........79 B4
Pavilions The BS4....65 B1
Pawlett Rd BS13 .....79 B3
Pawlett Wlk BS13....79 B3
Paxton BS16.........40 A4
Paybridge Rd BS13 ..78 B4
Payne Dr BS5 ....57 A3
Paynes Orchard Pk
 BS10 ....14 B1
Peache Ct BS16......42 A2
Peache Rd BS16 .....42 B2
Peacocks La BS15 ...59 B3
Pearces Hill BS16....41 A1
Pearl St BS3.........63 A3
Pearsall Rd BS30 ....68 A2
Peart Cl BS13........70 A1
Peart Dr BS13 ....78 A4
Peartree Cl BS13 ....79 A4
Peartree La
 Bristol, Lower
 Soundwell BS15 .....53 A2
 Bristol, St George
 BS5 ....59 A2
Pear Tree Rd BS32 ....9 A2
Peel St BS5..........86 C4
Pegasus Pk BS34.....16 A2
Pegasus Rd BS34 ....16 A2
Pemberton Ct BS16..41 B1
Pembery Rd BS3.....63 A3
Pembroke Ave BS11 .34 A2
Pembroke Gate BS8 .47 B1
Pembroke Gr BS8....84 A3
Pembroke Lodge
 BS8 ....84 A3
Pembroke Mans
 BS8 ....84 A4
Pembroke Pl BS8....85 A1
Pembroke Rd
 Bristol BS8 ....84 A4
 Bristol, Kingswood
 BS15 ....52 C2
 Bristol, Shirehampton
 BS11 ....34 A2
 Bristol, Southville
 BS3 ....63 B4

Pembroke St BS2....86 B4
Pembroke Vale BS8 ..84 A4
Penard Way BS15....60 B3
Pendennis Ave BS16 .52 B4
Pendennis Ho **5**
 BS16 ....41 C1
Pendennis Pk
 Bristol, Brislington
 BS4 ....65 C2
 1 Bristol, Staple Hill
 BS16 ....52 B4
Pendennis Rd BS16 ..41 C1
Pendock Cl BS30 ....69 B1
Pendock Ct BS16 ....43 A3
Pendock Rd
 Bristol BS16 ....41 B2
 Winterbourne BS36 ..18 C1
Penfield Cl BS2......49 B2
Penfield Rd BS2 .....49 B2
Penlea Ct BS11 ......33 C3
Pennard Ct BS14....73 A1
Penn Dr BS16 ....30 A1
Penngrove BS30.....68 C3
Pennine Rd BS30 ....69 B4
Pennlea BS13 ....71 B3
Pennon Rise BS1 ....85 C1
Penn St BS1 ....86 B3
Pennyroyal Gr BS16..50 C4
Pennywell Ct **3**
 BS5 ....56 C4
Pennywell Rd BS2,
 BS5 ....56 C4
Pen Park Rd BS10 ..26 B2
Penpole Ave BS11 ...34 A2
Penpole Cl BS11.....33 C3
Penpole La BS11.....34 A3
Penpole Pk BS11.....34 A3
Penpole Pl BS11.....34 A2
Penrith Gdns BS10...37 C4
Penrose BS14 ....72 B3
Penrose Dr BS32 ....16 B3
Pensfield Pk BS10 ...26 B4
Pensford Ct BS14....73 C1
Pentagon The BS9 ...35 A1
Pentire Ave BS13 ....70 C2
Percival Rd BS8 .....54 B4
Percy St **8** BS3......63 C4
Percy Walker Ct
 BS16 ....41 B2
Perrett Ho **22** BS2 ..86 C3
Perretts Ct BS1......85 C1
Perrott Rd BS15 .....53 B1
Perry Cl BS36........30 B4
Perry Court Inf Sch
 BS14 ....72 C2
Perry Court Jun Sch
 BS14 ....72 C2
Perrycroft Ave BS13 .70 C4
Perrycroft Rd BS13 ..70 C2
Perrymans Cl BS16 ..40 C2
Perry Rd BS1 ....86 A3
Perrys Lea BS32......9 B2
Perry St BS5.........56 C4
Pesley Cl BS13.......78 C4
Petercole Dr BS13 ...70 C2
Peterson Sq BS13 ...79 B3
Peter's Terr BS5 .....57 A3
Petersway Gdns
 BS5 ....58 C2
Petherbridge Way
 BS7 ....38 C1
Petherton Cl BS15 ...60 A3
Petherton Gdns
 BS14 ....73 A3
Petherton Rd BS14 ..73 A3
Pethick Ho BS4......72 B4
Pettigrove Gdns
 BS15 ....60 A3
Pettigrove Rd BS15 ..60 A2
Pevensey Wlk BS4 ...71 C3
Peverell Cl BS10.....25 A3
Peverell Dr BS10.....25 A3
Philippa Cl BS14.....72 C3
Philips Ho **2** BS2...86 B4

Philip St
 Bristol, St Philip's
 Marsh BS2 ....57 A1
 Bristol, Windmill Hill
 BS3 ....63 C4
Phippen St **1** BS1 ..87 B3
Phipps Barton BS15..59 A4
Phipps St BS3 ....63 A4
Phoenix Bsns Pk
 BS3 ....62 C2
Phoenix Gr BS6......37 B1
Phoenix Ho BS5 .....57 A2
Picton La BS6 ....48 C1
Picton Mews 6
 BS6 ....48 C1
Picton St BS6........48 C1
Pigeon House Dr
 BS13 ....79 C4
Pigott Ave BS13 .....78 C4
PILE MARSH 57 C3
Pilemarsh BS5 ......57 C3
Pilgrims Way
 Avonmouth BS11 ....33 B3
 Bristol BS16 ....41 C4
Pilgrims Wharf BS4..58 A3
Pilkington Cl BS34...28 A2
PILL 45 B4
Pillingers Gdns BS6..47 C2
Pillingers Rd BS15 ..59 B3
Pill St BS20..........45 C4
PILNING 3 B3
Pilning Prim Sch
 BS35 ....3 C2
Pimpernel Mead
 BS32 ....16 C3
Pinecroft BS14 ......72 B3
Pine Ct BS31 ....82 A4
Pine Gr BS7 ....27 B1
Pine Grove Pl BS7 ..48 B3
Pine Rd BS10 ....25 C3
Pine Ridge Cl BS9 ...46 A4
Pines Rd BS30 ......69 B1
Pines The
 Bristol, Lower
 Soundwell BS15 .....53 B3
 Bristol, Sneyd Park
 BS9 ....46 B3
Pinewood BS15......53 A1
Pinewood Cl BS9 ....37 A3
Pinhay Rd BS13......71 B2
Pinkers Mead BS16 ..43 B2
Pinkhams Twist
 BS14 ....72 C1
Pinnell Gr BS16......43 B3
Pioneer Pk BS4......57 B1
Pipe La BS1 ....85 C2
Pippin Ct **4** BS30 ..68 B4
Pitchcombe Gdns
 BS9 ....35 C3
Pitch La BS6.........48 B1
Pitch & Pay La BS9 ..46 C3
Pitch & Pay Pk BS9 ..46 C3
Pithay Ct BS1........86 A3
Pithay The BS1 ......86 A3
Pitlochry Cl BS7.....27 A1
Pitt Rd BS7..........38 A1
Pitville Pl **15** BS6 ...47 C1
Pixash Bsns Ctr
 BS31 ....77 A1
Pixash La BS31 ......77 B1
Pixash Works BS31 ..77 B1
Players Cl BS16......29 C3
Playford Gdns BS11..34 A4
Plaza The BS2 ....87 C2
Pleasant Ho **4**
 BS16 ....41 C1
Pleasant Rd BS16....41 C1
Plimsoll Ho
 Bristol BS1 ....87 B1
 5 Bristol, Woolcott Park
 BS6 ....47 C1
Plowright Ho **8**
 BS15 ....59 A1

Plummer's Hill BS5 . . .58 A4
Plumpton Ct BS16 . . .31 A1
Poets' Cl BS5 . . . . .57 C4
Polden Ho BS3 . . . . . . .63 C3
Polly Barnes Cl 6
 BS15 . . . . .59 A1
Polly Barnes Hill
 BS15 . . . . .59 A1
Polygon Rd BS8 . . . . . .85 A2
Polygon The
 Avonmouth BS11 . . . . .22 B1
 16 Bristol BS8 . . . . . .54 B2
Pomfrett Gdns BS14 .74 A1
Pond Head BS20 . . . . .45 C4
Ponsford Rd BS4 . . . . .65 A1
Ponting Cl BS5 . . . . . . .51 B1
Poole St BS11 . . . . . . .33 A4
Pooles Wharf BS8 . . .85 A1
Pooles Wharf Ct
 BS8 . . . . .85 A1
Pool Ho BS34 . . . . .15 B4
Pool Rd BS15 . . . . .55 C2
Poplar Ave BS9 . . . . . . .35 C2
Poplar Cl BS30 . . . . . . .61 B2
Poplar Fields BS30 . .61 C2
Poplar Gardens Ho 3
 BS15 . . . . .60 A4
Poplar Pl BS16 . . . . . . .51 B3
Poplar Rd
 Bristol, Hanham
  BS15 . . . . .58 C1
 Bristol, Highridge
  BS13 . . . . .70 B3
 Bristol, North Common
  BS30 . . . . .61 C2
 Bristol, Speedwell
  BS5 . . . . .51 A1
Poplar Rdbt BS11 . . . .10 C1
Poplars The BS20 . . . .45 A4
Poplar Terr BS15 . . . . .60 B4
Poplar Way E BS11 . . .23 A4
Poplar Way W BS10,
 BS11 . . . . .10 B2
Pople Walk BS7 . . . . . .49 A3
Poppy Mead BS32 . . . .16 C3
Porlock Rd BS3 . . . . . . .63 C3
PORTBURY 44 A3
Portbury Gr BS11 . . . .33 C2
Portbury Way BS20 . .32 A1
Portbury Wlk BS11 . . .33 C2
Port Elizabeth Ho
 BS10 . . . . .25 C1
Portishead Way BS3 .62 A3
Portland Ct
 Bristol BS1 . . . . .85 B1
 Bristol, Upper Soundwell
  BS16 . . . . .52 B3
Portland Lofts 8
 BS2 . . . . .86 B4
Portland Mans 9
 BS2 . . . . .86 B4
Portland Pl BS16 . . . . .52 B3
Portland Sq BS2 . . . . .86 B4
Portland St
 Bristol, Clifton BS8 . . . .54 B3
 Bristol, Staple Hill
  BS16 . . . . .52 B3
Portmeirion Cl
 BS14 . . . . .73 A1
Port Side Cl 5 BS5 . .58 B2
Port View BS20 . . . . . .33 B1
Portview Rd BS11 . . . .33 A4
Portwall La BS1 . . . . . .87 B1
Portwall La E 10
 BS1 . . . . .87 B1
Portway
 Bristol BS8 . . . . .46 A3
 Bristol, Shirehampton
  BS11 . . . . .33 B2
Portway Com Sch
 BS11 . . . . .34 A3
Portway Rdbt BS11 . .33 B4
Potterswood Cl
 BS15 . . . . .59 C3

Pound Dr BS16 . . . . . .40 B1
Pound La BS16 . . . . . . .51 A4
Pound Rd BS15 . . . . . .53 A2
Pountney Dr 2 BS5 .57 A4
Pow's Rd BS15 . . . . . . .59 C3
Poyntz Ct BS30 . . . . . .68 B3
Poyntz Rd BS4 . . . . . . .72 B4
Pratten's La 2 BS16 .52 B4
Preacher Cl BS5 . . . . . .59 A2
Preddy's La BS8 . . . . . .58 C2
Press Moor Dr BS30 .68 B4
Preston Wlk BS4 . . . . .64 C1
Prestwick Cl BS4 . . . . .65 C1
Pretoria Rd BS34 . . . . .15 A4
Prewett St BS1 . . . . . . .87 B1
Priddy Cl BS14 . . . . . . .73 A1
Priddy Dr BS14 . . . . . . .73 A1
Priestwood Cl BS10. .25 B3
Primrose Cl
 Bristol BS32 . . . . .9 B2
 Bristol, St George
  BS15 . . . . .59 B4
Primrose La BS15 . . . .52 A1
Primrose Terr BS15 . .52 A1
Prince's Bldgs 19
 BS8 . . . . .54 B2
Princes Ct BS30 . . . . . .68 B4
Princes' La BS8 . . . . . .54 B2
Princes' Pl BS7 . . . . . . .48 C3
Princess Cl BS31 . . . .82 C4
Princess Gdns BS16. .39 C2
Princess Row BS2 . . .86 A4
Princess St
 Bristol, Newton
  BS2 . . . . .56 C3
 Bristol, Windmill Hill
  BS3 . . . . .64 A4
Prince's St BS2 . . . . . .86 C4
Princess Victoria St
 BS8 . . . . .54 B2
Prince St BS1 . . . . .87 A1
Prior's Hill 12 BS6 . .48 B1
Priory Ave BS9 . . . . . . .36 C3
Priory Court Rd BS9 .36 C3
Priory Ct
 Bristol, Hanham
  BS15 . . . . .67 B3
 Bristol, Upper Knowle
  BS4 . . . . .65 A2
Priory Dene BS9 . . . . .36 C3
Priory Gdns
 Bristol, Horfield
  BS7 . . . . .38 B4
 Bristol, Shirehampton
  BS11 . . . . .33 C3
 Easton-in-G BS20 . . . .45 A4
Priory Rd
 Bristol BS8 . . . . .84 C4
 Bristol, Shirehampton
  BS11 . . . . .33 C2
 Bristol, Upper Knowle
  BS4 . . . . .65 A2
 Keynsham BS31 . . . . . .76 A3
Pritchard St BS2 . . . . .86 B4
Privet Dr BS13 . . . . . . .71 B1
Probyn Cl BS16 . . . . . .40 C3
Pro-Cathedral BS8 . .84 B3
Proctor Cl BS4 . . . . . . .65 C1
Proctor Ho BS1 . . . . . .87 B1
Promenade The
 BS7 . . . . .48 B2
Prospect Ave BS15. . .51 C1
Prospect Cl
 Easter Compton
  BS35 . . . . .6 B2
 Frampton Cotterell
  BS36 . . . . .19 A4
 Winterbourne BS36 . . . .30 C4
Prospect Cres BS15 .53 A2
Prospect La BS36 . . . .19 A4
Prospect Pl
 1 Bristol, Montpelier
  BS6 . . . . .48 B2

Prospect Pl continued
 Bristol, Moorfields
  BS5 . . . . .57 B4
Prospect Rd BS35. . . . .2 B1
Prospect Terr 5
 BS3 . . . . .63 B3
Protheroes Ho BS1 . .85 C2
Providence Pl BS2 . . .87 C2
Prudham St 7 BS5 . .50 A1
Pullin Ct BS30 . . . . . . .69 C4
Pump La BS1 . . . . .87 B1
Pump Sq BS20 . . . . . . .33 C1
Purcell Wlk BS4 . . . . . .71 C3
Purdown Rd BS7 . . . . .38 B1
Purdy Ct BS16 . . . . . . .51 B4
Pursey Dr BS32 . . . . . .17 A2
Purton Cl BS15 . . . . . . .60 A2
Purton Rd BS7 . . . . . . .48 B2
Puxley Cl BS14 . . . . . . .74 A2
PYE CORNER 30 B3
Pye Croft BS32 . . . . . . .9 C3
Pyecroft Ave BS9 . . . .37 B3
Pylle Hill Cres BS3. . .64 B4
Pynne Cl BS14 . . . . . . .74 B1
Pynne Rd BS14 . . . . . .74 B1
Pyracantha Wlk
 BS14 . . . . .72 C2

Q
QEH Theatre ★ BS8 . .84 B3
Quadrant BS32 . . . . . . .8 C3
Quadrant E BS16 . . . . .52 A3
Quadrant The BS32 . . .8 B3
Quadrant The BS6 . . . .47 C3
Quadrant W BS16 . . . .52 A3
Quadrilles The BS35 . .2 B2
Quaker's Cl BS16 . . . .41 C4
Quakers' Friars BS1 .86 B3
Quaker's Rd BS16 . . . .42 A4
Quantock Cl BS30 . . . .61 B1
Quantock Ct BS16 . . . .28 C1
Quantock Rd BS3 . . . .63 C3
Quarrington Rd BS7 .38 A1
Quarry Barton BS16. .30 A4
Quarry La
 Bristol BS11 . . . . .24 A1
 Winterbourne BS36 . . . .30 C4
Quarry Rd
 Bristol BS8 . . . . .47 B2
 Bristol, Frenchay
  BS16 . . . . .41 B3
 Bristol, Kingswood
  BS15 . . . . .59 C2
Quarry Steps 8 BS8 .47 B2
Quarry The BS11 . . . . .24 A1
Quarry Way
 Bristol, Emerson's
  Green BS16 . . . . .31 B1
 Bristol, Fishponds
  BS16 . . . . .40 A1
Quayside La 4 BS5 . .58 B2
Quay St BS1 . . . . .86 A3
Quays The BS1 . . . . . . .85 C1
Queen Ann Rd BS5. . .57 A2
Queen Charlotte St
 BS1 . . . . .87 A2
Queen Elizabeth's
 Hospital Sch BS8 . . .84 B3
Queen Quay BS1 . . . . .87 A2
Queens Apartments
 BS8 . . . . .84 C3
Queen's Ave BS8 . . . . .84 B3
Queens Ct BS31 . . . . . .76 A1
Queen's Ct BS8 . . . . . .84 B3
Queensdale Cres
 BS4 . . . . .64 C1
Queens Down Ct
 BS4 . . . . .65 B3
Queensdown Gdns
 BS4 . . . . .65 B3
Queens Down Gdns
 BS4 . . . . .65 B3
Queens Dr BS15 . . . . .67 A4

Queen's Dr BS7 . . . . . .37 B1
Queens Gate BS9 . . . .35 C1
Queenshill Rd BS4. . .64 C1
Queensholm Ave
 BS16 . . . . .30 C1
Queensholm Cl
 BS16 . . . . .30 C1
Queensholm Cres
 BS16 . . . . .30 C1
Queensholm Dr
 BS16 . . . . .30 C1
Queens Mans BS8 . . .84 B3
Queens Par BS1 . . . . . .85 C2
Queen Sq BS1 . . . . . . .87 A2
Queen Square Ave 10
 BS1 . . . . .87 A2
Queen Square Ho
 BS1 . . . . .87 A2
Queens Rd
 Bristol BS4 . . . . .65 B2
 Keynsham BS31 . . . . . .82 B4
Queen's Rd
 Bristol, Ashley Down
  BS7 . . . . .38 B1
 Bristol, Bishopsworth
  BS13, BS41 . . . . .78 B4
 Bristol BS8 . . . . .84 B3
 Bristol, Cadbury Heath
  BS30 . . . . .69 A4
 Bristol, Crew's Hole
  BS5 . . . . .58 B3
Queen St
 Avonmouth BS11 . . . . .21 B1
 Bristol BS2 . . . . .86 B3
 Bristol, Eastville BS5 . .50 B3
 Bristol, St George
  BS15 . . . . .59 A4
Queensway BS34 . . . . .16 B2
Queen Victoria Rd
 BS6 . . . . .47 A4
Queen Victoria St
 BS2 . . . . .56 C2
Quickthorn Cl BS14. .72 C2
Quilter Gr BS4 . . . . . . .71 C3

R
Rackham Cl BS7 . . . . .39 C3
Rackhay BS1 . . . . .87 A2
Radley Rd BS16 . . . . . .51 C4
Radnor Bsns Ctr
 BS7 . . . . .38 A1
Radnor Rd
 Bristol, Horfield
  BS7 . . . . .38 A1
 Bristol, Westbury on Trym
  BS9 . . . . .37 A1
Raeburn Rd BS5 . . . . .59 A2
Raglan La BS5 . . . . . . .58 C3
Raglan Pl BS7 . . . . . . .48 B3
Raglan Rd BS7 . . . . . . .48 B3
Raglan Wlk BS31 . . . .82 B4
Railton Jones Cl
 BS34 . . . . .28 C3
Railway Arches BS2 .87 C2
Railway Terr BS16. . . .52 A4
Raleigh Rd BS3 . . . . . .63 A4
Ralph Rd BS7 . . . . .49 A4
Ram Hill Bsns Pk
 BS36 . . . . .20 B1
Ramsey Rd BS7 . . . . . .38 B3
Randall Cl BS15 . . . . . .53 A2
Randall Rd BS8 . . . . . .85 B2
Randolph Ave BS13 . .71 A1
Randolph Cl BS13. . . .71 A1
Rangers Wlk BS15 . . .67 B4
Rannoch Rd BS7 . . . . .27 A1
Raphael Ct BS1 . . . . . .87 B1
Ratcliffe Dr BS34 . . . .16 C1
Rathbone Cl BS36 . . .20 A1
Raven Ct BS9 . . . . .36 B4
Ravendale Dr BS30 . .69 A2
Ravenglass Cres
 BS10 . . . . .26 B2

Ravenhead Dr BS14. .73 A4
Ravenhill Ave BS3 . . .64 B2
Ravenhill Rd BS3 . . . .64 B3
Ravenscourt Rd
 BS34 . . . . .15 C3
Ravenswood BS30 . . .69 A3
Ravenswood Rd
 BS6 . . . . .48 A1
Rawnsley Ho 15 BS5 .49 B1
Rayleigh Rd BS9 . . . . .36 A3
Raymend Rd BS3 . . . .64 A3
Raymend Wlk BS3 . . .64 A2
Raymill BS4 . . . . .66 C2
Raymond Ho BS16 . . .53 A4
Raynes Rd BS3 . . . . . . .62 C3
Reading Ct BS15 . . . . .59 A4
Rectory Gdns BS10 . .24 C2
Rectory La BS34 . . . . .27 B3
Rectory Rd
 Easton-in-G BS20 . . . .45 A3
 Frampton Cotterell
  BS36 . . . . .19 B4
Redcar Ct BS16 . . . . . .31 A1
Redcatch Rd BS4 . . . .64 B1
Redcliff Backs BS1 . .87 B2
Redcliff Cres BS3 . . . .64 A4
Redcliffe Par E BS1. .87 A1
Redcliffe Par W BS1 .87 A1
Redcliffe Way BS1 . . .87 B1
Redcliff Hill BS1 . . . . .87 B1
Redcliff Mead La
 BS1 . . . . .87 B1
Redcliff St BS1 . . . . . . .87 B2
Redcross Mews 14
 BS2 . . . . .86 C3
Redcross St BS2 . . . . .86 C3
Reddings The BS15 . .53 A2
REDFIELD 57 B3
Redfield Edge Prim
 Sch BS30 . . . . .69 C4
Redfield Rd BS34 . . . .15 C3
Redford Cres BS13 . . .78 B3
Redford Wlk BS13 . . .78 B3
Redhill Cl BS16 . . . . . .50 C3
Redhill Dr BS16 . . . . . .50 C3
Red House La
 Almondsbury BS32 . . . .8 C4
 Bristol BS9 . . . . .36 A2
REDLAND 48 A3
Redland Ave BS20 . . .32 B2
Redland Court Rd
 BS6 . . . . .48 A2
Redland Gr BS6 . . . . . .48 A2
Redland Green Rd
 BS6 . . . . .47 C3
Redland High Sch
 BS6 . . . . .48 A2
Redland Hill BS6 . . . . .47 C2
Redland Pk BS6 . . . . . .47 C2
Redland Rd BS6 . . . . . .48 A2
Redland Sta BS6 . . . . .48 A2
Redland Terr 8
 BS6 . . . . .47 C2
Red Lodge The ★
 BS8 . . . . .84 C3
Redlynch La BS31. . . .82 B2
Red Maids Jun Sch The
 BS9 . . . . .36 C2
Red Maids Sch The
 BS9 . . . . .36 C2
Redshelf Wlk BS10. . .26 A3
REDWICK 2 C4
Redwick Cl BS11 . . . . .24 A2
Redwick Crossroads
 BS35 . . . . .3 A3
Redwick Gdns BS35. . .3 A3
Redwick Rd
 Pilning BS35 . . . . .3 A4
 Redwick BS35 . . . . .2 C4
Redwing Gdns BS16 .40 A2
Redwood Cl BS30 . . . .68 C3

Redwood Ho BS13 . . .**79** C3
Redwoods The BS31 .**75** C2
Reed Cl BS10 . . . .**37** C2
Reed Ct BS30 . . . .**68** B3
Reedley Rd BS9. . . . . . .**36** B1
Reedling Cl BS16 . . . . .**40** A2
Regency Dr BS4 . . . . . .**66** C2
Regent Apartments
BS6 . . . .**48** A3
Regent Rd BS3 . . . .**63** C4
Regents St BS8 . . . .**85** A2
Regent St BS15 . . . .**59** C4
Regents The BS31. . . . .**76** B2
Remenham Dr BS9 . .**37** A1
Remenham Pk BS9 . .**37** A1
Rendle Ho BS16 . . . . . .**53** A4
Rene Rd **12** BS5. . . . . . .**49** C1
Repton Hall BS10 . . . .**25** C2
Repton Rd BS4 . . . .**65** C3
Retort Rd BS11 . . . .**22** A3
Reubins The BS5. . . . . .**51** B2
Reynolds Cl BS31 . . . . .**76** C1
Reynold's Wlk BS7. .**38** C3
Rhode Cl BS31 . . . .**83** B3
Richeson Cl BS10 . . .**25** A2
Richeson Wlk BS10 . .**25** A2
Richmond Apartments
BS6 . . . .**48** A3
Richmond Ave
Bristol, Montpelier
BS6 . . . .**49** A2
Bristol, Stoke Gifford
BS34 . . . .**16** C1
Richmond Cl BS31. . .**82** B4
Richmond Ct
Bristol BS34 . . . .**8** A1
7 Bristol, Clifton
BS8 . . . .**47** B2
2 Bristol, Windmill Hill
BS3 . . . .**64** B3
Richmond Dale **6**
BS8 . . . .**47** B2
Richmond Hill BS8. .**84** B3
Richmond Hill Ave
BS8 . . . .**84** B3
Richmond Hts BS8. .**84** A3
Richmond La BS8. . .**84** A3
Richmond Mews
BS8 . . . .**84** A3
Richmond Park Rd
BS8 . . . .**84** A3
Richmond Rd
Bristol, Mangotsfield
BS16 . . . .**42** C1
Bristol, Montpelier
BS6 . . . .**48** C1
Bristol, Pile Marsh
BS5 . . . .**58** A3
Richmond St BS3 . . .**64** B4
Richmond Terr
Avonmouth BS11 . . . .**21** C1
Bristol BS8 . . . .**84** A3
Ride The BS11 . . . .**53** B2
Ridgehill BS9. . . . .**37** B2
Ridgemeade BS14 . . .**81** A4
Ridgemount Gdns
BS14 . . . .**73** A1
Ridge The
Bristol, Hengrove
BS14 . . . .**73** B1
Bristol, Shirehampton
BS11 . . . .**34** A3
Frampton Cotterell
BS36 . . . .**20** A3
RIDGEWAY **51** A3
Ridgeway BS36 . . . . . .**20** B3
Ridgeway Ct
Bristol BS14 . . . .**73** B1
Bristol, Henbury
BS10 . . . .**25** B1

Ridgeway Gdns
BS14 . . . .**73** B1
Ridgeway Ind Ctr
BS5 . . . .**50** C2
Ridgeway La BS14 . . .**73** A1
Ridgeway Par BS5 . . .**50** C3
Ridgeway Rd BS16. . .**51** A3
Ridgeway The BS10 . .**25** B1
Ridgewood BS9 . . . . . .**46** B3
Ridingleaze BS11 . . . .**23** B1
Ridings High Sch The
Frampton Cotterell
BS36 . . . .**20** A2
Ridings The
Bristol BS13 . . . .**78** A4
Frampton Cotterell
BS36 . . . .**20** A2
Ridings Rd BS36 . . . . .**20** A2
Ridley Ave BS15,
BS16 . . . .**53** C3
Ringwood Cres
BS10 . . . .**26** A1
Ripley Rd BS5 . . . .**51** B1
Ripon Ct BS16 . . . .**31** A2
Ripon Rd BS4. . . . .**58** A2
Risdale Rd BS3 . . . .**62** B1
Risedale Ho BS15. . . .**59** C1
Rivergate BS1 . . . .**87** C2
Riverland Dr BS13 . . .**70** B1
Riverleaze BS9 . . . .**35** B1
River Rd BS20 . . . .**32** B4
Riverside Bsns Pk
BS4 . . . .**57** C2
Riverside Cl BS11. . . .**34** B1
Riverside Cotts
BS15 . . . .**57** A1
Riverside Dr BS16 . . .**41** B3
Riverside Mews BS4 .**58** B2
Riverside Pk BS35 . . . . .**2** A2
Riverside Steps BS4 .**58** A3
Riverside Way BS15. .**67** B3
Riverside Wlk 6
BS5 . . . .**58** B2
River St BS2. . . . .**86** C3
River Terr BS31 . . . .**76** B1
River View BS16 . . . . .**40** A1
Riverwood Ho BS16. .**30** A1
Riverwood Rd BS16. .**30** A1
Riviera Cres BS16. . . .**44** C4
Riviera Way BS34 . . . .**29** B4
Road Two BS10 . . . .**4** B3
Robbins Cl BS32 . . . . .**17** A2
Robbins Ct BS16 . . . . .**43** A2
Robel Ave BS36. . . . . . .**19** B4
Robert Ct BS16 . . . . . .**43** A3
Robertson Dr BS4 . . .**58** B2
Robertson Rd BS5 . . .**50** A2
Robert St
Bristol, Baptist Mills
BS5 . . . .**49** C2
16 Bristol, Russell Town
BS5 . . . .**57** A3
Robin Cl
Bristol, Brentry
BS10 . . . .**25** C2
Bristol BS14 . . . .**73** C2
Robinia Wlk BS14. . . .**72** C3
Robinson Dr BS5 . . . . .**56** C4
Rochester Rd BS4 . . .**58** B1
Rock Cl BS4 . . . .**66** A2
Rockhill Est BS31. . . .**83** A4
Rock Ho BS10 . . . .**26** A3
Rockingham Gdns
BS11 . . . .**34** C4
Rockingham Rdbt
BS11 . . . .**10** B2
Rock La BS34 . . . .**29** A4
Rockland Gr BS16 . . .**39** C1
Rockland Rd BS16. . .**41** C3
Rockleaze BS9 . . . .**46** C2
Rockleaze Ave BS9 . .**46** C3
Rockleaze Ct BS9 . . . .**46** C3
Rockleaze Rd BS9 . . .**46** C3
Rock Rd BS31 . . . .**76** A1

Rockside Ave BS16 . .**42** B4
Rockside Dr BS9. . . . . .**37** B2
Rockside Gdns
Bristol BS16 . . . .**42** B4
Frampton Cotterell
BS36 . . . .**20** A4
Rockstowes Way
BS10 . . . .**26** B3
Rock The BS4. . . . .**66** A3
Rockwell Ave BS11 . .**23** C1
Rodborough Way
BS15 . . . .**60** C3
Rodbourne Rd BS10 .**38** A2
Rodfords Mead
BS14 . . . .**72** C3
Rodmead Wlk BS13 . .**78** C4
Rodney Ave BS15 . . . .**58** C4
Rodney Cres BS34 . . .**27** B4
Rodney Pl BS8 . . . .**84** A3
Rodney Rd BS15 . . . . .**58** C4
Rodney Wlk BS15 . . . .**51** B1
Rodway Cl BS16 . . . . .**42** C1
Rodway Hill BS16. . . .**53** C3
Rodway Hill Rd
BS16 . . . .**53** B4
Rodway Rd
Bristol BS34 . . . .**15** B4
Bristol, Mangotsfield
BS16 . . . .**42** C1
Bristol, Patchway
BS34 . . . .**15** A3
Rodway View BS15. . .**53** A3
Roegate Dr BS4 . . . . . .**58** A2
Roegate Ho BS5. . . . . .**51** B1
Rogers Cl BS30 . . . . . .**61** A1
Rogers Wlk BS30 . . . .**61** C3
Rokeby Ave BS6 . . . . .**48** A1
Roman Farm Ct
BS11 . . . .**24** A2
Roman Farm Rd
BS4 . . . .**72** A3
Roman Rd BS5 . . . . . .**49** C1
Roman Way BS9 . . . . .**46** A4
Roman Wlk
Bristol, Kensington Park
BS4 . . . .**65** B3
Bristol, Stoke Gifford
BS34 . . . .**16** C1
Romney Ave BS7. . . . .**39** A2
Romo Ct BS16 . . . .**52** A4
Ronald Rd BS16 . . . . .**40** B2
Ronaldson BS30 . . . . .**69** B2
Ronayne Wlk BS16. . .**41** B2
Ron Jones Ho 3
BS1. . . . .**86** B4
Rookery Rd BS4 . . . . .**64** C3
Rookery Way BS14. . .**80** B4
Rope Walk Ho 23
BS2 . . . .**86** C3
Rosary Rdbt The
BS16 . . . .**43** C3
Rosary The BS16. . . . .**43** C3
Rose Acre BS16 . . . . . .**25** B3
Rosebay Mead BS16 .**40** A1
Roseberry Pk BS5 . . .**57** C4
Roseberry Rd BS5 . . .**57** B3
Rosebery Ave BS2 . . .**49** B1
Rosebery Ct **7** BS2. .**49** B1
Rosebery Terr BS8 . . .**85** B2
Rose Cl BS36 . . . .**30** C4
Rosedale Rd BS16 . . .**52** A3
ROSE GREEN **50** C1
Rose Green Cl BS5. . .**50** C2
Rose Green Rd BS5 . .**50** B2
Rose La BS36 . . . .**20** B2
Roselarge Gdns
BS10 . . . .**25** B2
Rosemary Cl BS32 . . .**17** A3
Rosemary La BS5. . . .**50** A2
Rose Mead BS7. . . . . .**38** C3
Rose Meare Gdns
BS13 . . . .**70** A3
Rosemont Terr BS8 . .**85** A2
Rosemount Ct BS15. .**59** A4

Rose Oak Dr BS36 . . .**20** B3
Rose Oak Gdns
BS36 . . . .**20** B3
Rose Oak La BS36. . . .**20** B3
Rose Rd BS5 . . . .**58** A3
Rosery Cl BS9 . . . .**36** C4
Rosery The BS16. . . . .**52** A3
Rose Terr BS8 . . . .**84** B3
Rose Tree Ho BS16. . .**53** A4
Rosevear BS2 . . . .**56** C3
Roseville Ave BS30. . .**68** C2
Rose Wlk BS16 . . . .**52** A3
Roshni Gar E **16**
BS5 . . . .**49** C1
Roshni Gar W **15**
BS5 . . . .**49** C1
Rosling Rd BS7 . . . . . .**38** A2
Roslyn Rd BS6. . . . .**48** A1
Rossall Ave BS34 . . . .**16** A2
Rossall Rd BS4 . . . .**65** C3
Rossiter Grange 5
BS13 . . . .**78** B4
Rossiter's La BS5 . . . .**58** C2
Rossiter Wood Ct
BS11 . . . .**23** C2
Roundmoor Gdns
BS14 . . . .**73** C3
Roundways BS36 . . . .**20** B2
Rousham Rd BS5 . . . .**49** B3
Rowacres BS14 . . . . . .**72** B2
Rowan Cl BS16 . . . . . .**51** B2
Rowan Ct **10** BS5 . . . .**57** A3
Rowan Ho BS13. . . . . .**79** C4
Rowans The BS16. . . .**29** C1
Rowan Tree Ho
BS16 . . . .**53** A4
Rowan Way BS15 . . . .**67** A3
Rowan Wlk BS31 . . . .**82** A4
Rowberrow BS14 . . . .**72** B3
Rowland Ave BS16 . . .**50** B4
Rowlandson Gdns
BS7 . . . .**39** A2
Rowley St BS3 . . . .**63** B3
Rownham Cl BS3 . . . .**62** A4
Rownham Ct BS8 . . . .**85** A1
Rownham Hill BS8. . .**54** A2
Rownham Mead
BS8 . . . .**85** A1
Roxburgh BS8 . . . .**54** B4
Royal Albert Rd BS6 .**47** B4
Royal Cl BS10. . . . .**24** B3
Royal Fort Rd BS2,
BS8 . . . .**84** C3
Royal Par BS8 . . . .**84** B3
Royal Park Mews
BS8 . . . .**84** A3
Royal Pk BS8 . . . .**84** A3
Royal Portbury Dock
Rd BS20. . . . .**32** A1
Royal Prom BS8 . . . . .**84** B3
Royal Rd BS16 . . . .**42** C2
Royal Victoria Pk
BS10 . . . .**25** C2
Royal West of England
Acad * BS8. . . . .**84** B3
Royal York Cres
BS8 . . . .**54** B2
Royal York Ho 7
BS8 . . . .**85** A2
Royal York Mews 6
BS8 . . . .**85** A2
Royal York Villas
BS8 . . . .**85** A2
Royate Hill BS5. . . . . .**50** B2
Roycroft Rd BS34 . . . .**37** A2
Roy King Gdns BS30 .**61** B2
Royston Wlk BS10 . . .**26** B2
Rozel Rd BS7 . . . .**38** A1
Rubens Cl BS31. . . . . .**76** C1
Ruby St BS3 . . . .**63** A3
Rudford Cl BS34 . . . . . .**8** C1
Rudge Cl BS15. . . . . . .**53** A2
Rudgewood Cl BS13 .**79** C4
Rudgleigh Ave BS20 .**45** B4

Rudgleigh Rd BS20 . .**45** B4
Rudhall Gr BS10 . . . . .**38** A1
Rudthorpe Rd BS7 . . .**38** B1
Ruffet Rd BS36 . . . . . .**31** C4
Rugby Rd BS4 . . . .**65** C3
Runnymead Ave
BS4 . . . .**65** C2
Runnymede BS15. . . .**52** C1
Runswick Rd BS4 . . . .**65** B3
Rupert Ho BS2 . . . . . .**84** C4
Rupert St
Bristol BS1 . . . .**86** A3
Bristol, Redfield BS5 . .**57** B3
Rusham BS13. . . . .**78** B4
Rush Cl BS32 . . . .**9** B2
Rushton Dr BS36 . . . .**20** B3
Rushy BS30. . . . .**68** C4
Rushy Way BS16 . . . . .**31** B1
Ruskin Gr BS7 . . . .**38** C4
Ruskin Ho BS34. . . . . .**15** A4
Russell Ave BS15 . . . .**60** A3
Russell Gr BS6. . . . .**37** B1
Russell Rd
Bristol, Chester Park
BS16 . . . .**51** C2
Bristol, Westbury Park
BS6 . . . .**47** C4
RUSSELL TOWN **57** A3
Russell Town Ave
BS5 . . . .**57** A4
Russell Town Ind Pk **18**
BS5 . . . .**57** B3
Russ St BS2 . . . .**87** C2
Rustic Pk BS35 . . . .**2** B2
Rutherford Cl BS30 . .**68** C3
Ruthven Rd BS4 . . . . .**72** A4
Rutland Ave BS30. . . .**68** C2
Rutland Rd BS7 . . . . . .**48** C3
Rydal Ho BS34. . . . . . .**15** B4
Ryde Rd BS4 . . . .**65** A2
Rye Cl BS13 . . . .**70** A2
Ryecroft Ct BS36. . . . .**20** A3
Ryecroft Rd BS36. . . .**20** A4
Ryedown La BS30. . . .**69** C2
Ryland Pl **1** BS2 . . . . .**49** B2
Rylestone Gr BS9. . . .**36** B1
Rylestone Gr BS9 . . . .**36** B1
Rysdale Rd BS9 . . . . . .**36** B2

S

Sabrina Way BS9 . . . .**46** A4
Saco Ho BS1 . . . .**87** B2
Saddlers Ct BS15 . . . .**52** B1
Sadlier Cl BS11. . . . . . .**34** C4
Sages Mead BS32. . . .**16** C4
St Agnes Ave BS4 . . . .**64** B2
St Agnes Gdns BS4 . .**64** B2
St Agnes Wlk BS4. . . .**64** B2
St Aidan's Cl BS5 . . . .**59** A2
St Aidan's Rd BS5 . . .**59** A2
St Alban's Rd BS6 . . .**47** C4
St Aldwyn's Cl BS7. . .**38** B4
St Andrews BS30 . . . .**61** A2
St Andrews Gate Rdbt
BS11 . . . .**21** C2
Saint Andrews Mews
BS6 . . . .**48** C3
St Andrew's Rd
Avonmouth BS11 . . . .**21** C1
Bristol BS6 . . . .**48** C2
St Andrews Road Sta
BS11 . . . .**21** C4
St Andrews Trad Est
BS11 . . . .**22** A2
ST ANNE'S **58** A1
St Anne's Ave BS31 . .**75** C2
St Anne's CE Prim Sch
BS30 . . . .**69** B3
St Annes Cl **7** BS5. . .**58** B2
St Anne's Cl BS30. . . .**69** A4
St Annes Ct BS4 . . . . .**57** C1
St Anne's Ct BS31. . . .**75** C2
St Annes Dr BS30 . . . .**69** B2

St Anne's Dr BS36 . . .20 A1
St Anne's Inf Sch
 BS4 . . . . .57 C1
St Anne's Jun Sch
 BS4 . . . . .57 C1
ST ANNE'S PARK 58 A2
St Anne's Park Prim
 Sch BS4 . . . . .58 A1
St Anne's Park Rd
 BS4 . . . . .58 A1
St Anne's Rd
 Bristol, St Anne's Park
 BS4 . . . . .57 C2
 Bristol, St George
 BS5 . . . . .59 A2
St Anne's Terr BS4 . .58 A1
St Aubin's Ave BS4. . .66 B3
St Augustines of
 Canterbury RC Sch
 BS16. . . . . .42 B3
St Augustine's Par
 BS1 . . . . .87 A2
St Augustine's Pl **1**
 BS1 . . . . .87 A2
St Barnabas CE Prim
 Sch
 Bristol, Montpelier
 BS6 . . . . .49 A1
 Bristol, North Common
 BS30 . . . . .61 B2
St Barnabas Cl
 Bristol, Lower Knowle
 BS4 . . . . .64 B1
 Bristol, Warmley
 BS30 . . . . .61 B3
St Barnabas Ho
 BS30 . . . . .61 B3
St Bartholomew's Rd
 BS7. . . . . .49 A3
St Bede's RC Coll
 BS11 . . . . .23 C2
St Bede's Rd BS15 . . .52 B2
St Bernadette RC Prim
 Sch BS14 . . . . .73 A2
St Bernadette RC Sch
 BS14 . . . . .73 A2
St Bernard's RC Prim
 Sch BS11 . . . . .34 A2
St Bernard's Rd
 BS11 . . . . .34 A2
St Bonaventure's RC
 Prim Sch BS7 . . . . . .48 B4
St Brelades Gr BS4 . .58 B1
St Brendans Rdbt
 BS11 . . . . .22 A1
St Brendan's Sixth
 Form Coll BS4 . . . . . .66 C1
St Brendan's Way
 BS11 . . . . .21 C1
St Brenda's Ct BS8. . .84 A3
St Cadoc Ho BS31 . . .76 B1
St Catherines Ct
 BS4 . . . . .64 C2
St Catherine's Ind Est
 BS3 . . . . .63 C3
St Catherine's Mead
 BS20. . . . . .45 C3
St Catherines Pl **7**
 BS3 . . . . .63 C4
St Catherine's Terr
 BS3 . . . . .63 C3
St Christopher's Sch
 BS6 . . . . .47 C4
St Clements Ct
 Bristol, St Pauls
 BS2 . . . . .86 C4
 5 Bristol, Upper
 Soundwell BS16 . . . . .52 B3
 Keynsham BS31 . . . . .82 C4
St Clements Rd
 BS31. . . . . .83 A4
St David's Ave BS30. .61 A1
St David's Cres BS4 . .58 B2

St Davids Mews
 BS1. . . . . .85 C2
St Dunstans Cl BS13 .78 A4
St Dunstan's Rd BS3 63 B2
St Edward's Rd BS8. . .85 B2
St Edyth's Rd BS9. . . .35 B2
SS Peter & Paul RC
 Cath* BS8 . . . . .84 A4
SS Peter & Paul RC
 Prim Sch BS8 . . . . . .84 C4
St Fagans Ct BS30 . . .69 A2
St Francis Dr BS36. . .19 A2
St Francis Rd
 6 Bristol BS3 . . . . . .62 C4
 Keynsham BS31 . . . . .75 C2
St Gabriel's Bsns Pk **24**
 BS5 . . . . .57 A4
St Gabriel's Rd BS5 . .57 A4
ST GEORGE 58 C3
St George CE Prim Sch
 BS1 . . . . .85 B2
St George's* BS1 . . .85 C2
St Georges Ave **10**
 BS5 . . . . .58 B2
St George's Hill
 BS20 . . . . .44 C3
St Georges Ho BS5 . .58 A4
St George's Ho BS8. .85 B2
St George's Hts **12**
 BS5 . . . . .57 C3
St Georges Ind Est
 BS11 . . . . .21 C3
St Georges Rd BS1. . .85 C2
St George's Rd
 Keynsham BS31 . . . . .75 C2
 Portbury BS20 . . . . . .32 A3
St Gregory's Rd BS7 .38 B4
St Helena Rd BS6. . . .47 C4
St Helens Dr BS30 . . .69 B2
St Helen's Wlk BS5 . .51 B1
St Helier Ave BS4. . . .66 B3
St Hilary Cl BS9. . . . .35 C1
St Ivel Way BS30. . . . .61 B2
St James' Barton
 BS1 . . . . .86 B4
St James Ct BS32. . . . .9 A3
St James Pl BS16 . . . .42 C1
St James's Ct BS8 . . .47 C1
St James's St BS16 . .42 C1
St John's Bridge **5**
 BS1 . . . . .86 A3
St John's CE Prim Sch
 BS8 . . . . .47 B2
St John's CE Prim Sch
 BS31. . . . . .76 A1
St John's Cres BS3 . .64 A2
St Johns Ct
 Bristol, Bedminster
 BS3 . . . . .63 C2
 Bristol BS16 . . . . .51 B3
 Keynsham BS31 . . . . .76 A1
St John's Ho BS5 . . . .57 C4
St John's La BS3. . . . .64 A2
St John's Rd
 Bristol, Bedminster
 BS3 . . . . .63 B3
 Bristol, Clifton BS8 . . .47 B1
 Bristol, Southville
 BS3 . . . . .63 C4
St John's St BS3 . . . .63 B3
St Joseph's RC Prim
 Sch BS16. . . . . .51 C3
St Joseph's Rd BS10 .25 C3
St Judes Ho **21** BS2 . .86 C3
St Kenya Ct BS31 . . . .76 B1
St Keyna Ct BS31 . . . .76 B1
St Keyna Rd BS31. . . .76 A1
St Ladoc Rd BS31. . . .75 C2
St Laud Cl BS9. . . . . .35 C1
St Leonard's Rd
 Bristol, Horfield
 BS7 . . . . .38 A1
 Bristol, Lower Easton
 BS5 . . . . .50 A2

St Loe Cl BS14. . . . . .80 B3
St Lucia Cl BS7 . . . . .38 A3
St Lucia Cres BS7 . . .38 A3
St Lukes Cl BS16. . . . .43 B3
St Luke's Cres BS3. . .64 B4
St Luke's Ct BS3 . . . .64 A4
St Luke's Gdns BS4 . .66 A2
St Luke's Mews BS4 .66 A2
St Luke's Rd BS3. . . . .64 A4
St Luke St **13** BS5 . . . .57 A3
St Margaret's Cl
 BS31. . . . . .75 C2
St Margaret's Dr
 BS9 . . . . .37 B1
St Mark's Ave **1**
 BS5 . . . . .49 C1
St Marks Church Ho **4**
 BS5 . . . . .49 C1
St Marks Cl BS31 . . . .76 A2
St Mark's Gr **8** BS5. .49 C1
St Mark's Ho **13** BS5 .49 C1
St Mark's Rd BS5 . . . .49 C1
St Mark's Terr **11**
 BS5 . . . . .49 C1
St Martins Cl BS4. . . .65 A1
St Martin's Gdns
 BS4 . . . . .65 A1
St Martins Ind Pk
 BS11 . . . . .11 A1
St Martin's Rd BS4. . .65 A1
St Martin's Wlk BS4 .65 A1
St Mary Redcliffe CE
 Prim Sch BS3 . . . . . .64 A4
St Mary Redcliffe &
 Temple Sch BS1 . . . .87 B1
St Mary's CE Prim Sch
 BS20. . . . . .44 A3
St Marys Cl BS30 . . . .61 A1
St Mary's Hospl BS8 84 B4
St Mary's Prim Sch
 BS20. . . . . .44 A3
St Marys RC Prim Sch
 BS34. . . . . .36 B3
St Mary's Rd BS11 . . .33 C3
St Mary's Wlk BS11 . .33 C2
St Matthew's Ave **11**
 BS6 . . . . .49 B4
St Matthews Hall **20**
 BS5 . . . . .57 A4
St Matthew's Rd
 BS6 . . . . .86 A4
St Matthias & Dr Bell's
 CE Prim Sch BS16 . .51 B4
St Matthias Ho BS2 . .86 C4
St Matthias Pk BS2 . .86 C3
St Michael on the
 Mount CE Prim Sch
 BS2 . . . . .84 C3
St Michaels CE Prim
 Sch BS36. . . . . .18 C2
St Michael's CE Prim
 Sch BS34. . . . . .16 C1
St Michaels Cl BS7. . .48 C4
St Michaels Cl BS36 .18 C3
St Michaels Ct BS15 .59 A4
St Michael's Hill
 BS2 . . . . .84 C4
St Michael's Hospl
 BS2 . . . . .84 C4
St Michael's Pk BS2 .84 C4
St Monica Ct BS9 . . . .36 C1
St Nicholas
 Almshouses **7**
 BS1 . . . . .87 A2
St Nicholas of
 Tolentine RC Prim
 Sch BS5. . . . . .56 C4
St Nicholas Pk **10**
 BS5 . . . . .49 C1
St Nicholas Rd
 Bristol BS2 . . . . .86 C4
 Whitchurch BS14 . . . .81 B4
St Nicholas' Rd BS2. .49 A1
St Nicholas St BS1. . .87 A2

St Oswald's Ct BS13 .70 C4
St Oswald's Ct BS6 . .47 C3
St Oswald's Rd BS6 . .47 C3
St Patricks Ct BS31 . .76 A1
St Patrick's RC Prim
 Sch BS5. . . . . .57 C3
St Paul St BS2 . . . . . .86 B4
ST PAULS. 86 C4
St Pauls Ho **18** BS3 . .63 C4
St Paul's Rd
 Bristol BS8 . . . . .84 B4
 2 Bristol, Southville
 BS3 . . . . .63 C4
St Paul St BS2 . . . . . .86 B4
St Peter's Cres BS36 .19 C4
St Peters Ct **12** BS3 . .63 C4
St Peter's Ho BS8. . . .85 B2
St Peter's Rise BS13 .71 B3
St Peter's Wlk **3**
 BS9 . . . . .37 A2
St Philips Central
 BS2 . . . . .56 C1
St Philips Cswy BS2. .57 A1
ST PHILIP'S
 MARSH. 57 A1
St Philips Rd BS2 . . . .86 C3
St Philips Trad Pk
 BS2 . . . . .65 A4
St Phillips Rd BS2 . . .56 C1
St Pias X RC Prim Sch
 BS13 . . . . .70 C1
St Pierre Dr BS30 . . . .61 A2
St Ronan's Ave BS6 . .48 A1
St Saviours Ho BS4 . .64 B2
St Saviour's Rise
 BS36 . . . . .19 C2
St Stephen's Ave **3**
 BS1 . . . . .87 A2
St Stephens Bsns Ctr
 BS30 . . . . .61 B1
St Stephen's CE Jun
 Sch BS15. . . . . .52 B2
St Stephens Cl
 Bristol, Brentry
 BS10 . . . . .26 A2
 Bristol, Upper Soundwell
 BS16. . . . . .52 C3
St Stephen's Rd
 BS16. . . . . .52 B2
St Stephen's St BS1. .87 A2
St Teresa's RC Prim
 Sch BS7. . . . . .26 C1
St Thomas Pl BS1. . . .87 B2
St Thomas St E BS1. .87 B2
St Thomas St BS1. . . .87 B2
St Ursula's High Sch
 BS9 . . . . .36 C2
St Vincent's Hill **1**
 BS6 . . . . .47 B2
St Vincent's Rd BS8. .85 A2
St Vincents Trad Est
 BS2 . . . . .57 C2
Saint Way BS34. . . . . .29 B4
St Werburgh's Pk
 BS2 . . . . .49 B2
St Werburgh's Prim
 Sch BS2. . . . . .49 B2
St Werburgh's Rd
 BS2 . . . . .49 A2
St Whytes Rd BS4. . . .71 C4
St Wulfstans Ave
 BS10 . . . . .36 C4
Salcombe Rd BS4. . . .64 C1
Salem Rd BS36 . . . . . .19 A3
Salisbury Ave BS15 . .59 A4
Salisbury Dr BS16 . . .42 A2
Salisbury Gdns
 BS16. . . . . .42 A1
Salisbury Pk BS16 . . .42 A2
Salisbury Rd
 Bristol, Mangotsfield
 BS16. . . . . .42 A2
 Bristol, Redland BS6. .48 B2
 Bristol, St Anne's
 BS4 . . . . .57 C1

Salisbury St
 Bristol, Pile Marsh
 BS5 . . . . .58 A3
 Bristol, Russell Town
 BS5 . . . . .57 A2
Sallybarn Cl BS30. . . .68 A2
Sallysmead Cl BS13. .79 A4
Sallys Way BS36 . . . . .19 A3
Salmon Cl BS35 . . . . . .2 B2
Salmons Way BS16 . .43 A4
Salthouse Farm Pk
 BS35 . . . . .2 B3
Salthrop Rd BS7 . . . . .48 C4
Saltmarsh Dr BS11. . .23 B1
Saltwell Ave BS14. . . .73 B1
Sambourne La BS20 .45 B4
Samian Way BS34 . . . .16 C1
Sampson House Bsns
 Pk BS10. . . . . .12 B3
Sampsons Rd BS13 . .79 C4
Samuel St **3** BS5. . . .57 B4
Samuel White Rd
 BS15 . . . . .67 B4
Samuel White's Inf Sch
 BS15 . . . . .67 B4
Samuel Wright Cl
 BS30 . . . . .61 C1
San Andreas BS34 . . .14 C2
Sanctuary Gdns BS9 .46 B3
Sandbach Rd BS4. . . .65 C4
Sandbed Rd BS2. . . . .49 B2
Sandburrows Rd
 BS13 . . . . .70 B2
Sandburrows Wlk
 BS13 . . . . .70 B2
Sandcroft BS14 . . . . . .72 B2
Sandford Rd BS8 . . . .85 A1
Sandgate Rd BS4 . . . .65 C3
Sand Hill BS4. . . . . . . .65 B4
Sandholme Cl BS16. . .42 A4
Sandholme Rd BS4 . .65 C4
Sandhurst Cl BS34. . . .8 C1
Sandhurst Rd BS4 . . .65 C4
Sandling Ave BS7. . . .38 C3
Sandown Cl BS16. . . . .31 A1
Sandown Rd
 Bristol, Filton BS34. . . .28 A3
 Bristol, Kensington Park
 BS4 . . . . .65 C4
Sandringham Ave
 BS16. . . . . .42 A4
Sandringham Pk
 BS16. . . . . .42 A4
Sandringham Rd
 Bristol, Kensington Park
 BS4 . . . . .65 C4
 Bristol, Longwell Green
 BS30 . . . . .68 C2
 Bristol, Stoke Gifford
 BS34 . . . . .28 B4
Sandstone Rise
 BS36 . . . . .30 C4
Sandwich Rd BS4. . . .65 C4
Sandy Cl BS32 . . . . . .16 C2
Sandy La BS5. . . . . . . .50 A3
Sandyleaze BS9 . . . . .36 A3
Sandy Park Rd BS4 . .65 B3
Saracens The BS7 . . .38 A1
Sarah St BS5 . . . . .57 A3
Sargent St BS3 . . . . . .64 A4
Sarum Cl BS16 . . . . . .43 B2
Sarum Cres BS10 . . . .26 A1
Sassoon Ct BS30. . . . .60 B1
Satchfield Cl BS10 . . .25 A1
Satchfield Cres
 BS10 . . . . .25 A2
Satellite Bsns Pk
 BS5 . . . . .57 C2
Sates Way BS9 . . . . . .37 B2
Saunders Rd BS16. . .52 C4
Saunton Wlk BS4. . . .72 A4

Savages Wood BS32 .16 C4
Savages Wood Rd
BS32 . . . . .16 B4
Saville Gate CI BS9 . .47 A4
Saville Mews BS6 . . .86 A4
Saville PI BS8 . . . . . . .85 A2
Saville Rd BS9 . . . . . . .47 A3
Savoy Rd BS4 . . . . . .65 C4
Savoy The BS11 . . . . .34 A2
Saxon Rd BS2 . . . . . .49 B2
Saxon Way BS32 . . . . . .9 A1
Say Wlk BS30 . . . . . . .61 C3
SBI Ctr BS15 . . . . .59 A1
Scandrett CI BS10 . .24 C2
Scantleberry CI
BS16 . . . . .41 C4
School CI
Bristol BS14 . . . . .80 B4
Bristol, Eastville BS5 . .50 B2
Bristol, Patchway
BS34 . . . . .16 A4
School Ct BS34 . . . . . .17 B1
School La ☑ BS16 . . . .40 A1
**School of Christ the
King RC Prim** BS4 . .72 A4
School Rd
Bristol, Broom Hill
BS4 . . . . .66 A3
Bristol BS15 . . . . .59 B4
Bristol, Cadbury Heath
BS30 . . . . .68 C4
Bristol, Oldland Common
BS30 . . . . .69 B3
Bristol, Totterdown
BS4 . . . . .64 C3
Frampton Cotterell
BS36 . . . . .19 B4
School Way BS35 . . . . . .2 B2
School Wlk BS5 . . . . .50 B1
Scotland La BS4,
BS14 . . . . .74 C3
Scott CI BS30 . . . . . . .60 B1
Scott Lawrence CI
BS16 . . . . .40 C3
Scott Wlk BS30 . . . . . .61 C3
Seagry CI BS10 . . . . . .26 C1
SEA MILLS 35 A2
Sea Mills Inf Sch
BS9 . . . . .35 B3
Sea Mills Jun Sch
BS9 . . . . .35 A1
Sea Mills La BS9 . . . . .35 B1
Searle Court Ave
BS4 . . . . .66 A4
Seaton CI BS3 . . . . . . .63 C1
Seaton Rd BS5 . . . . . .50 A1
Seawalls BS9 . . . . . . .46 B2
Seawalls Rd BS9 . . . . .46 B2
Second Ave BS14 . . . .73 A3
Second Way BS11 . . . .22 B1
Seddon Rd ☑ BS2 . .49 B2
Sedgefield Gdns
BS16 . . . . .31 A1
Sedgewick Ho BS11 .34 A3
**Sefton Park Jun & Inf
Schs** BS7 . . . . .49 A3
Sefton Park Rd BS7 . .49 A3
Selborne Rd BS7 . . . .38 B1
Selbrooke Cres
BS16 . . . . .41 B2
Selby Rd BS5 . . . . .51 A1
Selden Rd BS14 . . . . .74 A1
Selkirk Rd BS15 . . . . .52 A1
Selley Wlk BS13 . . . . .70 C1
Selworthy BS15 . . . . . .60 A3
Selworthy CI BS31 . .75 C1
Selworthy Rd BS4 . . .65 A2
Seneca PI ☑ BS5 . . .57 C3
Seneca St BS5 . . . . . . .57 C3
Septimus Bldgs
BS14 . . . . .71 C1

Seventh Ave
Bristol BS14 . . . . .72 C3
Bristol, Filton BS7 . . . . .27 C1
SEVERN BEACH 2 C2
Severn Beach Prim Sch
BS35 . . . . .2 B2
Severn Beach Sta
BS35 . . . . .2 B2
**Severn Bridges Visitor
Ctr★** BS35 . . . . .2 A2
Severn Grange BS10 .24 B3
Severn Ho BS10 . . . . .24 B3
Severnleigh Gdns
BS9 . . . . .47 A3
Severnleigh Ho BS9 .47 A3
Severn Rd
Avonmouth BS11 . . . . .22 A4
Bristol BS11 . . . . .33 C2
Hallen BS10 . . . . .11 B3
Pill BS20 . . . . .33 B1
Severn Beach BS35 . . . . .4 A3
Severnside Trad Est
BS11 . . . . .10 A1
Severn View BS10 . . . .24 A1
Severn View Ind Pk
BS10 . . . . .4 A3
Severn Way
Bristol BS34 . . . . .8 A1
Keynsham BS31 . . . . . .76 C1
Severnwood Gdns
BS35 . . . . .2 B1
Sevier St BS2 . . . . . . .49 A2
Seymour Ave BS7 . . .48 C4
Seymour Rd
Bristol, Ashley Down
BS7 . . . . .48 C4
Bristol, Kingswood
BS15 . . . . .52 A1
Bristol, Staple Hill
BS16 . . . . .52 A4
Bristol, Upper Easton
BS5 . . . . .49 B1
Seyton Wlk BS34 . . . .16 C1
Shackel Hendy Mews
BS16 . . . . .43 A1
Shadwell Rd BS7 . . . .48 B3
Shaftesbury Ave
BS6 . . . . .48 C1
Shaftesbury Crusade
BS2 . . . . .56 C2
Shaftesbury Terr ☑
BS5 . . . . .57 C3
Shaft Rd BS35 . . . . . . .2 B4
Shakespeare Ave
BS7 . . . . .38 C4
Shaldon Rd BS7 . . . . .49 B4
Shamrock Rd BS5 . . .50 B3
Shanklin Dr BS34 . . . .27 C3
Shapcott CI BS4 . . . . .65 A1
Shaplands BS9 . . . . . .47 A4
Sharland CI BS9 . . . . .46 C3
Sharland Br BS13 . . . .79 B4
Shaw CI
Bristol BS16 . . . . .53 C3
☑ Bristol, Upper Easton
BS5 . . . . .57 A4
Shaw Gdns BS14 . . . .72 C4
Shaymoor La BS35 . . . .6 B4
Shearmore CI BS7 . . .38 C3
Shearwater CI BS16 .40 B2
Sheene Ct Ind Est ☑
BS3 . . . . .63 B3
Sheene Rd BS3 . . . . . .63 B3
Sheene Way BS3 . . . . .63 B3
Sheephouse Cvn Pk
BS20 . . . . .32 A3
Sheeps Croft BS13 . . .70 C1
Sheepwood CI BS10 .25 B2
Sheepwood Rd
BS10 . . . . .25 B2
Sheldare Barton
BS5 . . . . .59 A3
Sheldrake Dr BS16 . .40 A2
Shellard Rd BS34 . . . .27 B2

Shellards Rd BS30 . . .68 B3
Shelley CI BS5 . . . . . . .58 B4
Shelley Ho BS34 . . . . .8 B1
Shelley Way BS7 . . . . .38 C4
Shellmor Ave BS34 . . .8 A1
Shellmor CI ☑ BS32 . .9 B1
Shepherds CI BS16 . .42 A1
Shepherds Wlk
☑ Bristol BS32 . . . . . . .9 B1
Bristol BS32 . . . . .16 B4
Sheppard Rd BS16 . . .41 B2
Shepton Wlk BS3 . . . .63 B2
Sherbourne Ave
BS32 . . . . .16 C3
Sherbourne CI BS15 .53 A2
Sherbourne's Brake
BS32 . . . . .16 C2
Sherbourne St BS5 . .58 A3
Sheridan Rd BS7 . . . . .38 A4
Sheridan Way BS30 . .68 C2
Sherrings The BS34 . .15 C4
Sherrin Way BS13 . . .78 A3
Sherston CI BS16 . . . .41 A1
Sherston Rd BS7 . . . . .38 A4
Sherwell Rd BS4 . . . . .66 A3
Sherwood Dr BS31 . . .76 A1
Sherwood Rd
Bristol BS15 . . . . .51 C1
Keynsham BS31 . . . . . .76 A1
Shetland Rd BS10 . . . .26 B1
Shield CI BS15 . . . . . . .59 C1
Shield Ret Ctr BS34 . .27 B3
Shield Road Prim Sch
BS7 . . . . .27 B1
Shields Ave BS7 . . . . .27 B1
Shiels Dr BS32 . . . . . . .16 B3
Shilton CI BS15 . . . . . .60 B3
Shimsey CI ☑ BS16 . .41 B2
Shipham CI BS14 . . . .73 A1
Ship La BS1 . . . . .87 B1
Shipley Mow BS16 . . .43 A2
Shipley Rd BS9 . . . . . .36 C4
Shipman Ct BS16 . . . .52 C4
Shire Gdns BS11 . . . . .33 C4
SHIREHAMPTON 34 A3
**Shirehampton Prim
Sch** BS11 . . . . .33 C2
Shirehampton Rd
BS9 . . . . .35 B2
Shirehampton Sta
BS11 . . . . .33 C1
Shirreff Ct ☑ BS6 . . .47 C1
Shorland Ho BS8 . . . .47 B1
Shortlands Rd BS11 . .23 B1
Short St BS2 . . . . .56 C1
Shortwood Rd BS13 . .80 A3
Shortwood View
BS15 . . . . .60 B4
Shortwood Wlk
BS13 . . . . .80 A3
Showering CI BS14 . .73 C1
Showering Rd BS14 . .73 C1
Shrubbery Cotts ☑
BS6 . . . . .47 C2
Shrubbery Ct ☑
BS16 . . . . .41 C1
Shrubbery Rd BS16 . .41 C1
Shuter Rd BS13 . . . . . .70 A1
Sidcot BS4 . . . . .66 C2
Sideland CI BS14 . . . .74 A2
Sidelands Rd BS16 . . .41 B2
Sidings The
Bristol, Lower
Soundwell BS16 . . . . . .53 C2
Bristol, Newleaze
BS34 . . . . .28 A2
Sidmouth Ct BS3 . . . .63 C1
Sidmouth Gdns BS3 .63 C2
Sidmouth Rd BS3 . . . .64 A2
Signal Rd BS16 . . . . . .53 A4
Silbury Rd BS3 . . . . . . .62 A2
Silbury Rise BS31 . . . .82 B2
Silcox Rd BS13 . . . . . .79 B4
Silklands Gr BS9 . . . . .35 B2

Silver Birch CI BS34. .16 B3
Silverhill Rd BS10 . . . .24 C4
Silverhill Sch BS36 . .18 C3
Silver St BS1 . . . . .86 A3
Silverthorne La BS2 .56 C2
Silverthorne Wharf
BS2 . . . . .57 A2
Silverton Ct BS4 . . . . .64 B1
Simmonds Bldgs
BS16 . . . . .30 A3
Simmonds View
BS34 . . . . .17 A1
Sinclair Ho
Bristol BS8 . . . . .85 A2
Bristol, Filton BS34. . . . .27 B2
Sion Hill BS8 . . . . .54 B3
Sion La BS8 . . . . .54 B3
Sion PI BS8 . . . . .54 B3
Sion Rd ☑ BS3 . . . . . .63 B3
Sir Bernard Lovell Sch
BS30 . . . . .69 B4
**Sir Bernard Lovell Sch
(annexe)** BS30 . . . . . .61 C1
Sir John's La
Bristol BS7 . . . . .39 A1
Bristol, Eastville BS5 . .49 C4
Siston CI BS15 . . . . . . .53 B2
Siston Comm BS15 . .53 B2
Siston Common
BS30 . . . . .53 C1
Siston Ctr The BS15. .53 B2
Siston Hill BS30 . . . . . .53 C1
Siston Hill Rdbt
BS15 . . . . .53 C2
Siston Pk BS15 . . . . . .53 B2
Sixth Ave
Bristol BS14 . . . . .72 C3
Bristol, Filton BS7. . . . . .27 C1
Skippon Ct BS15 . . . . .60 A1
Skypark Rd BS3 . . . . . .63 B3
Sleep La BS14 . . . . . . .81 C3
Sloan St BS5 . . . . .57 C4
Slymbridge Ave
BS10 . . . . .25 B3
Small La BS16 . . . . . . .40 A1
Small St
Bristol BS1 . . . . .86 A3
Bristol, St Philip's Marsh
BS2 . . . . .57 B3
Smeaton Rd BS1. . . . . .54 B1
Smithcourt Dr BS34. .16 B2
Smithmead BS13 . . . . .71 A1
Smiths Ct BS34 . . . . . .15 B4
Smoke La BS11 . . . . . .10 B2
Smythe Croft BS14. . .80 C3
Smyth Ho BS8 . . . . . . .54 A2
Smyth Rd BS3 . . . . . . .62 C3
Smyths CI BS11 . . . . . .21 C1
Smyth Terr ☑ BS3 . .63 B4
SNEYD PARK 46 B3
Sneyd Park Ho BS9 . .46 B3
Snowberry CI BS32 . .16 C4
Snowberry Wlk BS5. .50 C1
Snowdon CI BS16 . . . .51 A4
Snowdon Ho BS16 . . .40 B1
Snowdon Rd BS16 . . .51 A4
Soaphouse Ind Est
BS5 . . . . .58 A4
Solon Ct BS13 . . . . . . .70 B1
Somerby CI BS32 . . . .16 B3
SOMERDALE 76 A3
Somerdale Ave BS4 . .64 C1
Somerdale Rd BS31. .76 B3
Somerdale Rd N BS30,
BS31 . . . . .76 B4
Somerford Ct BS10 . .25 A1
Somermead BS3 . . . . .63 B1
Somerset Cres BS34 .17 A1
Somerset Ho ☑
BS2 . . . . .86 C3
Somerset Rd BS4 . . . .65 A3
Somerset Sq BS1 . . . .87 B1
Somerset St
Bristol BS1 . . . . .87 B1

Somerset St continued
Bristol, Kingsdown
BS2 . . . . .86 A4
Somerset Terr BS3. . .63 C3
Somerton CI BS15 . . .60 A3
Somerton Rd BS7. . . . .38 A2
Somerville Ho BS10. .36 C4
Somerville Rd
BS7 . . . . .48 C3
Sommerville Rd S ☑
BS6 . . . . .49 A2
Soper Gdns BS4 . . . . .71 C3
Soundwell Rd BS15,
BS16 . . . . .52 B2
Southampton Gdns
BS7 . . . . .38 B1
Southampton Mews
BS7 . . . . .38 B1
Southbow Ho ☑
BS3 . . . . .62 C3
South Bristol Bsns Pk
BS4 . . . . .72 A3
South Bristol Ret Pk
BS3 . . . . .62 C3
South Bristol Trad Pk
BS3 . . . . .62 C3
South Croft BS9 . . . . .37 B3
South Ct BS32 . . . . . . .9 B3
South Dene BS9 . . . . .36 B4
Southdown Rd BS9 . .36 B4
Southernhay
Bristol BS8 . . . . .85 A2
Bristol, Staple Hill
BS16 . . . . .52 B4
Southernhay Ave
BS8 . . . . .85 B2
Southernhay Cres
BS8 . . . . .85 B2
Southey Ave BS15 . . .52 C1
Southey CI BS15 . . . . .52 B1
Southey St BS2 . . . . . .49 A2
Southfield Ave BS15 .52 C1
Southfield Ct BS9 . . . .36 C3
Southfield Rd
Bristol, Cotham
BS6 . . . . .48 B1
Bristol, Westbury on Trym
BS9 . . . . .36 C3
**South Gloucestershire
Central Teaching
Unit** BS16 . . . . .42 C1
South Gr
Bristol BS6 . . . . .37 B1
Pill BS20 . . . . .45 B4
South Green St ☑
BS8 . . . . .54 B2
South Hayes BS5 . . . .49 C4
Southlands
Bristol, Clifton BS8 . . . .47 B1
Bristol, Knowle Park
BS4 . . . . .65 A1
Southleigh Mews
BS8 . . . . .84 B4
Southleigh Rd BS8. . .84 B4
South Liberty La
Bristol BS3 . . . . .62 C1
☑ Bristol BS3 . . . . . . .63 A2
SOUTHMEAD 26 B1
Southmead Hospl
BS10 . . . . .38 A4
Southmead Rd BS10,
BS34 . . . . .26 C1
Southmead Way
BS10 . . . . .37 C4
Southover CI BS9 . . . .36 C4
South Parade Mans
BS8 . . . . .84 B4
South Rd
☑ Bristol, Bedminster
BS3 . . . . .63 B3
Bristol, Kingswood
BS15 . . . . .59 C4
Bristol, Redland BS6. . .48 A2
Southsea Rd BS34 . . .15 B4

Southside CI BS9 . . . .35 A4
South St BS3 . . . . .63 A3
South Street Prim Sch
BS3 . . . . .63 A3
South Terr 6 BS6 . . . .47 C2
South View
Bristol BS16 . . . . .42 A1
Frampton Cotterell
BS36 . . . . .19 C3
South View Bsns Pk
BS16 . . . . .42 B1
South View Cres
BS36 . . . . .20 B2
South View Rise
BS36 . . . . .20 B2
SOUTHVILLE 63 B4
Southville PI BS3 . . . . .63 C4
Southville Prim Sch
BS3 . . . . .63 B4
Southville Rd BS3 . . . .63 B4
Southway Dr BS15 . . . .61 C1
Southwell St BS2 . . . .84 C4
Southwood Ave BS9 . .35 B4
Southwood Dr BS9 . . .35 A4
Southwood Dr E
BS9 . . . . .35 B4
Spalding CI BS7 . . . . .49 B3
Spaniorum View
BS35 . . . . .6 A2
Spar Rd BS11 . . . . .22 B4
Spartley Dr BS13 . . . .70 B2
Spartley Wlk BS13 . . .70 B2
SPEEDWELL 51 B2
Speedwell Ave 5
BS5 . . . . .57 C3
Speedwell Rd BS5,
BS15 . . . . .51 B1
Speedwell Tech Coll
BS15 . . . . .51 B1
Spencer Ho 6 BS1 . . .87 B1
SPIKE ISLAND 85 B1
Spike Island Artspace *
BS1 . . . . .85 B1
Spinney Croft BS13 . .70 B1
Spinney The
Bristol BS32 . . . . .16 C3
Frampton Cotterell
BS36 . . . . .19 C3
Spires View 4 BS16. .40 A1
Springfield Ave
Bristol, Horfield
BS7 . . . . .38 B1
Bristol, Mangotsfield
BS16 . . . . .42 C3
Bristol, Shirehampton
BS11 . . . . .33 C2
Springfield CI BS16 . .42 C3
Springfield Gr BS6 . . .37 B1
Springfield Ho BS6 . .84 C4
Springfield Lawns
BS11 . . . . .33 C2
Springfield Rd
Bristol, Cotham
BS6 . . . . .48 B1
Bristol, Mangotsfield
BS16 . . . . .42 C3
Pill BS20 . . . . .45 B4
Springfields BS34. . . .27 B2
Springfort BS9 . . . . . .47 A3
Spring Gdns BS4 . . . .64 C1
Spring Hill
Bristol BS2 . . . . .86 A4
Bristol, Upper Soundwell
BS15 . . . . .52 C2
Spring La BS41 . . . . . .78 C1
Springleaze
Bristol, Knowle Park
BS4 . . . . .64 C1
Bristol, Mangotsfield
BS16 . . . . .42 C3
Springly Ct BS15. . . . .60 C4
Spring St BS3 . . . . . . .64 A4
Spring Street PI
BS3 . . . . .64 A4

Springville CI BS30 . .68 C3
Springwater Pk Trad
Est BS5 . . . . .58 A3
Springwood Dr
BS10 . . . . .24 B3
Spruce Way BS34 . . . .15 A3
Square The
Bristol BS1 . . . . .87 C2
Bristol, Knowle Park
BS4 . . . . .64 C1
Bristol, Staple Hill
BS16 . . . . .52 C4
Squires Ct BS30 . . . . .68 B4
Stackpool Rd BS3 . . . .63 B4
Stadium Rd BS6 . . . . .37 B1
Stafford Rd BS2 . . . . .49 B2
Staffords CI BS30 . . . .60 C2
Stafford St BS3 . . . . . .63 C4
Stainer CI BS4 . . . . . .71 C3
Stanbridge CI BS16 . .42 B2
Stanbridge Prim Sch
BS16 . . . . .42 B2
Stanbridge Rd BS16 . .42 B2
Stanbury Ave BS16 . . .41 B1
Stanbury Rd BS3 . . . .64 A3
Standfast Rd BS10 . . .25 A3
Standish Ave BS34 . . . .9 A1
Standish CI BS10 . . . .25 A1
Standon Way BS10. . . .26 A2
Stane Way BS11 . . . . .33 B3
Stanfield CI BS7 . . . . .39 B2
Stanford CI BS36 . . . .19 A4
Stanford PI BS4 . . . . .71 C3
Stanhope Rd BS30 . . .68 B2
Stanhope St BS2. . . . .56 C1
Stanier Rd BS15,
BS16 . . . . .53 C3
Stanley Ave
Bristol, Bishopston
BS7 . . . . .48 C3
Bristol, Filton BS34. . .27 C2
Stanley Chase BS5. . . .50 C2
Stanley Cres BS34 . . .27 C2
Stanley Gdns BS30 . . .69 A4
Stanley Hill BS4 . . . . .64 A4
Stanley Mead BS32 . . .9 C2
Stanley Park Rd
BS16 . . . . .52 C3
Stanley Pk BS5 . . . . . .50 A1
Stanley Rd
Bristol, Cotham
BS6 . . . . .48 A1
Bristol, Warmley
BS15 . . . . .61 A4
Stanley St N 9 BS3 . .63 B3
Stanley St S BS3 . . . . .63 B2
Stanley St 4 BS3 . . . .63 B3
Stanshaw CI BS16 . . . .40 C3
Stanshaw Rd BS16 . . .40 C3
Stanshaws CI BS32 . . .9 A2
Stanton CI BS15 . . . . .53 A1
Stanton Rd BS10 . . . .26 C2
Stanway BS30 . . . . . . .69 B1
Staple Gr BS31 . . . . . .75 C1
Staple Grove Cres
BS5 . . . . .58 C3
STAPLE HILL 52 C4
Staple Hill Prim Sch
BS16 . . . . .52 B4
Staple Hill Rd BS16 . .51 C4
STAPLETON 50 B4
Stapleton CI BS16 . . .39 C1
Stapleton Rd
Bristol, Baptist Mills
BS5 . . . . .49 C1
Bristol, Eastville BS5 . .50 A3
Stapleton Road Sta
BS5 . . . . .49 C1
Star Ave BS34 . . . . . . .29 B4
Star Barn Rd BS36 . . .18 C3
Star La
Bristol BS16 . . . . .51 A3
Pill BS20 . . . . .45 C4

Starveall CI BS5 . . . . .51 B1
Station Ave 3 BS16. .51 B4
Station Ave S 5
BS16 . . . . .51 B4
Station CI BS15 . . . . . .61 B4
Station Ct BS5 . . . . . . .58 A4
Station La BS7. . . . . . .49 B4
Station Rd
Bristol, Ashley Down
BS7 . . . . .49 A4
Bristol, Filton BS34. . . .27 B3
Bristol, Fishponds
BS16 . . . . .51 B4
Bristol, Henbury
BS10 . . . . .25 A4
Bristol, Montpelier
BS6 . . . . .48 C2
Bristol, Newleaze
BS34 . . . . .28 A2
Bristol, Patchway
BS34 . . . . .16 A3
Bristol, Shirehampton
BS11 . . . . .33 C1
Bristol, Shirehampton
BS11 . . . . .34 A2
Bristol, Staple Hill
BS15 . . . . .53 A3
Bristol, Upper Knowle
BS4 . . . . .65 C2
Bristol, Warmley
BS30 . . . . .61 B3
Frampton Cotterell
BS36 . . . . .20 A1
Keynsham BS31 . . . . .76 A2
Pill BS20 . . . . .45 B4
Pilning BS35 . . . . .6 A4
Severn Beach BS35 . . .2 B1
Winterbourne BS36 . . .30 C4
Station Road Bsns Ctr
BS15 . . . . .53 B3
Station Road Link
BS15 . . . . .53 B2
Station Road
Workshops BS15. . . .53 B3
Station Yd BS36 . . . . .30 C4
Staunton Fields
BS14 . . . . .81 B4
Staunton La BS14. . . .81 C3
Staunton Way BS14. . .81 C4
Staveley Cres BS10 . .26 A3
Staverton CI BS32 . . . .9 A1
Staverton Way BS15 . .60 C3
Stavordale Gr BS14 . .73 A2
Staynes Cres BS15. . . .52 A4
Steanbridge BS32 . . .16 B2
Stean Bridge Rd
BS32 . . . . .16 C2
Steel Ct BS30 . . . . . . .68 B3
Steel Mills BS31 . . . . .83 A4
Steevens Ho
(Almshouses) 13
BS2 . . . . .86 C3
Stella Gr BS3 . . . . .62 C2
Stephens Dr BS30 . . .60 B1
Stephen St BS5. . . . . .57 B4
Stepney Rd BS5 . . . . .50 A1
Stepney Wlk BS5 . . . .50 A1
Stepping Stones The
BS4 . . . . .58 A2
Sterncourt Rd BS16. .40 C3
Stevens Cres BS3. . . .64 B4
Stevens Wlk BS32 . . .16 B4
Stibbs Ct BS30. . . . . . .68 B4
Stibbs Hill BS5 . . . . . .58 C3
Stile Acres BS11 . . . . .23 B1
Stillhouse La BS3. . . .63 C4
Stillingfleet Rd
BS13 . . . . .71 B1
Stillman CI BS13 . . . . .78 A4
Stirling Rd BS4 . . . . . .65 B3
Stirling Way BS31. . . .82 C4
Stockton CI
Bristol BS14 . . . . .80 B1
Bristol, Oldland BS30 . .69 A3

Stockwell Ave BS16. .42 C2
Stockwell CI BS16 . . .42 B3
Stockwell Dr BS16 . . .42 C2
STOCKWOOD 74 C1
Stockwood Chambers
BS5 . . . . .57 B3
Stockwood Cres
BS4 . . . . .64 B2
Stockwood Hill
BS31 . . . . .75 B3
Stockwood La
Bristol BS14 . . . . .74 A1
Keynsham BS14,
BS31 . . . . .75 A3
Stockwood Mews
BS4 . . . . .58 B1
Stockwood Rd BS4 . .66 B1
STOCKWOOD VALE . .75 B2
Stockwood Vale
BS31 . . . . .75 B2
STOKE BISHOP 36 A1
Stoke Bishop CE Prim
Sch BS9 . . . . .35 C3
Stoke Bridge Ave
BS34 . . . . .16 B2
Stoke Cotts BS9 . . . . .46 C4
STOKE GIFFORD 29 A4
Stoke Gr BS9 . . . . .36 A2
Stoke Hamlet BS9 . . .36 B2
Stoke Hill BS9 . . . . . . .46 C3
Stoke La
Bristol, Broomhill
BS16 . . . . .40 A3
Bristol, Patchway
BS34 . . . . .16 A4
Bristol, Westbury on T
BS9 . . . . .36 B2
Stokeleigh Wlk BS9. .35 B1
Stoke Lodge Prim Sch
BS34 . . . . .16 A4
Stoke Mdws BS32. . . . .9 B1
Stokemead BS34 . . . .16 A4
Stoke Paddock Rd
BS9 . . . . .35 C2
Stoke Park Rd BS9. . .47 A4
Stoke Park Rd S
BS9 . . . . .46 C3
Stoke Rd BS8, BS9. . .47 A3
Stokes Croft BS1 . . . .86 B4
Stokes Ct 1 BS30. . . .68 C4
Stoke View Bsns Pk 6
BS16 . . . . .51 A4
Stoke View Rd BS16. .51 A4
Stoneberry Rd BS14 .81 A3
Stonebridge Pk BS5 . .50 C2
Stonechat Gdns
BS16 . . . . .40 A2
Stone CI BS36 . . . . . . .30 C4
STONE HILL 68 A4
Stonehill BS15. . . . . . .68 A4
Stonehill Ctr BS30. . . .68 A4
Stonehill Farm
BS15 . . . . .68 A4
Stone La BS36 . . . . . . .31 A3
Stoneleigh Cres
BS4 . . . . .64 C2
Stoneleigh Dr BS30 . .60 B1
Stoneleigh Ho BS8. . .84 B3
Stoneleigh Rd BS4 . . .64 C2
Stoneleigh Wlk BS4 . .64 C2
Stone Monolith
BS34 . . . . .14 C2
Stones Ct BS6 . . . . . . .47 C2
Stoneyfield CI BS20. . .33 A1
Stoneyfields BS20 . . .45 A4
Stores Rd BS11 . . . . . .22 A4
Stothard Rd BS7. . . . .39 A3
Stottbury Rd BS7 . . . .49 B3
Stoulton Gr BS10 . . . .25 B3
Stourden CI BS16. . . .40 C3
Stourton Dr BS30. . . .68 B4
Stow Ho BS11 . . . . . . .34 A1
Stowick Gdns BS11 . .24 C3

Stradbrook Ave BS5 . .59 A3
Stradling Rd BS11 . . .24 A2
Stradlings Yd BS2 . . .84 C4
Straight St BS2 . . . . . .87 C2
Straits Par BS16 . . . . .41 A1
Stratford CI BS14 . . . .80 B3
Stratford St BS9 . . . . .36 B4
Strathearn Dr BS10 . .25 C2
Strathmore Rd BS7 . .38 B1
Stratton CI BS34. . . . .16 A3
Stratton PI BS30. . . . .68 B2
Strawberry La
Bristol BS5 . . . . .58 A3
Dundry BS13, BS41. . .78 A3
Strawbridge Rd 11
BS5 . . . . .57 A3
Stream CI BS10 . . . . . .26 B3
Stream Side BS16. . . .42 B2
Streamside Wlk
BS4 . . . . .66 A3
Stream The BS16 . . . .29 C2
Stretford Ave BS5. . . .57 C4
Stretford Rd BS5 . . . .57 C4
Stride CI BS35 . . . . . . .2 B2
Stroud Rd
Bristol, Patchway
BS34 . . . . .15 A4
Bristol, Shirehampton
BS11 . . . . .34 A1
Stuart St BS5 . . . . .57 B3
Studland CI BS9 . . . . .37 B2
Sturden La BS16 . . . . .30 A3
Sturdon Rd BS3 . . . . .62 C3
Sturminster CI BS14 .73 C2
Sturminster Lodge
BS14 . . . . .73 C1
Sturminster Rd
BS14 . . . . .73 C3
Sullivan CI BS4 . . . . . .71 C2
Summer Ct BS8 . . . . .84 B3
Summer Ground Dr
BS13 . . . . .70 C1
Summerhayes BS30 . .61 C1
Summer Hill BS4 . . . .64 C4
Summerhill Jun & Inf
Schs BS5. . . . . .58 A4
Summerhill Rd BS5. . .58 B4
Summerhill Terr
BS5 . . . . .58 B3
Summer House Way
BS30 . . . . .61 A3
Summerleaze
Bristol BS16 . . . . .52 A3
Keynsham BS31 . . . . .76 A3
Summers Rd 4 BS2 . .49 B1
Summer St 4 BS3 . . .63 B4
Summers Terr 3
BS2 . . . . .49 B1
Sundays Hill BS32 . . . .8 B4
Sunderland PI BS8. . .84 B3
Sunningdale BS8 . . . .84 B4
Sunningdale Dr
BS30 . . . . .61 A2
Sunnybank BS16. . . . .42 A2
Sunny Bank BS15 . . . .51 C1
Sunnydene BS4 . . . . .65 C4
Sunny Hill BS9 . . . . . .35 B3
Sunnyhill Dr BS11 . . .34 A2
Sunnyhill Ho E BS11 .34 A2
Sunnyhill Ho W
BS11 . . . . .34 A2
Sunnymead
Bristol BS30 . . . . .61 C2
Keynsham BS31 . . . . .83 A3
Sunnyside
Bristol BS9 . . . . .36 A1
Frampton Cotterell
BS36 . . . . .19 C3
Sunnyside Farm Trad
Est BS20 . . . . .45 B2
Sunnyside La BS16. . .30 A2

Sunnyvale Dr BS30 ..69 A3
Sunny Wlk BS15 .....51 C1
Sunridge BS16 ....41 C2
Sunrise Gr BS4 ......65 C4
Surrey Rd BS7 ....48 C3
Surrey St BS2 ....86 B4
Sussex Pl BS2 ....49 A1
Sussex St BS2 ....56 C2
Sutherland Ave
BS16 ....42 A3
Sutherland Pl **9**
BS8 ....47 B2
Sutton Ave BS4 ......65 C4
Swainswick BS14 ....72 B2
Swallow Cl BS14 .....74 B2
Swallow Dr BS34 ....14 C4
Swallows Ct BS34...28 C4
Swane Rd BS14 ......74 B2
Swan La BS36 ....18 A4
Swanmoor Cres
BS10 ....25 B4
Sweets Cl BS15 ......52 C2
Sweets Rd BS15 .....52 C2
Swiss Dr BS3 ....62 B2
Swiss Rd BS3 ....62 B1
Sycamore Cl
Bristol, Hanham
BS15 ....67 A3
Bristol, Whitehall
BS5 ....50 C1
Sycamore Ct BS7 ...48 C3
Sycamore Dr BS34...15 A3
Sycamore Ho **6**
BS16 ....41 B2
Sydenham Hill BS6 ..48 B1
Sydenham La BS6 ...48 C1
Sydenham Pl **15**
BS6 ....48 C1
Sydenham Rd
Bristol, Cotham
BS6 ....48 C1
Bristol, Totterdown
BS4 ....64 C3
Sydenham Way
BS15 ....67 B3
Sydney Row BS1.....85 B1
Sylvan Way BS9 .....35 A3
Sylvia Ave BS3.......64 B3
Symes Ave BS13 .....79 B4
Symington Rd BS16..41 A1
Syston View BS15....60 C4
Syston Way BS15 ....52 B1

T

Tabernacle Rd BS15 .59 B2
Tackley Rd BS5 ......49 C3
Tailor's Ct **9** BS1...86 A3
Talbot Ave BS15 .....52 A1
Talbot Ct BS4.........65 A2
Talbot Rd BS4 ....65 B2
Talgarth Rd BS7 .....49 A4
Tallis Gr BS4..........71 C2
Tamar Dr BS31 ......83 B4
Tamar Rd BS2 ....57 B2
Tamsin Ct BS31......76 B1
Tamworth Rd BS31 ..82 C4
Tankard's Cl BS8 ....84 C3
Tanner Cl BS30 ......60 B1
Tanner St BS30 ......60 B1
Tanners Ct
Bristol, Frenchay
BS16 ....29 C1
4 Bristol, Two Mile Hill
BS15 ....52 A1
Tanorth Cl BS14 .....80 C3
Tanorth Rd BS14....80 B3
Tanyard The BS30....69 A2
Tapsters BS30 ....68 C4
Tarn Ho BS34 ....15 B4

Tarnock Ave BS14....72 C3
Tarragon Pl BS32 ....17 A3
Taunton Wlk BS7 ....38 C3
Taverner Cl BS4 .....71 C3
Tavistock Rd BS4 ....64 B1
Tavistock Wlk BS4 ..64 B1
Taylor Cl BS15 ....60 B4
Taylor Gdns BS13....78 B4
Taylors Bank **10**
BS1 ....86 A3
Tayman Cl BS10 .....38 A2
Tayman Ridge BS30..77 B4
Taynton Rd BS30.....69 B2
Teal Cl BS32..........9 B2
Teasel Mead BS32 ..16 C3
Teewell Ave BS16....52 C4
Teewell Cl BS16 .....52 C4
Teewell Ct BS16 .....52 C4
Teewell Hill BS16....52 C4
Teignmouth Rd BS4..64 B1
Telephone Ave BS1 ..87 A2
Telford Ho BS8 ......54 A3
Telford Wlk BS5 .....51 B1
Temple Back BS1....87 B2
Temple Back East
BS1 ....87 C2
Temple Church ★
BS1 ....87 B1
Temple Circus Giratory
BS1 ....87 B1
Temple Ct BS31......76 A1
Temple Gate BS1 ....87 B1
Temple Gate District
Ctr BS3 ....64 B2
Templeland Rd
BS13 ....70 B1
Temple Rose St BS1 .87 B2
Temple St
Bristol, Bedminster
BS3 ....63 A2
Bristol BS1 ....87 B2
Keynsham BS31......76 B1
Temple Trad Est
BS2 ....57 B1
Temple Way BS2.....87 B2
Temple Way Underpass
BS2 ....86 C3
Tenby Rd BS31.......82 B4
Tenby St BS5 ....57 A3
Tennessee Gr BS6 ...37 B1
Tenniscourt Rd
BS15 ....53 B1
Tennis Rd BS4 ....64 C2
Tennyson Cl BS31...76 B2
Tennyson Rd BS7....38 A1
Tenth Ave BS7........27 C1
Tereslake Gn BS10..26 B4
Terrell Gdns **14** BS5..57 C3
Terrell St BS2 ....86 A4
Terris Ct BS34 ....28 C4
Terry Ho BS1.........84 C3
Tetbury Cl BS34......16 A3
Tetbury Rd BS15.....59 A4
Teviot Rd BS31 ......83 B4
Tewkesbury Rd **12**
BS2 ....49 B2
Tewther Rd BS13 ....79 C3
Teyfant Com Sch
BS13 ....80 A4
Teyfant Rd BS13 ....80 A4
Teyfant Wlk BS13....80 A4
Thackeray BS7 ....38 C4
Thanet Rd BS3 ......63 A2
Thatchers Cl BS5 ....59 A3
Theatre Royal (Bristol
Old Vic) closed for
refurbishment
BS1 ....87 A2
There-and-Back-Again
La BS1 ....84 C3
Theresa Ave BS7.....48 C4
Thicket Ave BS16 ....52 A3
Thicket Rd BS16 .....52 A4
Thiery Rd BS4 ....65 B2

Thingwall Pk BS16...50 C3
Third Ave
Bristol BS14 ....73 A3
Bristol, Filton BS7...27 B1
Third Way BS11......22 A2
Thirlmere Ct BS30 ..61 C2
Thirlmere Rd BS34...15 B4
Thistle St **1** BS3 ....63 A3
Thomas Ave BS16....43 A4
Thomas Cl BS1.......87 B2
Thomas La BS1.......87 B2
Thomas Lane
Apartments BS1 ....87 B2
Thomas Pring Wlk **1**
BS5 ....51 B1
Thomas St N **13** BS2 ..48 B1
Thomas St
Bristol BS2 ....86 B4
8 Bristol, Russell Town
BS5 ....57 A3
Bristol, St Pauls BS2...49 A1
Thomas Way BS16 ...40 A3
Thompson Rd BS14..74 A2
Thomson Rd **7** BS5..57 A4
Thorndale BS8 ....84 A4
Thorndale Mews
BS8 ....84 A4
Thornhayes Cl BS36..19 B4
Thornhills The BS16..41 A2
Thornleigh Rd BS7 ..38 A1
Thornmead Gr BS10..25 B2
Thornycroft Cl BS7 ..39 A3
Thorpe Lodge **10**
BS6 ....48 B1
Three Brooks La
BS32 ....16 C4
Three Oaks Cl BS16..52 A4
Three Queens' La
BS1 ....87 B2
Three Wells Rd
BS13 ....78 B4
Thrissell St BS5 .....56 C4
Throgmorton Rd
BS4 ....72 B4
Thurlestone BS14....72 C2
Thurlow Rd BS5 .....50 A2
Thurston's Barton
BS5 ....50 C1
Tibberton BS15......60 C4
Tibbott Rd BS14 ....73 C1
Tibbott Wlk BS14....73 C1
Tichborne Rd BS5 ..57 B3
Tide Gr BS11 ....34 C4
Tidenham Way BS34..8 A1
Tiffany Ct BS1.......87 B1
Tilley Cl BS31........83 B2
Tilling Rd BS10 ......38 A3
Tilling Wlk BS10.....38 A3
Timber Dene BS16...50 B4
Timberscombe Wlk
BS14 ....73 B1
Timsbury Rd BS3 ...64 B2
Timsbury Wlk BS3 ..64 A2
Tindell Ct **12** BS30 ..68 B4
Tintagel Cl BS31.....82 B4
Tintern Ave BS5 .....57 C4
Tintern Cl BS30......60 B2
Tippetts Rd BS15 ...59 C2
Tirley Ho BS34.......8 A1
Tiverton Wlk BS16...51 B2
Toll House Ct **5**
BS3 ....62 C4
Tormarton Cres
BS10 ....25 A4
Toronto Rd BS7......38 C4
Torpoint Rd BS3.....63 C2
Torrance Cl BS30....61 C2
Torridge Rd BS31....83 B4
Torrington Ave BS4..72 B4
Tortworth Rd BS7....49 A1
Torwood House Sch
BS6 ....47 B3
Totshill Dr BS13 .....80 A4
Totshill Gr BS13 .....80 A4

Tottenham Pl BS8 ...84 B3
TOTTERDOWN 64 C4
Totterdown Bridge Ind
Est BS2 ....64 C4
Touchstone Ave
BS34 ....17 A1
Tower Hill BS2.......86 B3
Tower La
Bristol BS1 ....86 A3
Bristol, Cadbury Heath
BS30 ....61 A2
Towerleaze BS9 .....46 B3
Tower Rd BS15 ......52 A1
Tower Rd N BS30....61 A3
Tower Rd S BS30.....61 A1
Tower St BS1 ....87 B2
Tower The
Bristol BS1 ....87 B2
Bristol, Redland BS6...48 A2
Townsend BS32......8 A4
Townsend Cl BS14 ..74 B1
Townsend Rd BS14..74 B1
Tozers Hill BS4 ......65 B2
Tracy Cl BS14........72 B3
Trafalgar Terr **3**
BS3 ....63 A2
Tralee Wlk BS4 ......63 C1
Tramway Rd BS4.....65 B3
Tranmere Ave BS10..25 B4
Tranmere Gr BS10 ..25 B3
Transom Ho BS1.....87 B2
Tratman Wlk BS10...25 A3
Travers Cl BS4.......71 C2
Travers Wlk BS34....17 A1
Tredegar Rd BS16...51 C3
Treefield Pl **6** BS2...49 B2
Treetops Cvn Pk
BS16 ....40 C4
Tregarth Rd BS3 ....62 B1
Trelawney Ave BS5 ..57 C4
Trelawney Pk BS4 ...65 C3
Trelawney Rd BS6 ..48 A1
Trellick Wlk BS16....40 A4
Trenchard St BS1....84 C3
Trench La BS32 ......9 C2
Trendlewood Pk
BS16 ....40 A1
Trent Gr BS31........83 B4
Trentham Cl **7** BS2..49 B2
Trescothick Cl BS31..76 A2
Trescothick Dr
BS30 ....69 C4
Tresham Cl BS32.....9 B2
Trevanna Rd BS3 ...62 B1
Trevelyan Wlk
Bristol, Henbury
BS10 ....25 A3
Bristol, Stoke Gifford
BS34 ....17 B1
Treverdowe Wlk
BS10 ....24 B3
Trevethin Cl BS15....59 C3
Trevisa Gr BS10......26 A4
Trewint Gdns BS4....72 B4
Triangle S BS8.......84 B3
Triangle W BS8.......84 B3
Trident Cl BS16......31 B1
Trinder Rd BS20 ....45 A4
Trinity Coll BS9......46 C4
Trinity Ct
5 Bristol BS15 .....60 A4
Bristol, Horfield BS7...38 A1
Trinity Mews **15**
BS2 ....86 C3
Trinity Pl **3** BS8 .....85 A2
Trinity Rd BS2 ....56 C3
Trinity St BS2........56 C3
Trinity Wlk
Bristol BS2 ....86 C3
Bristol, Newton BS2...56 C3
Trin Mills BS1 ....87 A1
Troon Dr BS30.......61 A2
Troopers' Hill Rd
BS5 ....58 C3

Trowbridge Rd
BS10 ....26 A1
Trowbridge Wlk
BS10 ....26 A1
Trubshaw Cl BS7 ....38 B2
Trumpet La BS5 .....59 A3
Truro Rd BS3 ....63 A3
Trym Bank BS9 .....35 C3
Trym Cross Rd BS9..35 B3
Trymleaze BS9 ......35 B3
Trym Rd BS9 ....36 C3
Trym Side BS9.......35 B3
Trymwood Cl BS10...25 A2
Trymwood Par BS9 ..35 C2
Tucker St BS2 ....86 C3
Tuckett Ho BS16 ....41 B3
Tuckett La BS16 .....41 B3
Tudor Cl BS30 ....69 B3
Tudor Rd
Bristol, Hanham
BS15 ....59 B1
Bristol, Lower Easton
BS5 ....50 A1
Bristol, St Pauls BS2...49 A1
Tuffley Rd BS10 .....37 B4
Tufton Ave BS11 ....34 C4
Tugela Rd BS13......70 B3
Tunbridge Way
BS16 ....42 C4
Tunstall Cl BS9 ......46 C4
Turley Rd BS5 ....50 B1
Turnberry BS30......61 A2
Turnberry Wlk **3**
BS4 ....65 C1
Turnbridge Cl BS10..26 B4
Turnbridge Rd BS10..26 A3
Turner Cl BS31 ......76 C1
Turner Gdns BS7 ....39 A2
Turners Ct **9** BS30...68 B4
Turner Wlk BS30.....61 C3
Turtlegate Ave BS13..78 A4
Turtlegate Wlk
BS13 ....78 A4
Turville Dr BS7 ......38 C2
Tuscany Ho BS6 .....47 B3
Tweeny La BS30 .....61 C2
Twenty Acres Rd
BS10 ....25 C2
Twickenham Rd
BS6 ....37 B1
Twinnell Ho **5** BS5..56 C4
Two Acres Rd BS14..72 C3
Two Mile Ct BS15....59 B4
TWO MILE HILL 52 A1
Two Mile Hill Jun & Inf
Schs BS15............59 B4
Twomile Hill Rd
BS15 ....59 A4
Twynings The BS15..52 C2
Tybalt Way BS34.....16 C1
Tyler Cl BS15.........60 A1
Tyler's La BS16 ......41 C1
Tyler St BS2 ....56 C2
Tyndale Ave BS16...51 B4
Tyndale Rd **7** BS6...47 C1
Tyndale Rd BS15.....52 C2
Tyndall Ave BS8 .....84 C4
Tyndall Ho **5** BS2...86 C3
Tyndall Rd BS5 ......57 A4
Tyndalls Ct BS8......84 C4
Tyndalls Ho BS8 .....84 C4
TYNDALL'S PARK ...84 C4
Tyndalls Park Mews
BS2 ....84 C4
Tyndall's Park Rd
BS8 ....84 C4
Tyndalls Way BS10...38 A4
Tyne Rd BS7 ....48 B3
Tyne St BS2 ....49 B2
Tyning Cl BS14 ......72 C3
Tyning Rd BS3.......64 B3
Tynings Sch The
BS16 ....52 C4
Tynte Ave BS13......80 A3

Tyntesfield Rd BS13...70 C4
Tyrone Wlk BS4.......72 A4
Tyrrel Way BS34......16 C1

U

Ullswater Cl BS30...61 C2
Ullswater Rd BS10...26 A1
Underbanks BS20.....45 C4
Underdown Ho BS1..87 A1
Unicorn Bsns Pk
 BS4.................57 C1
Unicorn Pk BS4.....57 C1
Union Rd 2 BS2....56 C2
Union St BS1.........86 B3
Unite Ho BS1.........85 C2
Unity Ct BS31........76 C1
Unity Rd BS31........76 C2
Unity St
 Bristol, Brandon Hill
  BS1................85 C2
 Bristol BS2...........86 C3
 Bristol, Kingswood
  BS15...............59 B4
University Cl BS9 ...47 A4
University of Bristol
 Dorothy Hodgkin
 Bldg BS1...........86 A4
University Rd BS8 ...84 C3
University Wlk BS8 ..84 C3
Univ of Bristol BS8 .84 C3
Univ of Bristol Botanic
 Gdns★ BS9.........47 A4
Univ of the West of
 England BS3 ....62 A4
Univ of the West of
 England Faculty of
 Health & Social Care
 BS16...............40 A1
Univ of the West of
 England Frenchay
 Campus BS16......28 C1
Univ of the West of
 England, St Matthias
 Campus BS16......40 C1
Uphill Rd BS7 ......38 B1
Upjohn Cres BS13 ...79 C3
Uplands Rd BS16 ....52 B3
Upper Belgrave Rd
 BS8 ....47 B2
Upper Belmont Rd
 BS7 ....48 C3
Upper Berkeley Pl
 BS8 ....84 B3
Upper Byron Pl BS8..84 B3
Upper Chapel La
 BS36...............20 A3
Upper Cheltenham Pl
 BS6................48 C2
Upper Church La
 BS2................84 C3
Upper Conham Vale
 BS15...............58 C1
Upper Cranbrook Rd
 BS6................47 C4
UPPER EASTON...57 A4
UPPER EASTVILLE .50 C3
Upper Horfield Prim
 Sch BS7.............38 C1
UPPER KNOWLE 65 A2
Upper Maudlin St
 BS2................86 A3
Upper Myrtle Hill
 BS20...............45 B4
Upper Perry Hill
 BS3................63 B4
Upper Sandhurst Rd
 BS4................65 C4
UPPER
 SOUNDWELL 52 B3
Upper St BS4.........64 C4
Upper Station Rd
 BS16...............52 B4

V

Vale Ct BS8.........84 A4
Vale Foundry La
 BS3................62 B2
Vale La BS3..........71 B4
Valentine Cl BS4.....73 A1
Valerian Cl BS11.....34 B2
Vale St BS4..........64 C4
Valley Gdns BS16 ....42 B4
Valley Rd
 Bristol, Bedminster
 Down BS13 ....70 C4
 Bristol, Mangotsfield
  BS16...............42 C1
 Bristol, Warmley
  BS30...............61 C2
Valls The BS32.......17 A2
Valma Rocks BS5.....58 C2
Vanbrugh La BS16 ...40 A3
Vandyck Ave BS31...76 B2
Vantage Office Pk
 BS34...............17 B2
Vassall Ct BS16......41 A1
Vassall Rd BS16......41 A1
Vaughan Cl BS10 ....25 A3
Vauxhall Terr 3
 BS3................62 C4
Ventnor Ave 1 BS5..58 B4
Ventnor Rd
 Bristol, Filton BS34...27 C3
 Bristol, St George
  BS5................51 A1
Venton Ct 5 BS15 ..59 A1
Venture The BS4.....64 A1
Venue The BS10 .....14 A2
Vera Rd BS16........51 A2
Vernon St 5 BS2.....64 B4
Verrier Rd BS5 ......57 B3
Verwood Dr BS30....69 B2
Vicarage Cotts 12
 BS16...............41 C1
Vicarage Ct
 Bristol, Jefferies Hill
  BS15...............59 A1
 19 Bristol, Russell Town
  BS5................57 B3
Vicarage Rd
 Bristol, Bishopsworth
  BS13...............70 C2
 Bristol, Hanham
  BS15...............59 A1
 Bristol, Moorfields
  BS5................57 B4
 Bristol, Southville
  BS3................63 A4
 Frampton Cotterell
  BS36...............20 A2
 Pilning BS35 ....3 A3
Vicars Cl BS16.......51 C4
Victor Ho BS34.......16 A3
Victoria Ave BS5.....57 B3
Victoria Cres BS35....2 B2
Victoria Ct
 7 Bristol, Cotham
  BS6................48 B1
 Bristol, Redland BS6..47 B3
Victoria Gdns 8
 BS6................48 B1
Victoria Gr BS3......64 A4
Victoria Ho BS31.....83 A4
Victoria Par BS5.....57 B4
VICTORIA PARK.....84 B3

Victoria Park Com Inf
 Sch BS3............64 A3
Victoria Park Com Jun
 Sch BS3............64 A3
Victoria Park Ct
 BS3................64 B3
Victoria Pk
 Bristol, Fishponds
  BS16...............40 C1
 Bristol, Kingswood
  BS15...............52 B1
Victoria Pl BS3.......63 B3
Victoria Rd
 Avonmouth BS11 ....33 A3
 Bristol, Hanham
  BS15...............59 B1
 Bristol, St Philip's Marsh
  BS2................56 C1
 Bristol, Warmley
  BS30...............61 C1
Victoria Rooms★
 BS8................84 B3
Victoria Sq BS8......84 A3
Victoria St
 Bristol BS1..........87 B2
 Bristol, Staple Hill
  BS16...............41 C1
Victoria Terr
 15 Bristol, Clifton
  BS8................54 B2
 Bristol, St Philip's Marsh
  BS2................57 A1
Victoria Wlk BS6 ....48 B1
Victor Rd BS3 ....63 B3
Victor St
 9 Bristol, Russell
 Town BS5 ....57 A2
 Bristol, St Philip's Marsh
  BS2................64 C4
Vigor Rd BS13 ....71 A1
Village The BS16......43 B3
Villiers Rd BS5.......49 C1
Vimpany Cl BS10 ....25 A3
Vimpennys La BS35...5 C1
Vincent Cl BS11......24 A2
Vincent Ct 2 BS16...52 B3
Vining Wlk 4 BS5...57 A4
VINNEY GREEN 42 C3
Vinny Ave BS16......42 C3
Vintery Leys BS9.....37 A3
Vivian St BS3........63 C3
Vowell Cl BS13.......79 A4
Voyager Cl BS34.....29 A3
Vyvyan Rd BS8 ......84 A3
Vyvyan Terr BS8.....84 A3

W

Wadehurst Ind Pk
 BS2................56 C3
Wades Rd BS34......27 C3
Wade St BS2.........86 C3
Wadham Dr BS16....29 C1
Wadham Gr BS16....43 B1
Wainbridge Cres
 BS35...............3 B3
Wainbrook Dr BS5...50 B2
Wakeford Rd 1
 BS16...............42 C3
Wakeford Way BS30 .61 C3
Walden Rd BS31.....83 B4
Walker Cl
 Bristol, Downend
  BS16...............42 C3
 Bristol, Upper Easton
  BS5................57 A4
Walker Ct BS16......42 B1
Walker St BS2........84 C4
Wallcroft Ho BS6....47 B3
Wallingford Rd BS4..71 C3
Walliscote Ave BS9 ..37 B2
Walliscote Rd BS9 ...37 B2
Wallis Est BS2........49 A3
Wallscourt Rd BS34..27 C2

Wallscourt Rd S
 BS34...............27 C1
Walnut Cl
 Bristol BS15........53 A1
 Easton-in-G BS20 ....44 C3
 Frampton Cotterell
  BS36...............20 A2
 Keynsham BS31......82 A4
Walnut Cres BS15....60 B4
Walnut La BS15......60 C4
Walnut Wlk
 Bristol BS13........70 C2
 Keynsham BS31......82 A4
Walsh Ave BS14 .....72 C3
Walsingham Rd BS6 .48 C2
Walter St BS3........62 C4
Walton Ave BS4 .....57 C1
Walton Cl
 Bristol BS30........69 B1
 Keynsham BS31......82 B4
Walton Rd BS11......33 C2
Walton Rise BS9.....36 C3
Walton St BS5........49 C1
Walwyn Gdns BS13 ..79 B3
Wansbeck Rd BS31 ..83 B4
Wanscow Wlk BS9...37 A2
Wansdyke Rd BS14 ..73 A1
Wansdyke Prim Sch
 BS14...............80 B4
Wansdyke Workshops
 BS31...............76 C2
Wapping Rd BS1.....87 A1
Warden Rd BS3......63 B4
Wardour Rd BS4.....71 C4
Ware Ct BS36........18 B1
Waring Ho BS1......87 A1
Warman Cl BS14.....74 B2
Warman Rd BS14 ....74 B2
Warmington Rd
 BS14...............73 B4
Warminster Rd BS2..49 B2
WARMLEY..........61 A3
WARMLEY HILL.....60 A3
Warmley Park Sch
 BS30...............61 B3
WARMLEY TOWER .61 A2
Warner Cl BS15......60 B2
Warns The BS30.....68 C4
Warren Cl BS32......9 B3
Warren Gdns BS14...74 B1
Warren Rd BS34 .....27 C3
Warrington Rd BS4..65 C2
Warwick Ave 7
 BS5................49 C1
Warwick Cl BS30.....69 A2
Warwick Rd
 Bristol, Baptist Mills
  BS5................49 C1
 Bristol, Redland BS6..47 C1
 Keynsham BS31......82 B4
Washingpool La
 BS11...............11 A3
Washing Pound La
 BS14...............81 A4
Washington Ave
 BS5................50 A1
Watch Elm Cl BS32..16 C2
Watch House Rd
 BS20...............45 C4
Watchill Ave BS13....70 B2
Watchill Cl BS13......70 B2
Waterbridge Rd
 BS13...............78 B4
Watercress Rd BS2..49 A3
Waterdale Cl BS9....37 B3
Waterdale Gdns
 BS9................37 B3
Waterford Rd BS9 ...37 A2
Water La
 Bristol BS1..........87 B2
 Bristol, Hanham Green
  BS15...............67 A2
 Bristol, Upper Knowle
  BS4................65 C2

Water La continued
 Bristol, Windmill Hill
  BS3................64 B3
 Pill BS20............45 B4
Waterloo Ho BS20 ...33 C1
Waterloo Pl 10 BS2...86 C3
Waterloo Rd BS2 ....86 C3
Waterloo St
 Bristol BS2..........86 C3
 10 Bristol, Clifton
  BS8................54 B3
Watermore Cl BS36..20 A3
Watermore Gdns
 BS36...............20 A4
Watershed Media Ctr★
 BS1................87 A2
Waterside Dr BS32....8 B1
Water's La BS9 ......36 C3
Waters Rd BS15 .....59 B4
Wathen Rd BS6......44 B3
Watkins Yd BS9......36 C4
WATLEY'S END......19 A3
Watley's End Rd
 BS36...............19 A3
Watling Way BS11 ...33 C3
Watson Ave BS4.....65 C4
Watson's Rd BS30 ...68 B3
Watters Cl BS36......20 B2
Waveney Rd BS31....83 B3
Waverley Ho BS1.....85 C1
Waverley Rd
 Bristol, Cotham
  BS6................48 A1
 Bristol, Shirehampton
  BS11...............34 A2
Waverley St 9 BS5..49 B1
Waycroft Prim Sch
 BS14...............74 A1
Wayford Cl BS31.....83 B3
Wayland Ct 7 BS16..51 B4
Wayleaze BS36.......20 B3
Wayside BS36........19 C3
WCA Ho BS1 ....87 A2
Weare Ct BS1........85 A1
Webb St BS5.........56 C4
Webbs Wood BS32...17 A3
Webbs Wood Rd
 BS32...............17 A3
Wedgewood Rd
 BS16...............30 B1
Wedgwood Cl BS14..73 A1
Wedlock Way BS3 ...62 B3
Wedmore Cl BS15 ...60 B3
Wedmore Vale BS3...64 A2
Weedon Cl 6 BS2 ...49 B2
Weight Rd 2 BS5....57 B3
Welland Rd BS31.....83 A4
Wellgarth Ct BS4.....64 C2
Wellgarth Rd BS4....64 C2
Wellgarth Wlk BS4...64 C2
Well House Cl BS9 ...46 C3
Wellington Ave BS6..48 C1
Wellington Cres
 BS7................38 A2
Wellington Ct 11
 BS6................48 C1
Wellington Dr BS9 ...37 C2
Wellington Hill BS7 ..38 A2
Wellington Hill W
 BS9................37 C3
Wellington La BS6 ...48 C1
Wellington Mews
 BS11...............33 C1
Wellington Pk BS8...47 B2
Wellington Pl BS16 ..29 C1
Wellington Rd
 Bristol BS2..........86 C4
 Bristol, Kingswood
  BS15...............52 B2
Wellington Terr 20
 BS8................54 B2

Wellington Wlk
BS10 . . . . .37 B3
Wells Cl BS14 . . . . .73 B1
Wells Rd
Bristol, Hengrove
BS14 . . . . .73 B3
Bristol, Upper Knowle
BS4 . . . . .65 A2
Wells St BS3 . . . . .62 C4
Wellsway Rd BS31 . . . .83 A3
Wellsway Sch BS31 . .76 C1
Well The BS9 . . . . .46 C3
Welsford Ave BS16 . . . .50 B4
Welsford Rd BS16 . . . . .50 A4
Welsh Back BS1 . . . . . . .87 C2
Welton Wlk BS15 . . . . . .52 A2
Wenmore Cl BS16 . . . . .30 B1
Wentforth Dr 2
BS15 . . . . .52 A2
Wentworth BS30 . . . . .60 C2
Wentworth Rd BS7 . . .48 B3
Wescott Gr BS11 . . . . . .24 A2
Wesley Ave BS15 . . . . . .59 C1
Wesley Cl
6 Bristol, Upper
Soundwell BS16 . . . . .52 B3
Bristol, Whitehall
BS5 . . . . .50 B1
Wesley Hill BS15 . . . . .52 B1
Wesley La BS30 . . . . . . .61 A1
Wesley Pl BS8 . . . . .47 B2
Wesley Rd BS7 . . . . .48 C4
Wesley's Chapel ('The
New Room)* BS1 .86 B3
Wesley St BS3 . . . . .63 B3
Wesley Theological
Coll BS10 . . . . .25 A1
Wessex Ave BS7 . . . . . .38 B3
Wessex Ct BS7 . . . . .38 B3
Wessex Ho 10 BS2 . . . .86 C3
Westacre Cl BS10 . . . . .25 B2
Westbourne Ave
BS31 . . . . .76 A1
Westbourne Cl 2
BS16 . . . . .42 C3
Westbourne Ct BS5 . . .57 A4
Westbourne Gr 15
BS3 . . . . .63 B3
Westbourne Pl BS8 . . .84 B3
Westbourne Rd
Bristol, Downend
BS16 . . . . .42 B4
8 Bristol, Upper Easton
BS5 . . . . .57 A4
Westbourne Terr
BS16 . . . . .41 A3
West Broadway BS9 . .37 C2
Westbrooke Ct BS1 . .85 A1
Westbrook Rd BS4 . . . .73 C4
Westbury Court Rd
BS9 . . . . .36 C3
Westbury Ct BS9 . . . . .36 C3
Westbury Hill BS9 . . . .36 C3
Westbury La BS9 . . . . . .35 B3
Westbury Mews 6
BS9 . . . . .36 C3
**WESTBURY ON
TRYM** 36 B3
Westbury-on-Trym CE
Prim Sch BS9 . . . . . . .36 C4
WESTBURY PARK . .47 B3
Westbury Park Prim
Sch BS6 . . . . .47 C3
Westbury Pk BS6 . . . . .47 B4
Westbury Rd BS6 . . . . .47 B4
West Coombe BS9 . . . .35 C2
Westcourt Dr BS30 . . .69 A4
West Croft BS9 . . . . .37 B3
West Dene BS9 . . . . .36 A2
West Dundry La
BS41 . . . . .78 A2

West End
Bristol BS3 . . . . .85 C1
Bristol, Kingsdown
BS2 . . . . .86 A4
Westering Cl BS16 . . . .42 C1
Westerleigh Rd BS16 .42 B3
Westerleigh Rd
BS16 . . . . .42 B2
Western Approach
Distribution Pk
BS35 . . . . .5 A4
Western Ct BS34 . . . . . .29 B4
Western Dr BS14 . . . . . .72 A2
Western Grange
BS34 . . . . .27 B3
Western Rd BS7 . . . . . . .38 A2
Westfield Cl
Bristol BS15 . . . . .59 C1
Keynsham BS31 . . . . . .75 B1
Westfield Ho BS9 . . . . .36 B1
Westfield La BS34 . . . . .28 C3
Westfield Pk BS6 . . . . . .47 C1
Westfield Pl BS8 . . . . . .54 B3
Westfield Rd BS9 . . . . . .36 C4
Westfield Way BS32 . . .9 B2
Westgate BS1 . . . . .85 B1
West Gr BS6 . . . . .49 A1
Westland Ave BS30 . . .69 B4
West Leaze Pl BS32 . . .16 C2
Westleigh Cl BS10 . . . .26 B1
Westleigh Pk BS14 . . . .73 A4
Westleigh Rd BS10 . . . .26 B1
West Mall BS8 . . . . .54 B3
Westmead Ho BS11 . . . .21 C1
Westmead Rd BS5 . . . . .59 A3
Westminster Cl 1
BS9 . . . . .36 C3
Westminster Rd
BS5 . . . . .57 C4
Westmoreland Rd
BS6 . . . . .47 C3
Westmorland Ho
BS6 . . . . .47 B3
Weston Ave 4 BS5 . . .57 C3
Weston Cl BS9 . . . . .35 B3
Weston Cres BS7 . . . . . .38 A2
Westonian Ct BS9 . . . .46 A4
Weston Park Prim Sch
BS11 . . . . .34 B4
Westons Brake
BS16 . . . . .31 B1
Westons Hill Dr
BS16 . . . . .31 B1
Westons Way BS15 . . . .60 B3
Westover Cl BS9 . . . . . .25 A1
Westover Dr BS9 . . . . . .25 B1
Westover Gdns BS9 . . .36 B4
Westover Rd
Bristol BS9 . . . . .25 B1
Bristol BS9 . . . . .36 B4
Westover Rise BS9 . . . .25 B1
West Par BS9 . . . . .35 B3
West Park Rd BS16 . . . .42 A1
West Pk BS8 . . . . .84 B4
West Point Row BS32 .9 A3
Westpoint Trad Est
BS15 . . . . .59 C3
West Priory Cl BS9 . . .36 C3
West Ridge BS36 . . . . . .20 A3
West Rocke Ave
BS9 . . . . .35 C3
West Shrubbery 5
BS6 . . . . .47 C2
West St
Bristol, Bedminster
BS3 . . . . .63 B3
Bristol BS2 . . . . .86 C3
2 Bristol, Kingswood
BS15 . . . . .59 C4
Bristol, Oldland Common
BS30 . . . . .69 B4
West Town Ave BS4 . . .65 C1
West Town Dr 2
BS4 . . . . .65 C1

West Town Gr BS4 . . . .73 C4
West Town La BS4,
BS14 . . . . .65 C1
West Town Lane Prim
Sch BS4 . . . . .65 B1
West Town Pk BS4 . . . .65 B1
West Town Rd BS11 . . .33 B3
West View Rd BS16 . . . .42 C2
West View Rd
Bristol BS3 . . . . .63 A3
Keynsham BS31 . . . . . .76 A1
Westward Dr BS20 . . . .45 B4
Westward Rd BS13 . . . .70 B3
West Way BS10,
BS34 . . . . .26 C4
Westwood Cres BS4 . .57 C1
Westwood Rd BS4 . . . .73 C4
Wetherby Ct BS16 . . . .31 A1
Wetherby Gr 1
BS16 . . . . .31 A1
Wetherell Pl BS8 . . . . . .84 B3
Wexford Rd BS4 . . . . . .71 C4
Weymouth Rd BS3 . . .63 C2
Wharf Rd 5 BS16 . . . . .51 A4
Wharncliffe Cl
BS14 . . . . .73 A1
Wharncliffe Gdns
BS14 . . . . .73 A1
Whartons 8 BS4 . . . . . .65 C1
Whatley Ct 9 BS8 . . . .47 C1
Whatley Rd BS8 . . . . . .47 C1
Wheatfield Dr BS32 . . .9 B1
Wheatfield Prim Sch
BS32 . . . . .9 B1
Wheathill Cl BS31 . . . .75 C1
Wheelers Patch
BS16 . . . . .43 A1
Whinchat Gdns
BS16 . . . . .40 B2
Whippington Ct BS1 .86 B3
Whistle Rd BS16 . . . . . .53 C2
Whitby Rd BS4 . . . . . . .65 B4
WHITCHURCH 81 C4
Whitchurch District Ctr
BS14 . . . . .72 C1
Whitchurch La
Bristol, Bishopsworth
BS13 . . . . .71 A1
Bristol BS14 . . . . .72 A1
Bristol, Hartcliffe
BS13 . . . . .71 B1
Dundry BS41 . . . . .79 B1
Whitchurch Prim Sch
BS14 . . . . .81 B4
Whitchurch Rd
BS13 . . . . .70 C2
Whitebeam Cl BS5 . . .58 A4
Whitebeam Ho 7
BS16 . . . . .41 B2
Whitecroft Way
BS15 . . . . .60 C3
Whitecross Ave
BS14 . . . . .73 B2
Whitefield Ave
Bristol, Hanham
BS15 . . . . .59 C1
Bristol, Speedwell
BS5 . . . . .51 B1
Whitefield Cl 7
BS16 . . . . .52 B3
Whitefield Fishponds
Com Sch BS16 . . . . . .51 A4
Whitefield Rd BS5 . . . .51 B1
Whitegates BS36 . . . . .18 B2
WHITEHALL 50 B1
Whitehall Ave BS5 . . . .50 C1
Whitehall Gdns BS5 . .50 B1
Whitehall Prim Sch
BS5 . . . . .50 B1
Whitehall Rd BS5 . . . . .57 B4
Whitehall Trad Est 4
BS5 . . . . .57 B4
Whitehorn Vale
BS10 . . . . .26 A3

White House Bsns Ctr
The BS15 . . . . .59 C3
Whitehouse Ctr (PRU)
BS13 . . . . .71 B1
Whitehouse La
Bristol BS3 . . . . .63 C4
Pilning BS35 . . . . .3 A3
Whitehouse Pl BS3 . . .64 A4
Whitehouse St BS3 . . .64 A4
Whiteladies Rd BS8 . .84 B4
Whiteleaze BS10 . . . . . .37 B4
White Lodge Rd
BS16 . . . . .53 A4
Whitemead Ho 3
BS3 . . . . .62 C3
WHITESHILL 30 B3
Whiteshill BS16 . . . . . .30 B3
Whites Hill BS5 . . . . . . .58 C2
White St BS5 . . . . .86 C4
White Tree Rdbt
BS6 . . . . .47 B4
White Tree Rd BS9 . . . .47 C4
WHITEWAY 51 B1
Whiteway Cl
Bristol, St Anne's Park
BS4 . . . . .58 A2
Bristol, St George
BS5 . . . . .58 C4
Whiteway Ct 1 BS5 .58 C4
Whiteway Mews
BS5 . . . . .58 C4
Whiteway Rd BS5,
BS15 . . . . .51 B1
Whitewood Rd BS15 . .51 A1
Whitfield Ho 7
BS15 . . . . .59 C4
Whiting Rd BS13 . . . . . .78 C4
Whitland Ave BS13 . . . .71 A1
Whitland Rd BS13 . . . . .71 A1
Whitley Mead BS34 . . .28 C3
Whitmead Gdns
BS13 . . . . .79 B4
Whitmore Ave BS4 . . .66 C3
Whitson Ho 1 BS2 . . .86 C3
Whitson St BS1 . . . . . . .86 A4
Whittington Rd
BS16 . . . . .41 B2
Whittock Rd BS14 . . . .73 C2
Whittock Sq BS14 . . . .73 C3
Whittucks Cl BS15 . . . .67 C4
Whittucks Rd BS15 . . .67 B4
Whitwell Rd BS14 . . . . .73 A4
Whytes Cl BS9 . . . . .36 C4
Wick Cres BS4 . . . . .65 C3
Wickets The
Bristol, Filton BS7 . . . . .27 A1
Bristol, Upper Soundwell
BS15 . . . . .52 B2
Wicketts The BS7 . . . . .27 A2
Wickham Ct BS16 . . . . .39 C1
Wickham Glen BS16 . .39 C1
Wickham Hill BS16 . . . .39 C1
Wickham Theatre*
BS8 . . . . .84 C3
Wickham View BS16 . .50 B4
Wicklow Rd BS4 . . . . . .72 A4
Wick Rd
Bristol BS4 . . . . .65 C4
Pilning BS35 . . . . .3 C3
Wick Rdbt BS16 . . . . . .31 B2
Wick Wick Cl BS16,
BS36 . . . . .31 B3
Widcombe BS14 . . . . . .72 C2
Widcombe Cl 3
BS5 . . . . .58 C3
Widmore Gr BS13 . . . . .71 A1
Wigton Cres BS10 . . . .26 A2
Wilbye Gr BS4 . . . . .71 C3
Wilcox Cl BS15 . . . . .59 B2
Wildcroft Ho BS9 . . . . .47 C4
Wildcroft Rd BS9 . . . . .47 C4
Wilder Ct BS2 . . . . .86 B4
Wilder St BS2 . . . . .86 B4
Willada Cl BS3 . . . . .63 A2

William Mason Cl 19
BS5 . . . . .57 A3
Williams Cl BS30 . . . . .68 B3
Williamson Rd BS7 . . .49 A3
William St
Bristol, Fishponds
BS16 . . . . .51 C3
8 Bristol, Moorfields
BS5 . . . . .57 B4
Bristol, Newton BS2 . . .56 C2
Bristol, St Pauls BS2 . . .49 A4
Bristol, Totterdown
BS3 . . . . .64 B4
Bristol, Windmill Hill
BS3 . . . . .64 A4
Willinton Rd BS4 . . . . .72 B4
Willis Rd BS15 . . . . .53 A2
Willment Way BS11 . . .22 B1
Willmott Cl BS14 . . . . .80 B3
Willoughby Cl BS13 . .71 A3
Willoughby Rd BS7 . . .38 A1
Willow Bank BS10 . . . .37 B3
Willow Bed Cl BS16 . .41 A2
Willow Cl
Bristol, Patchway
BS34 . . . . .14 C3
Bristol, Warmley
BS30 . . . . .61 C2
Willow Ct BS7 . . . . .38 C3
Willow Gr 1 BS16 . . . .52 A2
Willow Ho BS13 . . . . . .79 C4
Willow Rd BS15 . . . . . . .67 B3
Willow Sh Ctr The
BS16 . . . . .42 A2
Willows The
Bristol, Bradley Stoke
BS32 . . . . .16 B4
Bristol BS16 . . . . .52 C4
Bristol, Frenchay
BS16 . . . . .29 C1
Keynsham BS31 . . . . . .76 A2
Willow Way BS36 . . . . .20 A2
Willow Wlk
Bristol BS10 . . . . .25 C3
Keynsham BS31 . . . . . .82 B4
WILLSBRIDGE 69 A1
Willsbridge Hill
BS30 . . . . .68 C2
Willsbridge Ho
BS30 . . . . .68 C2
Willsbridge Mill*
BS30 . . . . .69 A2
Wills Dr BS5 . . . . .56 C4
Wills Way BS4 . . . . .71 C2
Willway St BS3 . . . . . . .63 C4
Wilmot Ct BS30 . . . . . . .60 C2
Wilmots Way BS20 . . .45 C4
Wilshire Ave BS15 . . . .59 C1
Wilson Pl BS2 . . . . .86 C4
Wilson St BS2 . . . . .86 C4
Wilton Cl BS10 . . . . .26 A1
Wiltshire Pl BS15 . . . . .51 C1
Wilverley Ind Est
BS4 . . . . .66 A1
Wimbledon Rd BS6 . . .37 B1
Wimborne Rd BS3 . . . .63 B1
Winash Cl BS14 . . . . . . .73 C3
Wincanton Cl BS16 . . .31 A1
Winchcombe Gr
BS11 . . . . .34 B1
Winchcombe Rd
BS36 . . . . .19 C4
Winchester Ave BS4 . .65 C3
Winchester Cl BS16 . . .40 A2
Winchester Rd BS4 . . .65 C3
Wincombe Trad Est
BS2 . . . . .64 C4
Wincroft BS30 . . . . .69 B4
Windcliff Cres BS11 . .34 A3
Windermere Rd
BS34 . . . . .15 B4
Windermere Way
BS30 . . . . .61 C2
Windmill Cl BS3 . . . . . .64 A4

Windmill Farm Bsns
Ctr BS3 . . . . .63 C4
WINDMILL HILL. 64 A3
Windmill Hill BS3. . . .63 C3
Windmill La BS10. . . .24 B3
Windrush Gn BS31. . .83 B4
Windrush Rd BS31. . .83 B4
Windscreens Ave
BS2 . . . . .56 C3
Windsor Ave
Bristol BS5 . . . . .59 A2
Keynsham BS31 . . . . .82 C4
Windsor Cl BS34. . . . .28 C4
Windsor Cres BS10 . .24 A4
Windsor Ct
14 Bristol, Clifton
BS8 . . . . .54 B2
Bristol, Downend
BS16 . . . . .42 A3
Windsor Gr 20 BS5. .57 A4
Windsor Pl
Bristol, Clifton BS8 . . .54 B2
Bristol, Mangotsfield
BS16 . . . . .42 C1
Windsor Rd
Bristol, Longwell Green
BS30 . . . . .68 B3
Bristol, Montpelier
BS6. . . . . .48 C2
Windsor Terr
Bristol, Clifton BS8 . . .54 B2
Bristol, Windmill Hill
BS3 . . . . .64 B4
Windyridge BS16 . . . .52 C4
Wineberry Cl BS5. . . .50 B1
Wine St BS1 . . . . .86 A3
Winfield Rd BS30 . . . .61 B3
Winford Ct BS6 . . . . . .36 C1
Winford Gr BS13. . . . .70 C4
Wingfield Rd BS3. . . .64 A2
Winkworth Pl 4
BS2 . . . . .49 A1
Winsbury Way BS32. . . 9 B1
Winscombe Cl BS31 .75 C2
Winsford St 2 BS5 . .56 C4
Winsham Cl BS14. . . .73 A1
Winsley Rd BS6. . . . . .48 B1
Winstanley Ho 4
BS5 . . . . .57 A2
Winstone Ct BS2. . . .84 C3
WINTERBOURNE. 19 A2
WINTERBOURNE
DOWN. 31 A4
Winterbourne Hill
BS36 . . . . .18 B1
Winterbourne Rd
BS34 . . . . .16 C2
Winterstoke Cl 5
BS3 . . . . .63 A2
Winterstoke Ctr 1
BS3 . . . . .63 A2
Winterstoke Ho 1
BS3 . . . . .62 C3
Winterstoke Rd BS3 .62 C2

Winterstoke Underpass
BS3 . . . . .62 B4
Winton St BS2. . . . . . .64 B4
Wisemans Ho BS8 . .84 A4
Witchell Rd BS5 . . . . .57 B3
Witch Hazel Rd
BS13 . . . . .80 A3
Witcombe Cl BS15 . . .53 A1
Witham Rd BS31. . . . .83 B3
Witherlies Rd BS16 . .40 B2
Withey Cl E
Bristol BS9 . . . . .36 B2
Stoke Bishop BS9 . . . .36 B2
Withey Cl W BS9. . . . .36 B1
Witheys The BS14. . . .81 B4
Withington Cl BS30 . .69 B2
Withleigh Rd BS4. . . .65 A2
Withypool Gdns
BS14 . . . . .73 A1
Withys The BS20. . . . .45 C4
WITHYWOOD. 78 C4
Withywood Com Sch
BS13 . . . . .70 C1
Withywood Gdns 1
BS13 . . . . .78 B4
Withywood Rd BS13 .78 B4
Witney Mead BS36. . .19 C4
Woburn Cl BS30 . . . . .60 B1
Woburn Rd BS5. . . . . .49 C3
Wolferton Rd BS7 . . .49 A2
Wolfridge Gdns
BS10 . . . . .25 B4
Wolseley Rd BS7. . . .48 B3
Woodbine Rd BS5 . . .57 C4
Woodborough St
BS5 . . . . .49 C1
Woodbridge Rd BS4 .64 C2
Woodbury La BS8. . . .47 B2
Woodchester BS15 . .52 C3
Woodchester Rd
BS10 . . . . .37 B3
Woodcote BS15 . . . . .59 C2
Woodcote Rd BS16 . .51 C3
Woodcote Wlk BS16 .51 C2
Woodcroft Ave BS5 . .50 B1
Woodcroft Cl BS4. . . .66 A4
Woodcroft Rd BS4. . .66 A4
Woodend BS15 . . . . . .59 C2
Woodend Rd BS36 . . .20 A3
Wood End Wlk BS9 . .35 B2
Woodfield Rd BS6 . . .47 C2
Woodgrove Rd BS10 .24 B2
Woodhall Cl BS16. . . .42 B2
Woodhouse Gr BS7 . .38 A2
Woodington Ct 1
BS30 . . . . .68 B4
Woodland Ave BS15 .52 B2
Woodland Cl BS15 . . .52 A2
Woodland Ct
Bristol BS9 . . . . .46 A3
Bristol, Tyndall's Park
BS8 . . . . .84 C4
Woodland Gr BS9. . . .35 C2
Woodland Rd BS8 . . .84 C4

Woodlands
Bristol BS9 . . . . .46 C3
Bristol, Downend
BS16 . . . . .42 A2
Bristol, Patchway
BS32 . . . . 9 B3
Woodlands Ct
Bristol, Patchway
BS32 . . . . 8 C3
Bristol, Shirehampton
BS11. . . . . .34 A1
Woodlands La BS32. . . 9 A3
Woodlands Pk BS32 . . 9 A3
Woodlands Rise
BS16 . . . . .41 C2
Woodland Terr
Bristol, Kingswood
BS15 . . . . .60 A3
Bristol, Redland BS6. .47 C2
Woodland Way
BS15 . . . . .52 A2
Woodleaze BS9. . . . . .35 A2
Woodleigh Gdns
BS14 . . . . .73 B2
Woodmancote Rd 7
BS6 . . . . .49 C2
Woodmarsh Cl BS14 .80 C4
Woodmead Gdns
BS13 . . . . .79 B4
Woodnook The
BS10 . . . . .26 A2
Wood Rd BS15. . . . . . .59 C4
Woodside BS9. . . . . . .46 B3
Woodside Gr BS10 . . .24 B3
Woodside Rd
Bristol, Downend
BS16 . . . . .41 B3
Bristol, Kingswood
BS15 . . . . .59 B3
Bristol, St Anne's Park
BS4 . . . . .58 A2
Frampton Cotterell
BS36 . . . . .20 C4
Wood St BS5 . . . . .49 C2
WOODSTOCK. 60 B3
Woodstock Ave BS6 .48 A1
Woodstock Cl BS15 . .60 B4
Woodstock Rd
Bristol, Kingswood
BS15 . . . . .60 B3
Bristol, Redland BS6. .48 A2
Woodstock Sch
BS10 . . . . .24 C2
Woodview Cl BS11. . .34 A3
Woodward Dr BS30. . .68 B4
Woodwell Rd BS11. . .34 A1
Woodyleaze Dr
BS15 . . . . .59 C2
Woolcot St BS6. . . . . .47 C2
WOOLCOTT PARK. . . .47 C1
Woolley Rd BS14 . . . .74 A1
Wootton Cres BS4 . . .58 A2
Wootton Pk BS14,
BS4 . . . . .65 A1

Wootton Rd BS4 . . . . .58 B2
Worcester Cl BS16. . .51 C2
Worcester Cres BS8 .84 A4
Worcester Rd
Bristol BS8 . . . . .84 A4
Bristol, Kingswood
BS15 . . . . .52 B1
Worcester Terr BS8 . .84 A4
Wordsworth Ho
BS34 . . . . .15 B4
Wordsworth Rd BS7 .39 A3
Workshop Rd BS11 . .22 A4
World's End La BS31 77 B1
Worrall Mews 10
BS8 . . . . .47 B2
Worrall Pl 11 BS8. . . .47 B2
Worrall Rd BS8 . . . . . .47 B2
Worrel's La BS16,
BS36 . . . . .30 B3
Worsley St BS5 . . . . . .57 C3
Worthing Rd BS34 . . .15 A4
Worthy Cl BS15. . . . . .60 B2
Worthy Rd BS11 . . . . .10 B3
Worthys The BS34 . . .17 B2
Wraxall Gr BS13 . . . . .70 C4
Wraxall Rd BS30. . . . .60 C2
Wrenbert Rd BS16. . .41 C1
Wren Cl BS16. . . . . . . .40 A3
Wren Dr BS16 . . . . . . .40 C2
Wright Way BS16. . . .40 A4
Wrington Cl BS34. . . .16 A3
Wrington Cres BS13 .70 C3
Wroughton Dr BS13 .79 C4
Wroughton Gdns
BS13 . . . . .79 C4
Wroxham Dr BS34 . . .16 A4
Wyatt Ave BS13. . . . . .70 B1
Wyatt Cl BS13 . . . . . . .70 B1
Wyatts View BS4. . . . .58 A2
Wychwood BS15. . . . .60 A2
Wyck Beck Rd BS10. .25 B4
Wycliffe Rd BS9 . . . . .37 A3
Wycliffe Row 9
BS3 . . . . .64 B4
Wycombe Gr BS4 . . . .65 C2
Wye Croft Cl BS10 . . .26 B3
Wyedale Ave BS9 . . . .35 B3
Wykis Ct BS15 . . . . . . .60 A1
Wymbush Cres
BS13 . . . . .71 B1
Wymbush Gdns
BS13 . . . . .71 B1
Wyndam Ct BS2 . . . . .86 B4
Wyndham Cres
Bristol BS4 . . . . .66 C3
Easton-in-G BS20 . . . .45 A4
Wynstones The
BS15 . . . . .59 B3
Wyvern Villas BS9. . . .36 C4

Y

Yard The BS2 . . . . .49 B3
Yatton Cl BS13. . . . . . .70 B4

Yeaman's Ho BS1. . . .87 B1
Yelverton Rd BS4 . . . .66 A1
Yeomans Cl BS9 . . . . .35 C1
Yeomanside Cl
BS14 . . . . .73 B1
Yewcroft Cl BS14. . . .80 C4
Yew Tree Ct BS14 . . . .73 A1
Yew Tree Dr BS15 . . . .53 A3
Yew Tree Gdns
BS20. . . . . .45 B4
York Ave BS7 . . . . .49 A4
York Bldgs BS3 . . . . . .64 B4
York Cl
Bristol, Bromley Heath
BS16 . . . . .31 A1
Bristol, Stoke Gifford
BS34 . . . . .28 B4
York Ct BS2 . . . . .86 B4
York Gdns
Bristol BS8 . . . . .54 B2
Winterbourne BS36 . .19 A4
York Ho BS8. . . . . .84 A3
York Pl
Bristol, Brandon Hill
BS1 . . . . .85 C2
Bristol, Victoria Park
BS8 . . . . .84 B3
York Rd
Bristol BS2 . . . . .87 C1
Bristol, Lower Easton
BS5 . . . . .50 A1
Bristol, Montpelier
BS6 . . . . .48 C1
Bristol, Staple Hill
BS16 . . . . .52 C4
Bristol, Windmill Hill
BS3 . . . . .64 A4
York St
Bristol, Baptist Mills
BS2 . . . . .49 B2
Bristol BS2 . . . . .86 B4
2 Bristol, Clifton
BS8 . . . . .47 B2
9 Bristol, Redfield
BS5 . . . . .57 B3
Youngs Ct BS16. . . . . .43 A4

Z

Zetland Rd BS6. . . . . .48 B2
Zinc Rd BS11 . . . . .22 A3
Zone The 7 BS5. . . . .58 C4

List of numbered locations

In some busy areas of the maps it is not always possible to show the name of every place.

Where not all names will fit, some smaller places are shown by a number. If you wish to find out the name associated with a number, use this listing.

The places in this list are also listed normally in the Index.

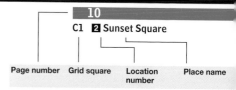

Page number	Grid square	Location number	Place name

9
B1 **1** Shellmor Cl
2 Hedgerows
3 Shepherds Wlk

31
A1 **1** Wetherby Gr
2 Kempton Cl
4 Britannia Cl

36
C3 **1** Westminster Cl
2 Carlton Ho
3 Carlton Ct
4 Ivy Lodge
5 Bellevue Cotts
6 Westbury Mews

37
A2 **1** Cranford Ct
2 Blandford Cl
3 St Peter's Wlk

40
A1 **1** Frome Pl
2 School La
3 Glenside Pk
4 Spires View
5 Blackberry Ave

41
B2 **1** Urfords Dr
2 Shimsey Cl
3 Bridges Dr
4 Grangewood Cl
5 Hornbeam Ho
6 Sycamore Ho
7 Whitebeam Ho
C1 **1** Britannia Ct
2 Overnhurst Ct
3 Garton Ho
4 Pleasant Ho
5 Pendennis Ho
6 Shrubbery Ct
7 Berkeley Ho
8 Nelson Ho
9 Pamela Ho
10 John Wesley Ct
11 Orchard Cotts
12 Vicarage Cotts

42
C3 **1** Wakeford Rd
2 Westbourne Cl

47
B2 **1** St Vincent's Hill

2 York St
3 Highland Cres
4 Highland Sq
5 Belgrave Hill
6 Richmond Dale
7 Richmond Ct
8 Quarry Steps
9 Sutherland Pl
10 Worrall Mews
11 Worrall Pl
12 Haydon Ct
13 Highland Pl
14 Mornington Rd
15 Anglesea Pl
16 Normanton Rd
C1 **1** King's Parade Ave
2 Grosvenor Ct
3 Compton Lodge
4 Collingwood Rd
5 Plimsoll Ho
6 Oakland Rd
7 Tyndale Ct
8 Imperial Rd
9 Whatley Ct
10 Clifton Metro
11 Clifton Down Sh Ctr
12 George Ct
13 Hopkins Ct
14 Shirreff Ct
15 Cotham Gdns
16 Pitville Pl
17 Hampton La
C2 **1** Fernleigh Ct
2 Lower Redland Mews
3 East Shrubbery
4 Shrubbery Cotts
5 West Shrubbery
6 South Terr
7 Fitzroy Terr
8 Redland Terr
9 Burlington Ct
10 Greenway Ho

48
A2 **1** Ermleet Rd
2 Fernbank Ct
3 Clyde Mews
B1 **1** Elmgrove Pk
2 Cheltenham Cres
3 Llanarth Villas
4 Arley Ct
5 Arley Cotts
6 Hillside Ho
7 Victoria Ct
8 Victoria Gdns
9 Fremantle La
10 Thorpe Lodge
11 St Matthew's Ave
12 Prior's Hill
13 Thomas St N
B2 **1** Prospect Pl

2 Brookfield La
3 Brookfield Rd
4 Gillham Ho
5 Elton Mans
6 New Sandringham Ho
C1 **1** Montpelier Central
2 Mont The
3 Millbook Ct
4 Armidale Ave
5 Armidale Cotts
6 Picton Mews
7 Woodmancote Rd
8 Norrisville Rd
9 Barnabas St
10 Dalrymple Rd
11 Wellington Ct
12 Brighton St
13 Catherine Ct
14 Catherine Pl
15 Nine Tree Hill

49
A1 **1** Ashley Ct
2 Cary Ct
3 Carr Ho
4 Winkworth Pl
5 Corey Cl
6 Langsdown Ho
7 Davey Terr
8 Franklyn La
9 Dermot St
10 Cairns' Cres
11 Lower Ashley Rd
12 Gordon Rd
13 Mary Carpenter Pl
A2 **1** Sommerville Rd S
2 Ashley Court Rd
3 Balmoral Mans
4 Falkland Rd
5 Cumberland Gr
6 Ashley Trad Est
7 Ashley Grove Rd
8 Parkway Trad Est
9 Newland Hts
A4 **1** Carlton Ct
2 Coulson Ho
3 Athena Ct
B1 **1** Ashley Grove Rd
2 Conduit Pl
3 Summers Terr
4 Summers Rd
5 Byron St
6 Newfoundland Rd
7 Rosebery Ct
8 Gable Rd
9 Waverley St
10 Millpond St
11 Mill Ho
12 Kensington Pk
13 Rawnsley Ho
B2 **1** Ryland Pl
2 Boucher Pl

3 Lynmouth Rd
4 Seddon Rd
5 Treefield Pl
6 Weedon Ct
7 Trentham Cl
8 Mary Seacole Ct
9 Minto Road Ind Ctr
10 Dorset Gr
11 Durham Rd
12 Tewkesbury Rd
13 Merstham Rd
C1 **1** St Mark's Ave
2 Chapel Rd
3 Church Ave
4 St Marks Church Ho
5 Henrietta St
6 Manor Ho
7 Warwick Ave
8 St Mark's Gr
9 Manor Ct
10 St Nicholas Pk
11 St Mark's Terr
12 Rene Rd
13 St Mark's Ho
14 Oxford Pl
15 Roshni Gar W
16 Roshni Gar E
17 Moorhill St
18 Northcote St
19 Normanby Rd
20 Graham Rd

50
A1 **1** Devon Road Trad Est
2 Colwyn Rd
3 Lena Ave
4 Littleton St
5 Greenhaven
6 Cartledge Rd
7 Prudham St
A2 **1** Freeland Bldgs
2 Juniper Ct
3 Fountaine Ct
4 Boswell St
5 Argyle St
C3 **1** Ashman Ct
2 Burton Ct
3 Colstone Ct
4 Daines Ct
5 Ellyott Ct
6 Franklyn Ct
7 Goldney Ct
8 Haythorne Ct
9 Jeffreys Ct
10 Kyngstone Ct
11 Langton Ct
12 Martin Ct
13 Marlborough Ave

51
A4 **1** Marshall Ho
2 Collard Ho
3 Grove Ave
4 Featherstone Rd
5 Wharf Rd
6 Stoke View Bsns Pk
B1 **1** Thomas Pring Wlk
B4 **1** Adelaide Terr
2 Annie Scott Cl
3 Station Ave
4 Elmdale Gdns
5 Station Ave S
6 Lower Station Rd
7 Wayland Ct
C1 **1** Claymore Cres
2 Clarence Ho
3 Clarence Ct
4 Lindon Ct
C4 **1** Chasefield La
2 Bridges Ct
3 Maywood Ave
4 Parkhurst Ave

52
A1 **1** High Point Ho
2 Hill View Ho
3 Handel Cossham Ct
4 Tanners Ct
A2 **1** Willow Gr
2 Wentforth Dr
A4 **1** Eclipse Ct
2 Eclipse Office Pk
B1 **1** Morley Terr
2 Gladstone Rd
3 Kennington Ave
4 Alsop Rd
5 Maple Ct
6 Oatley Trad Est
7 Hicking Ct
B3 **1** Hayward Ind Est
2 Vincent Ct
3 Gardens The
4 Beazer Cl
5 St Clements Ct
6 Wesley Cl
7 Whitefield Cl
8 Church Ct
9 Montreaux Ct
10 Mulberry Gdns
B4 **1** Pendennis Pk
2 Pratten's La
3 Haynes Ho
4 Nelson Rd
5 Acacia Mews
6 Brookridge Ct
7 Kensington Rd

54
B1 **1** Bristol Gate
2 Faraday Rd
3 Dowry Pl